G H O
WOR

GHOST WORLD

T. F. THISELTON DYER

SENATE

Ghost World

First published in 1893 by Ward & Downey, London

This edition published in 2000 by Senate,
an imprint of Senate Press Limited,
34 York Street, Twickenham,
Middlesex TW1 3LJ, United Kingdom

Cover design © Senate Press Limited 2000

1 3 5 7 9 10 8 6 4 2

ISBN 1 85958 547 7

Printed and bound in the UK by
Mackays of Chatham plc, Chatham, Kent

CONTENTS

CHAPTER   PAGE

   I. THE SOUL'S EXIT AT DEATH . . . 1

  II. TEMPORARY EXIT OF SOUL 17

 III. THE NATURE OF THE SOUL 24

 IV. THE UNBURIED DEAD 43

  V. WHY GHOSTS WANDER 50

 VI. GHOSTS OF THE MURDERED 64

VII. PHANTOM BIRDS 85

VIII. ANIMAL GHOSTS 102

 IX. PHANTOM LIGHTS 127

  X. THE HEADLESS GHOST 144

 XI. PHANTOM BUTTERFLIES 159

XII. RAISING GHOSTS 163

XIII. GHOST LAYING 179

XIV. GHOSTS OF THE DROWNED 206

 XV. GHOST SEERS 214

XVI. GHOSTLY DEATH-WARNINGS 219

XVII. 'SECOND SIGHT' 233

XVIII. COMPACTS BETWEEN THE LIVING AND DEAD . 245

XIX. MINERS' GHOSTS 257

CHAPTER		PAGE
XX.	THE BANSHEE	273
XXI.	SEA PHANTOMS	284
XXII.	PHANTOM DRESS	303
XXIII.	HAUNTED HOUSES	310
XXIV.	HAUNTED LOCALITIES	335
XXV.	CHECKS AND SPELLS AGAINST GHOSTS	354
XXVI.	WRAITH-SEEING	363
XXVII.	GHOSTLY TIMES AND SEASONS	382
XXVIII.	SPIRIT-HAUNTED TREES	391
XXIX.	GHOSTS AND HIDDEN TREASURES	397
XXX.	PHANTOM MUSIC	411
XXXI.	PHANTOM SOUNDS	426

THE GHOST WORLD

CHAPTER I

THE SOUL'S EXIT

In the Iliad,[1] after the spirit of Patroclus has
visited Achilles in his dream, it is described as
taking its departure, and entering the ground like
smoke. In long after years, and among widely scattered communities, we meet with the same imagery;
and it is recorded how the soul of Beowulf the
Goth 'curled to the clouds,' imaging the smoke
which was curling up from his pyre. A similar
description of the soul's exit is mentioned in one
of the works of the celebrated mystic, Jacob
Boehme,[2] who observes: 'Seeing that man is so

---

[1] xxiii. 100; Keary's *Outlines of Primitive Belief*, p. 284.

[2] *The Three Principles*, chap. xix. 'Of the Going Forth of
the Soul.'

B

very earthly, therefore he hath none but earthly
knowledge; except he be regenerated in the gate
of the deep. He always supposeth that the soul
—at the deceasing of the body—goeth only out at
the mouth, and he understandeth nothing concerning its deep essences above the elements.
When he seeth a blue vapour go forth out of the
mouth of a dying man, then he supposeth that is
the soul.' The same conception is still extensively
believed throughout Europe, and the Russian peasant often sees ghostly smoke hovering above
graves. The Kaffirs hold that at death man leaves
after him a sort of smoke, 'very like the shadow
which his living body will always cast before it,' [1]
reminding us of the hero in the Arabian romance
of Yokdnan, who seeks the source of life and
thought, and discovers in one of the cavities of the
heart a bluish vapour—the living soul. Among
rude races the original idea of the human soul
seems to have been that of vaporous materiality,
which, as Dr. Tylor observes,[2] has held so large
a place in modern philosophy, and in one shape

[1] Letourneau's *Sociology*, p. 252.
[2] *Primitive Culture*, 1873, i. p. 457.

or another crops up in ghost stories. The Basutos, speaking of a dead man, say that his heart has gone out, and the Malays affirm that the soul of a dying man escapes through the nostrils.

Hogarth has represented the figure of Time breathing forth his last—a puff of breath proceeding from his mouth; and a correspondent of 'Notes and Queries'[1] relates that, according to a popular belief, a considerable interval invariably elapses between the first semblance of death and what is considered to be the departure of the soul. about five minutes after the time when death, to all outward appearances, has taken place, 'the last breath' may be seen to issue with a vapour 'or steam' out of the mouth of the departed. According to some foreign tribes, the soul was said to dwell mainly in the left eye; and in New Zealand men always ate the left eye of a conquered enemy. At Tahiti, in the human sacrifices, the left eye of the victim was always offered to the chief presiding over the ceremony. It was further believed in New Zealand that 'in eating the left eye they doubled their own soul by incorporating with it

[1] 1st S. ii. p. 51.

that of the conquered man. It was also thought
by some people in the same archipelago that a
spirit used to dwell in both eyes.' [1]

The supposed escape of the soul from the
mouth at death gave rise to the idea that the
vital principle might be transferred from one
person to another; and, among the Seminoles
of Florida, when a woman died in childbirth, the
infant was held over her face to receive her
parting spirit. Algonquin women, desirous of
becoming mothers, flocked to the bed of those
about to die, in the hope that they might receive
the last breath as it passed from the body; and
to this day the Tyrolese peasant still fancies a
good man's soul to issue from his mouth at death
like a little white cloud.[2] We may trace the same
fancy in our own country, and it is related [3] that
while a well-known Lancashire witch lay dying,
'she must needs, before she could " shuffle off this
mortal coil," transfer her familiar spirit to some
trusty successor. An intimate acquaintance

[1] Letourneau's *Sociology*, p. 257.

[2] Tylor's *Primitive Culture*, i. p. 433; Brinton's *Myths of the
New World*, p. 253.

[3] Harland and Wilkinson's *Lancashire Folk-lore*, 1867, p. 210.

from a neighbouring township was sent for in all
haste, and on her arrival was immediately closeted
with her dying friend. What passed between them
has never fully transpired; but it is asserted
that at the close of the interview the associate
received the witch's last breath into her mouth,
and with it her familiar spirit. The powers for
good or evil were thus transferred to her companion.'

In order that the soul, as it quits the body, may
not be checked in its onward course, it has long
been customary to unfasten locks or bolts, and to
open doors, so that the struggle between life and
death may not be prolonged—a superstition common in France, Germany, Spain, and England. A
correspondent of 'Notes and Queries' tells how for
a long time he had visited a poor man who was
dying, and was daily expecting death. Upon calling
one morning to see his poor friend, his wife informed him that she thought he would have died
during the night, and hence she and her friends
unfastened every lock in the house; for, as she
added, any bolt or lock fastened was supposed to
cause uneasiness to, and hinder, the departure of

the soul.[1] We find the same belief among the
Chinese, who make a hole in the roof to let
out the departing soul; and the North American
Indian, fancying the soul of a dying man to go
out at the wigwam roof, would beat the sides
with a stick to drive it forth. Sir Walter Scott,
in 'Guy Mannering,' describes this belief as deep
rooted among 'the superstitious eld of Scotland;'
and at the smuggler's death in the Kaim of
Derncleugh, Meg Merrilies unbars the door and
lifts the latch, saying—

> Open lock, end strife,
> Come death, and pass life.

A similar practice exists among the Esquimos,
and one may often hear a German peasant express
his dislike to slam a door, lest he should pinch a
soul in it. It has been suggested that the un-
fastening of doors and locks at death may be
explained by analogy and association. Thus,
according to a primitive belief, the soul, or the
life, was thought to be tied up,[2] so that the
unloosing of any knot might help to get rid of it

[1] 1st S. i. p. 315.
[2] Cf. 'Nexosque resolveret artus,' Virgil on the death of Dido.
Æneid iv. 695.

at death. The same superstition 'prevailed in Scotland as to marriage. Witches cast knots on a cord; and in a Perthshire parish both parties, just before marriage, had every knot or tie about them loosened, though they immediately proceeded in private to tie them each up again.'[1] Another explanation suggests that the custom is founded on the idea that, when a person died, the ministers of purgatorial pains took the soul as it escaped from the body, and flattening it against some closed door—which alone would serve the purpose —crammed it into the hinges and hinge openings; thus the soul in torment was likely to be miserably squeezed. By opening the doors, the friends of the departed were at least assured that they were not made the unconscious instruments of torturing the departed.[2]

There is a widespread notion among the poor that the spirit will linger in the body of a child a long time when the parent refuses to part with it, an old belief which, under a variety of forms, has existed from a primitive period. In Denmark one

[1] See Dalyell's *Darker Superstitions of Scotland*, p. 302, and *Notes and Queries*, 1st S. iv. p. 350.   [2] *Ibid.* i. p. 467.

must not weep over the dying, still less allow tears
to fall on them, for it will hinder their resting in
the grave. In some parts of Holland, when a child
is at the point of death, it is customary to shade
it by the curtains from the parents' gaze, the soul,
it is said, being detained in the body so long as a
compassionate eye is fixed upon it. A German
piece of folk-lore informs us that he who sheds tears
when leaning over an expiring friend increases the
difficulty of death's last struggle. A correspondent
of 'Notes and Queries' alluding to this superstition
in the North of England writes: 'I said to Mrs.
B——, "Poor little H—— lingered a long time; I
thought when I saw him that he must have died
the same day, but he lingered on!" "Yes," said
Mrs. B——, "it was a great shame of his mother.
He wanted to die, and she would not let him die;
she couldn't part with him. There she stood fret-
ting over him, and couldn't give him up; and so we
said to her, 'He'll never die till you give him up,'
and then she gave him up, and he died quite peacefully." ' [1]

Similarly, it is not good to weep for the dead, as

[1] 1st S. iii. p. 84.

it disturbs the peace and rest of the soul. In an
old Danish ballad of Aage and Else, a lover's ghost
says to his mistress :

> Every time thou weepest, for each tear in that flood,
> The coffin I am laid in is filled with much blood.

Or, as another version has it :

> Every time thou'rt joyful,
>   And in thy mind art glad,
> Then is my grave within
>   Hung round with roses' leaves.

> Every time thou grievest,
>   And in thy mind are sad,
> Then is within my coffin
>   As if full of clotted blood.

A German song tells us how a sister wept incessantly over her brother's grave, but at last her
tears became intolerable to the deceased, because
he was detained on earth by her excessive weeping,
and suffered thereby great torment. In a fit of
desperation he cursed her, and in consequence of
his malediction, she was changed into a cuckoo, so
that she might always lament for herself.[1] Mann-
hardt relates a pretty tale of a young mother who

---

[1] Kelly's *Indo-European Folk-lore*, pp. 127-128.

wept incessantly over the loss of her only child, and would not be comforted. Every night she went to the little grave and sobbed over it, till, on the evening preceding the Epiphany, she saw Bertha pass not far from her, followed by her troop of children. The last of these was one whose little shroud was all wet, and who seemed exhausted by the weight of a pitcher of water she carried. It tried in vain to cross a fence over which Bertha and the rest had passed; but the fond mother, at once recognising her child, ran and lifted it over. ' Oh, how warm are mother's arms ! ' said the little one ; ' but don't cry so much, mother, for I must gather up every tear in my pitcher. You have made it too full and heavy already. See how it has run over and wet all my shift.' The mother cried again, but soon dried her tears.

We may compare a similar superstition among the natives of Alaska, when, if too many tears were shed by the relatives during the burial ceremonies, it was thought that the road of the dead would be muddy, but a few tears were supposed just to lay the dust.[1] The same idea is found in a Hindu

[1] Dorman's *Primitive Superstitions*, p. 43.

dirge : ' The souls of the dead do not like to taste the tears let fall by their kindred; weep not, therefore;' and, according to the Edda, every tear falls as blood upon the ice-cold bosom of the dead. We may trace the belief in Ireland, and Sir Walter Scott says[1] it was generally supposed throughout Scotland that ' the excessive lamentation over the loss of friends disturbed the repose of the dead, and broke even the rest of the grave.'

The presence of pigeon or game feathers is said to be another hindrance to the exit of the soul; and, occasionally, in order to facilitate its departure, the peasantry in many parts of England will lay a dying man on the floor. A Sussex nurse once told the wife of a clergyman that ' never did she see anyone die so hard as Master Short; and at last she thought—though his daughter said there were none—that there must be game feathers in the bed. So she tried to pull it from under him, but he was a heavy man, and she could not manage it alone, and there was none with him but herself, and so she got a rope and tied it round him, and

---

[1] In a note to *Redgauntlet*, Letter xi.

pulled him right off the bed, and he went off in a minute quite comfortable, just like a lamb.'[1]   In Lancashire, this belief is so deep-rooted that some persons will not allow sick persons to lie on a feather-bed ; while in Yorkshire the same is said of cocks' feathers.   Shakespeare alludes to the practice where Timon says[2]—

> Pluck stout men's pillows from below their heads.

And Grose remarks : ' It is impossible for a person to die whilst resting on a pillow stuffed with the feathers of a dove, for he will struggle with death in the most exquisite torture.'   This is also a Hindu and Mohammedan belief, and in India ' the dying are always taken from their beds and laid on the ground, it being held that no one can die peaceably except when laid on mother earth.[3]   In Russia, too, there is a strong feeling against the use of pigeon feathers in beds.

The summons for the soul to quit its earthly tenement has been thought to be announced, from early times, by certain strange sounds, a belief which Flatman has embodied in some pretty lines :

[1] *Folk-lore Record*, i. pp. 59–60.   [2] *Timon of Athens*, iv. 3.
[3] Henderson's *Folk-lore of Northern Counties*, pp. 60–61.

> My soul, just now about to take her flight
> Into the regions of eternal night,
> Methinks I hear some gentle spirit say,
> ' Be not fearful, come away ! '

Pope speaks in the same strain :

> Hark ! they whisper, angels say,
> ' Sister spirit, come away ! '

And in ' Troilus and Cressida ' (iv. 4), the former says :

> Hark ! you are called ; some say, the Genius so
> Cries ' Come ! ' to him that instantly must die.

As in days gone by so also at the present time, there is, perhaps, no superstition more generally received than the belief in what are popularly known as ' death-warnings,' [1] reference to which we shall have occasion to make in a later chapter.

It has been urged again, that at the hour of death the soul is, as it were, on the confines of two worlds, and hence may possess a power which is both prospective and retrospective. In ' Richard II.' (ii. 1), the dying Gaunt exclaims, alluding to his nephew, the young and self-willed king :

> Methinks I am a prophet, new inspired,
> And thus expiring do foretell of him.

[1] See Tylor's *Primitive Culture*, i. p. 145.

Nerissa says of Portia's father in 'Merchant of Venice' (i. 2): 'Your father was ever virtuous; and holy men at their death have good inspirations.' This idea may be traced up to the time of Homer,[1] and Aristotle tells us that the soul, when on the point of death, foretells things about to happen; the belief still lingering on in Lancashire and other parts of England. According to another notion, it was generally supposed that when a man was on his death-bed, the devil or his agents tried to seize his soul, if it should happen that he died without receiving the 'Eucharist,' or without confessing his sins. In the old office books of the Church, these 'busy meddling fiends' are often represented with great anxiety besieging the dying man; but on the approach of the priest and his attendants they are represented as being dismayed. Douce[2] quotes from a manuscript book of devotion, of the time of Henry VI., the following prayer to St. George: 'Judge for me when the most hedyous and damnable dragons of helle shall be redy to take my poore soule and engloute it into theyr

---

[1] *Iliad*, ii. 852.
[2] *Illustrations of Shakspeare*, 1839, pp. 324-326.

infernall belyes.'   One object, it has been urged, of
the 'passing bell' was to drive away the evil
spirit that might be hovering about to seize the
soul of the deceased, such as the king speaks of in
2 Henry VI. (iii. 3) :

> O, beat away the busy meddling fiend,
> That lays strong siege unto this wretch's soul,
> And from his bosom purge this black despair.

We may find the same idea among the Northern
Californians, who affirmed that when the soul first
escaped from the body an evil spirit hovered near,
ready to pounce upon it and carry it off.[1]

It is still a common belief with our seafaring
community on the east coast of England, that the
soul takes its departure during the falling of the
tide.   Everyone remembers the famous scene in
'David Copperfield,' where Barkis's life 'goes out
with the tide.'   As Mr. Peggotty explained to David
Copperfield by poor Barkis's bedside, 'People
can't die along the coast except when the tide's
pretty nigh out.   He's a-going out with the tide—
he's a-going out with the tide.   It's ebb at half
arter three, slack water half an hour.   If he lives

---

[1] Dorman's *Primitive Superstitions*, p. 40.

till it turns he'll hold his own till past the flood, and go out with the next tide.' In the parish register of Heslidon, near Hartlepool, the subjoined extract of old date alludes to the state of the tide at the time of death : ' The xith daye of Maye, A.D. 1595, at vi of ye clocke in the morninge, being full water, Mr. Henrye Mitford, of Hoolam, died at Newcastel, and was buried the xvi daie, being Sondaie. At evening prayer, the hired preacher made ye sermon.' Mrs. Quickly in ' Henry V.' (ii. 3) speaking of Falstaff's death says : ' 'A made a finer end and went away an it had been any christom child; 'a parted even just between twelve and one, even at the turning o' the tide.' In Brittany, death claims its victim at ebb of the tide, and along the New England coast it is said a sick man cannot die until the ebb-tide begins to run. It has been suggested that there may be some slight foundation for this belief in the change of tempera-ture which takes place on the change of tide, and which may act on the flickering spark of life, ex-tinguishing it as the ebbing sea recedes.

CHAPTER II

TEMPORARY EXIT OF SOUL

MANY of the conceptions of the human soul formed by savage races arose from the phenomena of everyday life. According to one of the most popular dream theories prevalent among the lower races, the sleeper's soul takes its exit during the hours of slumber, entering into a thousand pursuits. Now, as it is well known by experience 'that men's bodies do not go on these excursions, the explanation is that every man's living self, a soul, is his phantom or image, which can go out of his body and see, and be seen itself, in dreams.'[1] In the opinion of the savage, therefore, dreams have always afforded a convincing proof of the soul's separate existence, and Dr. Tylor considers that

[1] Tylor's *Anthropology*, 1881, p. 343.

c

'nothing but dreams and visions could ever have put into men's minds such an idea as that of souls being ethereal images of bodies.'

Thus the Dayaks of Borneo believe that in the hours of sleep the soul travels far away, and the Fijians think that the spirit of a living man during sleep can leave the body and trouble some one else. But Mr. E. im Thurn, in his 'Indians of Guiana' (344–346), gives some very striking instances of this strange phase of superstitious belief: 'One morning, when it was important to me to get away from a camp on the Essequibo River, at which I had been detained for some days by the illness of some of my Indian companions, I found that one of the invalids, a young Macusi Indian, though better in health, was so enraged against me that he refused to stir, for he declared that, with great want of consideration for his weak health, I had taken him out during the night, and had made him haul the canoe up a series of difficult cataracts. Nothing could persuade him that this was but a dream, and it was some time before he was so far pacified as to throw himself sulkily into the bottom of the canoe. At that time we were all suffering from a great scarcity of food, and, hunger having its usual effect in producing vivid dreams, similar events frequently occurred. More than once the men declared in the morning that some absent men whom they named had come during the night, and had beaten, or otherwise maltreated them; and they insisted on much rubbing of the bruised parts of their bodies.' [1]

Another evidence in savage culture of the soul's having its own individuality, independently of the body, is the fact that a person through some accident may suddenly fall into a swoon, remaining to all outward appearance dead. When such a one, however, revives and is restored to consciousness, the savage is wont to exclaim that he died for a time until his soul was induced to return.

Hence Mr. Williams informs us [2] how the Fijians believe, when anyone dies or faints, that the soul may sometimes be brought back by calling after it; and in China, when a child is at the point of death, the mother will go into the garden and call its

---

[1] See further instances in Tylor's *Primitive Culture*, i. pp. 440, 441.

[2] *Fiji and the Fijians*, i. p. 242.

name, thinking thereby to bring back the wandering spirit. On this account divination and sorcery are extensively employed, and certain ' wise men' profess to have a knowledge of the mystic art of invoking souls that for some reason or other may have deserted their earthly tenement.[1]

The Rev. W. W. Gill, in his ' Myths and Songs from the South Pacific' (171–172), gives a curious instance of the wandering of the soul during life. ' At Uea, one of the Loyalty Islands, it was the custom formerly, when a person was very ill, to send for a man whose employment it was to restore souls to forsaken bodies. The soul doctor would at once collect his friends and assistants, to the number of twenty men, and as many women, and start off to the place where the family of the sick man was accustomed to bury their dead. Upon arriving there, the soul doctor and his male companions commenced playing the nasal flutes with which they had come provided, in order to entice back the spirit to its old tenement. The women assisted by a low whistling, supposed to be

[1] See Sir John Lubbock's *Origin of Civilisation and the Primitive Condition of Man*, 1870, p. 141.

irresistibly attractive to exile spirits. After a time
the entire procession proceeded towards the dwelling
of a sick person, flutes playing and the women
whistling all the time, leading back the truant
spirit. To prevent its possible escape, with their
palms open, they seemingly drove it along with
gentle violence and coaxing. On entering the
dwelling of the patient, the vagrant spirit was
ordered in loud tones at once to enter the body of
the sick man.'

In the same way, too, according to a popular
superstition among rude tribes, some favoured
persons are supposed to have the faculty of sending
forth their own souls on distant journeys, and
of acquiring, by this means, information for their
fellow creatures. Thus the Australian doctor
undergoes his initiation by such a journey, and
those who are not equally gifted by nature subject
themselves to various ordeals, so as to possess the
supposed faculty of releasing their souls for a time
from the body. From this curious phase of
superstition have arisen a host of legendary stories,
survivals of which are not confined to uncivilised
communities, but are found among the folk-tales

of most countries.   Mr. Baring Gould,[1] for instance, quotes a Scandinavian story in which the
Norse Chief Ingimund shut up three Finns in a
hut for three nights so that their souls might make
an expedition to Iceland, and bring back information of the nature of the country where he was
eventually to settle.   Accordingly their bodies soon
became rigid, they dismissed their souls on the
errand, and on awakening after three days, they
gave Ingimund an elaborate description of the
country in question.   We may compare this phase
of belief with that which is commonly known in
this country as second sight.[2]

Among the Hervey Islanders, Mr. Gill says: 'The
philosophy of sneezing is that the spirit having
gone travelling about—perchance on a visit to the
homes or burying-places of its ancestors—its return
to the body is naturally attended with some
difficulty and excitement, occasionally a tingling
and enlivening sensation all over the body.
Hence the various customary remarks addressed
to the returned spirit in different islands.   At

---

[1] *Werewolves*, p. 29.
[2] See Chapter on Second Sight.

Rarotonga, when a person sneezes, the bystanders exclaim, as though addressing a spirit, " Ha ! you have come back." '

Then there is the widespread Animistic belief, in accordance with which each man has several souls;—some lower races treating the breath, the dream ghost, and other appearances as being separate souls. This notion seems to have originated in the pulsation of the heart and arteries, which rude tribes regard as indications of independent life. Thus this fancy is met with in various parts of America and exists also in Madagascar. It prevails in Greenland, and the Fijians affirm that each man has two souls. This belief, too, is very old, evidences of its existence being clearly traceable among the ancient Greeks and Romans.[1] Indeed, classic literature affords ample proof of how the beliefs of modern savages are in many cases survivals of similar notions held in olden times by nations that had made considerable progress in civilisation.

[1] See Tylor's *Anthropology*, p. 345 ; and Sir John Lubbock's *Origin of Civilisation and the Primitive Condition of Man*, p. 141 ; and H. Spencer's *Principles of Sociology*, 1885, i. p. 777.

CHAPTER III

THE NATURE OF THE SOUL

It has from time immemorial been a widely recognised belief among mankind that the soul after death bears the likeness of its fleshly body, although opinions have differed largely as to its precise nature. But it would seem to be generally admitted that the soul set free from its earthly tenement is at once recognised by anyone to whom it may appear, reminding us of Lord Tennyson's dictum in 'In Memoriam':

> Eternal form shall still divide
> The eternal soul from all beside;
> And I shall know him when we meet.

Despite the fact that the disembodied spirit has been supposed to retain its familiar likeness, we find all kinds of strange ideas existing in most parts of the world as to what sort of a thing it really is when its condition of existence is so completely changed. Thus, according to a conception which has received in most ages very extensive credence, the soul has substantiality. This was the Greek idea of ghosts, and 'it is only,' writes Bishop Thirlwall, 'after their strength has been repaired by the blood of a slaughtered victim, that they recover reason and memory for a time, can recognise their living friends, and feel anxiety for those they have left on earth.' A similar notion of substantiality prevailed among the Hebrews, and, as Herbert Spencer points out, 'the stories about ghosts accepted among ourselves in past times involved the same thought. The ability to open doors, to clank chains, and make other noises implies considerable coherence of the ghost's substance.'[1] That this conception of the soul was not only received but taught, may be gathered from Tertullian, who says : 'The soul is material, composed of a substance different to the body, and particular. It has all the qualities of matter, but it is immortal. It has a figure like the body. It is born at the same time as the flesh, and receives an individu-

---

[1] *Principles of Sociology*, 1885, i. p. 174.

ality of character which it never loses.' He further describes [1] a vision or revelation of a certain Montanist prophetess, of the soul seen by her corporeally, thin and lucid, aerial in colour, and human in form. It is recorded, too, as an opinion of Epicurus, that 'they who say the soul is incorporeal talk folly, for it could neither do nor suffer anything were it such. It was the idea of materiality that caused the superstitious folk in years gone by to attribute to ghosts all kinds of weird and eccentric acts which could not otherwise be explained. And yet it has always been a puzzle in Animistic philosophy, how a ghost could be possessed at one moment of a corporeal body, and immediately afterwards vanish into immateriality, escaping sight and touch. But this strange ghost phenomenon is clearly depicted in sacred history, where we find substantiality, now insubstantiality, and now something between the two, described. Thus, as Herbert Spencer remarks,[2] 'the resuscitated Christ was described as having wounds that admitted of tactual examination, and yet as passing unimpeded

---

[1] *De Anima*, p. 9 ; see Tylor's *Primitive Culture*, i. p. 456.
[2] *Principles of Sociology*, 1885, i. p. 174.

through a closed door or through walls.' And, as he adds, the supernatural beings of the Hebrews generally, 'whether revived dead or not, were similarly conceived: here, angels dining with Abraham, or pulling Lot into the house, apparently possess complete corporeity; there, both angels and demons are spoken of as swarming invisibly in the surrounding air, thus being incorporeal; while elsewhere they are said to have wings, implying motion by mechanical action, and are represented as rubbing against, and wearing out, the dresses of Rabbins in the Synagogue.' All kinds of strange theories have been suggested by perplexed metaphysicians to account for this duplex nature of the disembodied soul; Calmet having maintained that 'immaterial souls have their own vaporous bodies, or occasionally have such vaporous bodies provided for them by supernatural means to enable them to appear as spectres, or that they possess the power of condensing the circumambient air into phantom-like bodies to invest themselves in.' [1]

In Fiji the soul is regarded quite as a material

[1] See Tylor's *Primitive Culture*, i. p. 457.

object, subject to the same laws as the living body, and having to struggle hard to gain the paradisaical Bolotu. Some idea, too, of the hardships it has to undergo in its material state may be gathered from the following passage in Dr. Letourneau's 'Sociology' (p. 251) : 'After death the soul of the Fijian goes first of all to the eastern extremity of *Vanna Levou*, and during this voyage it is most important that it should hold in its hand the soul of the tooth of a spermaceti whale, for this tooth ought to grow into a tree, and the soul of the poor human creature climbs up to the top of this tree. When it is perched up there it is obliged to await the arrival of the souls of his wives, who have been religiously strangled to serve as escort to their master. Unless all these and many other precautions are taken, the soul of the deceased Fijian remains mournfully seated upon the fatal bough until the arrival of the good Ravuyalo, who kills him once and for all, and leaves him without means of escape.'

According to another popular and widely accepted doctrine, the soul was supposed to be composed of a peculiar subtle substance, a kind of

vaporous materiality. The Choctaws have their
ghosts or wandering spirits which can speak and
are visible, but not tangible.[1] The Tongans conceived it as the aeriform part of the body, related
to it as the perfume and essence of a flower;
and the Greenlanders speak of it as pale and soft,
without flesh and bone, so that he who tries to grasp
it feels nothing he can take hold of. The Siamese
describe the soul as consisting of some strange
matter, invisible and untouchable. While Dr.
Tylor quotes a curious passage from Hampole,[2] in
which the soul, owing to the thinness of its substance, suffers all the more intense suffering in
purgatory :

> The soul is more tendre and nesche (soft)
> Than the bodi that hath bones and fleysche ;
> Thanne the soul that is so tendere of kinde,
> Mote nedis hure penaunce hardere y-finde,
> Than eni bodi that evere on live was.

Then there is the idea of the soul as a shadow,
a form of superstition which has given rise to
many quaint beliefs among uncultured tribes. The

---

[1] Dorman's *Primitive Superstitions*, p. 20.
[2] Tylor's *Primitive Culture*, i. p. 456.

Basutos, when walking by a river, take care not
to let their shadow fall on the water, lest a croco-
dile seize it, and draw the owner in. The Zulu
affirms that at death the shadow of a man in some
mysterious way leaves the body, and hence, it
is said, a corpse cannot cast a shadow. Certain
African tribes consider that 'as he dies, man leaves
a shadow behind him, but only for a short time.
The shade, or the mind, of the deceased remains,
they think, close to the grave where the corpse has
been buried. This shadow is generally evil-minded,
and they often fly away from it in changing their
place of abode.' [1] The Ojibways tell how one of their
chiefs died,[2] but while they were watching the body
on the third night, his shadow came back into it.
He sat up, and told them how he had travelled to
the River of Death, but was stopped there, and sent
back to his people.

Speaking of the human shadow in relation to
foundation sacrifices, we are reminded [3] how, according to many ancient Roumenian legends, 'every

---

[1] Letourneau's *Sociology*, p. 253.

[2] See Tylor's *Anthropology*, 1881, p. 344.

[3] *Nineteenth Century*, July 1885, pp. 143–144, ' Transylvanian
Superstitions,' by Madame Emily de Laszowska Gerard.

new church or otherwise important building became a human grave, as it was thought indispensable to its stability to wall in a living man or woman,
whose spirit henceforward haunts the place. In
later times this custom underwent some modifica-
tions, and it became usual, in place of a living man,
to wall in his shadow. This is done by measuring
the shadow of a person with a long piece of cord, or
a ribbon made of strips of reed, and interring this
measure instead of the person himself, who, unconscious victim of the spell thrown upon him, will
pine away and die within forty days. It is an
indispensable condition to the success of this proceeding that the chosen victim be ignorant of the
part he is playing, therefore careless passers by
near a building may often hear the cry, warning,
" Beware, lest they take thy shadow ! " So deeply
engrained is this superstition, that not long ago
there were professional shadow-traders, who made
it their business to provide architects with the
necessary victims for securing their walls.' ' Of
course, the man whose shadow is thus interred
must die,' argues the Roumenian, ' but as he is
unaware of his doom, he does not feel any pain or

anxiety, and so it is less cruel than walling in a living man.'

At the present day in Russia, as elsewhere, a shadow is a common metaphor for the soul,[1] whence it arises that there are persons there who object to having their silhouettes taken, fearing that if they do, they will die before the year is out. In the same way, a man's reflected image is supposed to be in communion with his inner self, and, therefore, children are often forbidden to look at themselves in a glass, lest their sleep should be disturbed at night. It may be added, too, as Mr. Clodd points out, that in the barbaric belief of the loss of the shadow being baleful, 'we have the germ of the mediæval legends of shadowless men, and of tales of which Chamisso's "Story of Peter Schlemihl" is a type.'[2] Hence the dead in purgatory recognised that Dante was alive when they saw that, unlike theirs, his figure cast a shadow on the ground. But, as Mr. Fiske observes,[3] 'the theory which identifies the soul with the shadow, and supposes the shadow to depart with the sick-

[1] Ralston's *Songs of the Russian People*, p. 117.
[2] *Myths and Dreams*, 1885, p. 184.
[3] *Myths and Myth-makers*, 1873, p. 225.

ness and death of the body, would seem liable to be attended with some difficulties in the way of verification, even to the dim intelligence of the savage.'

. Again, another doctrine promulgated under various forms in Animistic philosophy is, that the existence and condition of the soul depend upon the manner of death. The Australian, for instance, not content with slaying his enemy, cuts off the right thumb of the corpse, so that the departed soul may be incapacitated from throwing a spear; and even the half-civilised Chinese prefer the punishment of crucifixion to that of decapitation, that their souls may not wander headless about the spirit world. Similarly the Indians of Brazil 'believe that the dead arrive in the other world wounded or hacked to pieces, in fact, just as they left this.' European folk-lore has preserved, more or less, the same idea, and the ghost of the murdered person often appears displaying the wounds which were the cause of the death of the body. Many a weird and ghastly ghost tale still current in different parts of the country gives the most blood-curdling details of such apparitions; and although, in certain cases, a century or so is said to

D

have elapsed since they first made their appearance,
they still bear the marks of violence and cruelty
which were done to them by a murderous hand
when in the flesh. An old story tells how, when
the Earl of Cornwall met the fetch of William
Rufus carried on a very large black goat, all black
and naked, across the Bodmin moors, he saw that
it was wounded through the breast. Robert ad-
jured the goat, in the name of the Holy Trinity, to
tell what it was he carried so strangely. He
answered, 'I am carrying your king to judgment;
yea, that tyrant, William Rufus, for I am an evil
spirit, and the revenger of his malice which he bore
to the Church of God. It was I that did cause this
slaughter.' Having spoken, the spectre vanished.
Soon afterwards Robert heard that at that very
hour the king had been slain in the New Forest by
the arrow of William Tirell.[1] This idea corresponds with what was believed in early times, for
Ovid [2] tells us how

> Umbra cruenta Remi visa est assistere lecto.

Again, some modes of death are supposed to

---

[1] See Hunt's *Popular Romances of the West of England*, p. 373.
[2] *Fasti*, v. 457.

kill not only the body but also the soul. 'Among
all primitive peoples,' writes Mr. Dorman,[1] 'where
a belief in the renewal of life, or the resurrection,
exists, the peace and happiness of the spirit, which
remains in or about the body, depend upon
success in preventing the body, or any part of it,
from being devoured or destroyed in any manner.'
The New Zealanders believed that the man who
was eaten was annihilated, both body and soul; and
one day a bushman, who was a magician, having put
to death a woman, dashed the head of the corpse
to pieces with large stones, buried her, and made a
large fire over the grave, for fear, as he explained,
lest she should rise again and trouble him.   The
same idea, remarks Sir John Lubbock,[2] evidently
influenced the Californian, who did not dispute the
immortality of the whites, who buried their dead,
but could not believe the same of his own people,
because they were in the habit of burning them,
maintaining that when they were burnt they
became annihilated.

It may be added, too, that the belief underlying

[1] *Primitive Superstitions*, p. 195.

[2] *The Origin of Civilisation, and the Primitive Condition of
Man*, 1870, p. 140; see Letourneau's *Sociology*, p. 263.

D 2

the burial customs of most American tribes was
to preserve the bones of the dead, the opinion
being that the soul, or a part of it, dwelt in the
bones. These, indeed, were the seeds which,
planted in the earth, or preserved unbroken in safe
places, would in time put on once again a garb of
flesh, and germinate into living human beings.[1]
This Animistic belief has been amply illustrated by
mythology and superstition. In an Aztec legend,
after one of the destructions of the world, Zoloti
descended to the realm of the dead, and brought
thence a bone of the perished race. This, sprinkled
with blood, grew on the fourth day into a youth,
the father of the present race. The practice of pul-
verising the bones of the dead, practised by some
tribes, and of mixing them with the food, was
defended by asserting that the souls of the dead
remained in the bones, and lived again in the
living.[2] The Peruvians were so careful lest any
of the body should be lost, that they preserved
even the parings of the nails and clippings of the
hair—expecting the mummified body to be inhabited by its soul; while the Choctaws maintain

---

[1] Brinton's *Myths of the New World*, 1868, p. 257.
[2] Dorman's *Primitive Superstitions*, 1881, p. 193.

that the spirits of the dead will return to the bones
in the bone mounds, and flesh will knit together
their loose joints. Even the lower animals were
supposed to follow the same law. 'Hardly any of
the American hunting-tribes,' writes Mr. Brinton,
'before their original manners were vitiated by
foreign influence, permitted the bones of game
slain in the chase to be broken, or left carelessly
about the encampment; they were collected in
heaps, or thrown into the water.' The Yuricares
of Bolivia carried this belief to such an inconvenient
extent that they carefully put by even small fish
bones, saying that unless this was done the fish
and game would disappear from the country. The
traveller on the western prairies often notices the
buffalo skulls, countless numbers of which bleach
on those vast plains, arranged in circles and
symmetrical piles by the careful hands of the
native hunters. The explanation for this practice
is that these osseous relics of the dead 'contain
the spirits of the slain animals, and that some
time in the future they will rise from the earth,
re-clothe themselves with flesh, and stock the
prairies anew.'

As a curious illustration of how every spiritual

conception was materialised in olden times, may
be quoted the fanciful conception of the weight
of the soul.   Thus in mediæval literature the
angel in the Last Judgment ' was constantly represented weighing the souls in a literal balance,
while devils clinging to the scales endeavoured to
disturb the equilibrium.' [1]   But how seriously such
tests of the weight of the soul have been received,
may be gathered from the cases now and then
forthcoming of this materialistic notion of its
nature.   These, writes Dr. Tylor,[2] range from the
' conception of a Basuto diviner that the late queen
had been bestriding his shoulders, and he never
felt such a weight in his wife, to Glanvil's story of
David Hunter, the neatherd, who lifted up the old
woman's ghost, and she felt just like a bag of
feathers in his arms; or the pathetic superstition
that the dead mother's coming back in the night
to suckle the baby she has left on earth, may be
known by the hollow pressed down in the bed
where she lay, and at last down to the alleged
modern spiritualistic reckoning of the weight of a

[1] See Lecky's *Rationalism in Europe*, 1870, i. p. 340; cf.
Maury's *Légendes Pieuses*, p. 124.

[2] *Primitive Culture*, i. p. 455.

human soul at from three to four ounces.' But
the heavy tread which occasionally makes the
stairs creak and boards resound has been in-
stanced as showing that, whatever may be the
real nature of the soul, it is capable of materialising
itself at certain times, and of displaying an amount
of force and energy in no way dissimilar to that
which is possessed when living in the flesh.

Just, too, as souls are possessed of visible forms,
so they are generally supposed to have voices.
According to Dr. Tylor,[1] 'men who perceive evidently that souls do talk when they present themselves in dream or vision, naturally take for
granted at once the objective reality of the ghostly
voice, and of the ghostly form from which it proceeds;' and this principle, he adds, 'is involved in
the series of narratives of spiritual communications
with living men, from savagery onward to civilisation.' European folk-lore represents ghostly
voices as resembling their material form during
life, although less audible. With savage races the
spirit voice is described 'as a low murmur, chirp,
or whistle.' Thus, when the ghosts of the New

---

[1] See Andrew Lang's *Myth, Ritual, Religion*, i. p. 108.

Zealanders address the living, they speak in whistling tones. The sorcerer among the Zulus 'hears the spirits who speak by whistlings speaking to him.' Whistling is the language of the Caledonians, and the Algonquin Indians of North America ' could hear the shadow souls of the dead chirp like crickets.' As far back as the time of Homer, the ghosts make a similar sound, 'and even as bats flit gibbering in the secret place of a wonderful cavern, even so the souls gibbered as they fared together.' [1]

Ghosts, when they make their appearance, are generally supposed, as already noticed, to have a perfect resemblance, in every respect, to the deceased person. Their faces appear the same —except that they are usually paler than when alive—and the ordinary expression is described by writers on the subject as ' more in sorrow than in anger.' Thus, when the ghost of Banquo rises and takes a seat at the table, Macbeth says to the apparition—

> Never shake
> Thy gory locks at me.

---

[1] *Odyssey*, xxiv.

And Horatio tells Marcellus how the ghost of Hamlet's father was not only fully armed, but—

> So frown'd he once, when in angry parle,
> He smote the sledded Polacks on the ice.

The folk-lore stories from most parts of the world coincide in this idea. It was recorded of the Indians of Brazil by one of the early European visitors that 'they believe that the dead arrive in the other world, wounded or hacked to pieces, in fact, just as they left this;'[1] a statement which reminds us of a ghost described by Mrs. Crowe,[2] who, on appearing after death, was seen to have the very small-pox marks which had disfigured its countenance when in the flesh.

As in life, so in death, it would seem that there are different classes of ghosts—the princely, the aristocratic, the genteel, and the common. The vulgar class, it is said, delight to haunt 'in grave-yards, dreary lanes, ruins, and all sorts of dirty dark holes and corners.' An amusing anecdote illustrative of this belief was related by the daughter of 'the celebrated Mrs. S.' [Siddons?] who told Mrs.

[1] Tylor's *Primitive Culture*, i. p. 451.
[2] *Night Side of Nature.*

Crowe that when her parents were travelling in
Wales they stayed some days at Oswestry, and
lodged in a house which was in a very dirty and
neglected state, yet all night long the noise of
scrubbing and moving furniture made it impossible to sleep. The servants did little or no
work, for they had to sit up with their mistress to
allay her fears. The neighbours said that this
person had killed an old servant, hence the
disturbance and her terror. Mr. and Mrs. S——
coming in suddenly one day, heard her cry out,
'Are you there again ? Fiend! go away !' But
numerous tales similar to the above are still current in different parts of the country; and from
time to time are duly chronicled in the local press.

CHAPTER IV

THE UNBURIED DEAD

THE Greeks believed that such as had not received funeral rites would be excluded from Elysium. The younger Pliny tells the tale of a haunted house at Athens, in which a ghost played all kinds of pranks owing to the funeral rites having been neglected. It is still a deep-rooted belief that when the mortal remains of the soul have not been honoured with proper burial, it will walk. The ghosts of unburied persons not possessing the *obolus* or fee due to Charon, the ferryman of Styx, and Acheron, were unable to obtain a lodging or place of rest. Hence they were compelled to wander about the banks of the river for a hundred years, when the portitor, or 'ferryman of hell,' passed them over *in formâ pauperis*. The famous tragedy of 'Antigone' by Sophocles owes much of its interest to this popular belief on the subject. In most countries all kinds of strange tales are told of ghosts ceaselessly wandering about the earth, owing to their bodies, for some reason or another, having been left unburied.

There is a well known German ghost, the Bleeding Nun. This was a nun who, after committing many crimes and debaucheries, was assassinated by one of her paramours and denied the rites of burial. After this, she used to haunt the castle where she was murdered, with her bleeding wounds. On one occasion, a young lady of the castle, willing to elope with her lover, in order to make her flight easier, personated the bleeding nun. Unfortunately the lover, whilst expecting his lady under this disguise, eloped with the spectre herself, who presented herself to him and haunted him afterwards.[1]

Comparative folk-lore, too, shows how very widely diffused is this notion. It is believed by the Iroquois of North America, that unless the rites of burial are performed, the spirits of the dead hover for a time upon the earth in great unhappiness. On this account every care is taken to procure the

[1] Yardley's *Supernatural in Fiction*, p. 93.

bodies of those slain in battle. Certain Brazilian
tribes suppose that the spirits of the dead have no
rest till burial, and among the Ottawas, a great
famine was thought to have been produced on
account of the failure of some of their tribesmen
to perform the proper burial rites. After having
repaired their fault they were blessed with abund-
ance of provisions. The Australians went so far as
to say that the spirits of the unburied dead became
dangerous and malignant demons. Similarly, the
Siamese dread, as likely to do them some harm, the
ghosts of those who have not been buried with
proper rites, and the Karens have much the same
notion. According to the Polynesians, the spirit of
a dead man could not reach the sojourn of his
ancestors, and of the gods, unless the sacred funereal rites were performed over his body. If he
was buried with no ceremony, or simply thrown
into the sea, the spirit always remained in the
body.[1]

Under one form or another, the same belief
may be traced in most parts of the world, and, as
Dr. Tylor points out,[2] 'in mediæval Europe the

[1] Letourneau's *Sociology*, p. 257.

[2] *Primitive Culture*, ii. p. 29; Douce's *Illustrations of
Shakespeare*, pp. 450, 451.

classic stories of ghosts that haunt the living till
laid by rites of burial pass here and there into new
legends where, under a changed dispensation, the
doleful wanderer now asks christian burial in consecrated earth.' Shakespeare alludes to this old
idea, and in 'Titus Andronicus' (i. 2) Lucius,
speaking of the unburied sons of Titus, says:

> Give us the proudest prisoner of the Goths,
> That we may hew his limbs, and on a pile
> *Ad manes fratrum* sacrifice his flesh,
> Before this earthly prison of their bones;
> That so the shadows be not unappeas'd,
> Nor we disturb'd with prodigies on earth.

Hence the appearance of a spirit, in times
past, was often regarded as an indication that
some foul deed had been done, on which account
Horatio in 'Hamlet' (i. 1) says to the ghost:

> If there be any good thing to be done
> That may to thee do ease, and grace to me,
> Speak to me.

In the narrative of the sufferings of Byron
and the crew of H.M. ship 'Wager,' on the
coast of South America, we find a good illustration
of the superstitious dread attaching to an unburied

corpse. ' The reader will remember the shameful
rioting, mutiny, and recklessness which disgraced
the crew of the " Wager," nor will he forget the
approach to cannibalism and murder on one
occasion. These men had just returned from a
tempestuous navigation, in which their hopes of
escape had been crushed, and now what thoughts
disturbed their rest—what serious consultations
were they which engaged the attention of these
sea-beaten men ? Long before Cheap's Bay had
been left, the body of a man had been found on a
hill named " Mount Misery." He was supposed
to have been murdered by some of the first gang
who left the island. The body had never been
buried, and to such neglect did the men now
ascribe the storms which had lately afflicted them ;
nor would they rest until the remains of their
comrade were placed beneath the earth, when each
evidently felt as if some dreadful spell had been
removed from his spirit.' Stories of this kind are
common everywhere, and are interesting as showing
how widely scattered is this piece of superstition.

In Sweden the ravens, which scream by midnight in forest swamps and wild moors, are held

to be the ghosts of murdered men, whose bodies
have been hidden in those spots by their undetected
murderers, and not had Christian burial.[1]   In
many a Danish legend the spirit of a strand
varsler, or coast-guard, appears, walking his beat
as when alive. Such ghosts were not always
friendly, and it was formerly considered dangerous
to pass along ' such unconsecrated beaches, believed
to be haunted by the spectres of unburied corpses
of drowned people.' [2]

The reason, it is asserted, why many of our
old castles and country seats have their traditional
ghost, is owing to some unfortunate person having
been secretly murdered in days past, and to his
or her body having been allowed to remain without the rites of burial. So long as such a crime
is unavenged, and the bones continue unburied,
it is impossible, we are told, for the outraged spirit
to keep quiet. Numerous ghost stories are still
circulated throughout the country of spirits wandering on this account, some of which, however,
are based purely on legendary romance.

[1] Henderson's *Folk-lore of Northern Counties*, p. 126, note.
[2] Thorpe's *Northern Mythology*, ii. p. 166.

But when the unburied body could not be found, and the ghost wandered, the missing man was buried in effigy, for, as it has been observed, 'according to all the laws of primitive logic, an effigy is every bit as good as its original. Therefore, when a dead man is buried in effigy, with all due formality, that man is dead and buried beyond a doubt, and his ghost is as harmless as it is in the nature of ghosts to be.' But sometimes such burial by proxy was premature, for the man was not really dead; and if he declined to consider himself as such, the question arose, was he alive, or was he dead? The solution adopted was that he might be born again and take a new lease of life. 'And so it was, he was put out to nurse, he was dressed in long clothes—in short, he went through all the stages of a second childhood. But before this pleasing experience could take place, he had to overcome the initial difficulty of entering his own house, for the door was ghost-proof. There was no other way but by the chimney, and down the chimney he came.' We may laugh at such credulity, but many of the ghost-beliefs of the present day are not less absurd.

E

CHAPTER V

WHY GHOSTS WANDER

A VARIETY of causes have been supposed to prevent
the dead resting in the grave, for persons 'dying
with something on their mind,' to use the popular
phrase, cannot enjoy the peace of the grave; oftentimes some trivial anxiety, or some frustrated com-
munication, preventing the uneasy spirit flinging
off the bonds that bind it to earth. Wickedness in
their lifetime has been commonly thought to cause
the souls of the impenitent to revisit the scenes
where their evil deeds were done. It has long been
a widespread idea that as such ghosts are too bad
for a place in either world, they are, therefore,
compelled to wander on the face of the earth
homeless and forlorn. We have shown in another
chapter how, according to a well-known superstition, the *ignes fatui*, which appear by night in

swampy places, are the souls of the dead—men who during life were guilty of fraudulent and other wicked acts. Thus a popular belief reminds us [1] how, when an unjust relative has secreted the title-deeds in order to get possession of the estate himself, he finds no rest in the other world till the title-deeds are given back, and the estate is restored to the rightful heir. Come must the spirit of such an unrighteous man to the room where he concealed the title-deeds surreptitiously removed from the custody of the person to whose charge they were entrusted. 'A dishonest milkwoman at Shrewsbury is condemned,' writes Miss Jackson in her ' Shropshire Folk-lore ' [2] (p. 120), 'to wander up and down "Lady Studley's Diche " in the Raven Meadow—now the Smithfield—constantly repeating:

" Weight and measure sold I never,
Milk and water sold I ever." '

The same rhyme is current at Burslem, in the Staffordshire Potteries. The story goes that ' Old Molly Lee,' who used to sell milk there, and had the reputation of being a witch, was supposed to be

[1] See Gregor's *Folk-lore of North-East of Scotland*, p. 68.
[2] Edited by C. S. Burne.

seen after her death going about the streets with
her milk-pail on her head repeating it.   Miss
Jackson further relates how a mid-Shropshire
squire of long ago was compelled to wander about
in a homeless state on account of his wickedness.
Murderers cannot rest, and even although they
may escape justice in this life, it is supposed that
their souls find no peace in the grave, but under a
curse are compelled to walk to and fro until they
have, in some degree, done expiation for their crimes.
Occasionally, it is said, their plaintive moans may
be heard as they bewail the harm done by them to
the innocent, weary of being allowed no cessation
from their ceaseless wandering—a belief which reminds us of the legend of the Wandering Jew, and
the many similar stories that have clustered round it.

In 'Blackwood's Magazine' for August 1818
this passage occurs: 'If any author were so mad
as to think of framing a tragedy upon the subject
of that worthy vicar of Warblington, Hants, who
was reported about a century ago to have strangled
his own children, and to have walked after his death,
he would assuredly be laughed to scorn by a London
audience.'   But a late rector of Warblington in-

formed a correspondent of 'Notes and Queries' (4th S. xi. 188), 'it was quite true that his house was said to be haunted by the ghost of a former rector, supposed to be the Rev. Sebastian Pitfield, who held the living in 1677.' A strong prejudice against hanging prevails in Wales, owing to troublesome spirits being let loose, and wandering about, to the annoyance of the living.

The spirits of suicides wander, and hence cross-roads in various parts of the country are oftentimes avoided after dark, on account of being haunted by headless and other uncanny apparitions. The same belief exists abroad. The Sioux are of opinion that suicide is punished in the land of spirits by the ghosts being doomed for ever to drag the tree on which they hang themselves; and for this reason they always suspend themselves to as small a tree as can possibly sustain their weight.

With the Chinese the souls of suicides are specially obnoxious, and they consider that the very worst penalty that can befall a soul is the sight of its former surroundings. Thus, it is supposed that, in the case of the wicked man, 'they only see their homes as if they were near them;

they see their last wishes disregarded, everything
upside down, their substance squandered, strangers
possess the old estate ; in their misery the dead
man's family curse him, his children become corrupt,
land is gone, the wife sees her husband tortured,
the husband sees his wife stricken down with
mortal disease; even friends forget, but some, perhaps, for the sake of bygone times, may stroke the
coffin and let fall a tear, departing with a cold
smile.' [1]   But, as already noticed, the same idea, in
a measure, extends to the West, for in this country
it has long been a popular belief that the ghosts of
the wicked are forced to periodically rehearse their
sinful acts.   Thus, the murderer's ghost is seen in
vain trying to wash out the indelible blood-stains,
and the thief is supposed to be continually counting
and recounting the money which came into his
possession through dishonest means.   The ghost
is dogged and confronted with the hideousness of
his iniquities, and the young woman who slew her
lover in a fit of jealous passion is seen, in an
agonised expression, holding the fatal weapon.   But

---

[1] Countess Evelyn Martinengo-Cesaresco, 1886, *Essays in the
Study of Folk-songs*, p. 8.

such unhappy spirits have, in most cases, been put to silence by being laid, instances of which are given elsewhere; and in other cases they have finally disappeared with the demolition of certain houses which for years they may have tenanted.

On the other hand, the spirits of the good are said sometimes to return to earth for the purpose of either succouring the innocent, or avenging the guilty.

'Those who come again to punish their friends' wrongs,' writes Miss Jackson, in her 'Shropshire Folk-lore' (p. 119), 'generally appear exactly as in life, unchanged in form or character. A certain well-to-do man who lived in the west of Shropshire within living memory, left his landed property to his nephew, and a considerable fortune to his two illegitimate daughters, the children of his house-keeper. Their mother, well provided for, was at his death turned adrift by the nephew. Her daughters, however, continued to live in their old home with their cousin. A maid-servant who entered the family shortly after (and who is our informant) noticed an elderly man often walking in the garden in broad daylight, dressed in old-fashioned clothes, with breeches and white stockings. He

never spoke, and never entered the house, though
he always went towards it. Asking who he was,
she was coolly told, "Oh, that is only our old father!"
No annoyance seems to have been caused by the
poor old ghost, with one exception, that the clothes
were every night stripped off the bed of the two
unnatural daughters.'

German folk-lore tells how slain warriors rise
again to help their comrades to victory, and how a
mother will visit her old home to look after her injured and forsaken children, and elsewhere the same
idea is extensively believed. In China, the ghosts
which are animated by a sense of duty are frequently seen : at one time they seek to serve virtue
in distress, and at another they aim to restore
wrongfully-held treasure. Indeed, as it has been
observed, 'one of the most powerful as well as the
most widely diffused of the people's ghost stories
is that which treats of the persecuted child whose
mother comes out of the grave to succour him.'[1]
And there perhaps can be no more gracious privilege
allotted to immortal spirits than that of beholding
those beloved of them in mortal life :

[1] *Study of Folk-songs*, p. 2.

I am still near,
Watching the smiles I prized on earth,
Your converse mild, your blameless mirth.[1]

As it has been observed, no oblivious draught
has been given the departed soul, but the remembrance of its earthly doings cleaves to it, and
this is why ghosts are always glad to see the places
frequented by them while on earth. In Galicia,
directly after a man's burial, his spirit takes to
wandering by nights about the old home, and
watching that no evil befalls his heirs.[2]

Occasionally the spirit returns to fulfil a promise
as in compacts, to which reference is made in
another chapter. The reappearance of a lover, ' in
whose absence his beloved has died, is a subject
that has been made use of by the folk-poets of
every country, and nothing,' it is added, ' can be
more characteristic of the nationalities to which
they belong than the divergences which mark their
treatment of it.[3] Another cause of ghosts wandering is founded upon a superstition as to the inter-

[1] *Study of Folk-songs*, p. 8.
[2] Ralston's *Songs of the Russian People*, p. 121.
[3] *Study of Folk-songs*, p. 21.

change of love-tokens, an illustration of which
we find in the old ballad of 'William's Ghost':

> There came a ghost to Marjorie's door,
>   Wi' many a grievous maen,
> And aye he tirl'd at the pin,
>   But answer made she nane.
>
> 'Oh, sweet Marjorie! oh, dear Marjorie!
>   For faith and charitie,
> Give me my faith and troth again,
>   That I gied once to thee.'
>
> 'Thy faith and troth I'll ne'er gie thee,
>   Nor yet shall our true love twin,
> Till you tak' me to your ain ha' house,
>   And wed me wi' a ring.'
>
> 'My house is but yon lonesome grave,
>   Afar out o'er yon lee,
> And it is but my spirit, Marjorie,
>   That's speaking unto thee.'[1]

She followed the spirit to the grave, where it
lay down and confessed that William had betrayed
three maidens whom he had promised to marry,
and in consequence of this misdemeanour he could
not rest in his grave until she released him of his
vows to marry her. On learning this, Marjorie at
once released him.

[1] *Folk-lore Record*, 1879, iii. pp. 111, 112.

> Then she'd taen up her white, white hand,
>   And struck him on the breist,
> Saying, 'Have ye again your faith and troth,
>   And I wish your soul good rest.'

In another ballad, 'Clerk Sanders,' there is a further illustration of the same belief. The instances, says Mr. Napier, differ, but 'the probability is that the ballad quoted above and "Clerk Sanders" are both founded on the same story. Clerk Sanders was the son of an earl, who courted the king's daughter, Lady Margaret. They loved each other even in the modern sense of loving too well. Margaret had seven brothers, who suspected an intrigue, and they came upon them together in bed and killed Clerk Sanders, whose ghost soon after came to Margaret's window. The ballad, which contains much curious folk-lore, runs thus :

> 'Oh! are ye sleeping, Margaret?' he says,
>   'Or are ye waking presentlie?
> Give me my faith and troth again,
>   I wot, true love, I gied to thee.
>
> 'I canna rest, Margaret,' he says,
>   'Down in the grave where I must be,
> Till ye give me my faith and troth again,
>   I wot, true love, I gied to thee.'

---

[1] *Folk-lore Record*, 1879, iii. pp. 111, 112.

‘ Thy faith and troth thou shalt na get,
    And our true love shall never twin,
Until ye tell what comes o’ women,
    I wot, who die in strong travailing.’

‘ Their beds are made in the heavens high,
    Down at the foot of our Lord’s knee,
Weel set about wi’ gilliflowers,
    I trow sweet company for to see.

‘ Oh, cocks are crowing a merry midnight,
    I wot the wild fowls are boding day;
The psalms of heaven will soon be sung,
    And I, ere now, will be missed away.’

Then she has ta’en a crystall wand,
    And she has stroken her throth thereon;
She has given it him out of the shot-window,
    Wi’ many a sigh and heavy goan.

‘ I thank ye, Margaret; I thank ye, Margaret;
    And aye, I thank ye heartilie;
Gin ever the dead come for the quick,
    Be sure, Margaret, I’ll come for thee.’

Then up and crew the milk-white cock,
    And up and crew the gray;
Her lover vanished in the air,
    And she gaed weeping away.

Madness, again, during life, is said occasionally
to produce restlessness after death. 'Parson
Digger, at Condover,' remarked an old woman to
Miss Jackson,[1] 'he came again. He wasn't right
in his head, and if you met him he couldn't speak
to you sensibly. But when he was up in the pulpit
he'd preach, oh! beautiful!' In Hungary, there
are the spirits of brides who die on their wedding-
day before consummation of marriage. They are
to be seen at moonlight, where cross-roads meet.
And it is a Danish tradition that a corpse cannot
have peace in the grave when it is otherwise than
on its back. According to a Scotch belief, excessive grief for a departed friend, 'combined with a
want of resignation to the will of Providence, had
the effect of keeping the spirit from rest in the
other world. Rest could be obtained only by the
spirit coming back, and comforting the mourner by
the assurance that it was in a state of blessedness.'[2]
The ghosts of those, again, who had some grievance
or other in life are supposed to wander. The
Droitwich Canal, in passing through Salwarpe,

[1] *Shropshire Folk-lore*, p. 119.
[2] Gregor's *Folk-lore of North-East of Scotland*, p. 69.

Worcestershire, is said to have cut off a slice of a
large old half-timbered house, in revenge for which
act of mutilation, the ghost of a former occupier
revisited his old haunts, and affrighted the domestics.

Once more, according to another Animistic
conception which holds a prominent place in the
religion of uncultured tribes, the soul at death
passes through some transitionary stages, finally
developing into a demon. In China and India
this theory is deeply rooted among the people,
and hence it is customary to offer sacrifices to
the souls of the departed by way of propitiation,
as otherwise they are supposed to wander to
and fro on the earth, and to exert a malignant
influence on even their dearest friends and relatives.
Diseases, too, are regarded as often being caused
by the wandering souls of discontented relatives,
who in some cases are said to re-appear as
venomous snakes.[1] Owing to this belief, a system
of terror prevails amongst many tribes, which is
only allayed by constantly appeasing departed
souls. Believing in superstitions of this kind,

[1] Sir John Lubbock's *Origin of Civilisation*, p. 134.

it is easy to understand how the uncivilised mind
readily lays hold of the doctrine that the souls
of the departed, angry and enraged at having
had death thrust on them, take every opportunity
of wandering about, and annoying the living, and
of wreaking their vengeance on even those most
nearly related to them. In this phase of savage
belief may be traced the notion of Manes worship
found under so many forms in foreign countries.
Indeed, once granted that the departed soul has
power to affect the living, then this power attributed to it is only one of degree. With this belief,
too, may be compared the modern one of worship of
the dead; and as Dr. Tylor remarks: 'A crowd of
saints, who were once men and women, now form an
inferior order of deities active in the affairs of men,
and receiving from them reverence and prayer,
thus coming strictly under the definition of
Manes.' [1] A further illustration may be adduced
in the patron deities of particular trades and
crafts, and in the imposing array of saints supposed to be specially interested in the particular
requirements of mankind.

[1] *Primitive Culture*, ii. p. 120.

CHAPTER VI

GHOSTS OF THE MURDERED

IT is commonly supposed that the spirits of those
who have suffered a violent or untimely death
are baneful and malicious beings; for, as Meiners
conjectures in his 'History of Religions,' they were
driven unwillingly from their bodies, and have
carried into their new existence an angry longing
for revenge.   Hence, in most countries, there is a
dread of such harmful spirits ; and, among the
Sioux Indians the fear of the ghost's vengeance
has been known to act as a check to murder.
The avenging ghost often comes back to convict
the guilty, and appears in all kinds of strange
and uncanny ways.   Thus the ghost of Hamlet's
father (i. 5) says :

> I am thy father's spirit,
> Doomed for a certain time to walk the night,
> And for the day confined to fast in fires,
> Till the foul crimes, done in my days of nature,
> Are burnt and purged away.

Till the crime has been duly expiated, not only is the spirit supposed to be kept from its desired rest, but it flits about the haunts of the living, that, by its unearthly molestation, it may compel them to make every possible reparation for the cruel wrong done. Any attempt to lay such a ghost is ineffectual, and no exorcist's art can induce it to discontinue its unwelcome visits. Comparative folk-lore proves how universal is this belief, for one of the most popular ghost stories in folk-tales is that which treats of the murdered person whose ghost hovers about the earth with no gratification but to terrify the living.

The Chinese have a dread of the wandering spirits of persons who have come to an unfortunate end. At Canton, in 1817, the wife of an officer of Government had occasioned the death of two female domestic slaves, from some jealous suspicion it was supposed of her husband's conduct towards the girls; and, in order to screen herself from the consequences, she suspended the bodies by the neck, with a view to its being construed into an act of suicide. But the conscience of the woman tormented her to such a degree that she became insane, and at times

F

personated the victims of her cruelty; or, as the Chinese supposed, the spirits of the murdered girls possessed her, and utilised her mouth to declare her own guilt. In her ravings she tore her clothes, and beat her own person with all the fury of madness; after which she would recover her senses for a time, when it was supposed the demons quitted her, but only to return with greater frenzy, which took place a short time previous to her death.[1] According to Mr. Dennys,[2] the most common form of Chinese ghost story is that wherein the ghost seeks to bring to justice the murderer who shuffled off its mortal coil.

The following tale is told of a haunted hill in the country of the Assiniboins. Many summers ago a party of Assiniboins pounced on a small band of Crees in the neighbourhood of Wolverine Knoll. Among the victors was the former wife of one of the vanquished, who had been previously captured by her present husband. This woman directed every effort in the fight to take the life of her first husband, but he escaped, and concealed himself on

[1] *The Chinese*: J. F. Davis, 1836, ii. pp. 139, 140.
[2] *Folk-lore of China*, p. 73.

this knoll.   Wolverine—for this was his name—fell
asleep, and was discovered by this virago, who
killed him, and presented his scalp to her Assini-
boin husband.   The knoll was afterwards called
after him.   The Indians assert that the ghosts of the
murderess and her victim are often to be seen from
a considerable distance struggling together on the
very summit of the height.[1]

The Siamese ' fear as unkindly spirits the souls
of such as died a violent death, or were not buried
with the proper rites, and who, desiring expiation,
invisibly terrify their descendants.'[2]   In the same
way, the Karens say that the ghosts of those who
wander on the earth are the spirits of such as died
by violence; and in Australia we hear of the souls
of departed natives walking about because their
death has not been expiated by the avenger of blood.

The Hurons of America, lest the spirits of the
victims of their torture should remain around the
huts of their murderers from a thirst of vengeance,
strike every place with a staff in order to oblige
them to depart.   An old traveller mentions the same

[1] See Dorman's *Primitive Superstitions*, p. 304.
[2] *Primitive Culture*, ii. p. 28.

custom among the Iroquois : ' At night we heard
a great noise, as if the houses had all fallen ; but it
was only the inhabitants driving away the ghosts
of the murdered ; ' with which we may compare the
belief of the Ottawas : On one occasion, when noises
of the loudest and most inharmonious kind were
heard in a certain village, it was ascertained that a
battle had been lately fought between the Ottawas
and Kickapods, and that the object of all this noise
was to prevent the ghosts of the dead combatants
from entering the village.[1]

European folk-lore still clings to this old belief,
and, according to the current opinion in Norway,[2]
the soul of a murdered person willingly hovers
around the spot where his body is buried, and
makes its appearance for the purpose of calling
forth vengeance on the murderer.

The idea that, in cases of hidden murder, the
buried dead cannot rest in their graves is often
spoken in our old ballad folk-lore. Thus, in the
ballad of the ' Jew's Daughter,' in Motherwell's
collection, a youth was murdered, and his body

[1] See Dorman's *Primitive Superstitions*, 1880, pp. 19, 20.
[2] Thorpe's *Northern Mythology*, ii. p. 19.

thrown into a draw-well, and he speaks to his
mother from the well:

> She ran away to the deep draw-well,
>   And she fell down on her knee,
> Saying, ' Bonnie Sir Hugh, oh, pretty Sir Hugh,
>   I pray ye, speak to me! '
> ' Oh! the lead it is wondrous heavy, mother,
>   The well, it is wondrous deep,
> The little penknife sticks in my throat,
>   And I downa to ye speak.
> But lift me out of this deep draw-well,
>   And bury me in yon churchyard;
> Put a Bible at my head,' he says,
>   ' And a Testament at my feet,
> And pen and ink at every side,
>   And I will lay still and sleep.
> And go to the back of Maitland town,
>   Bring me my winding sheet;
> For it's at the back of Maitland town
>   That you and I shall meet.'

The eye of superstition, we are told, sees such
ghosts sometimes as white spectres in the churchyard, where they stop horses, terrify people, and
make a disturbance; and occasionally as executed
criminals, who, in the moonlight, wander round the
place of execution, with their heads under their arms.
At times they are said to pinch persons while

asleep both black and blue, such spots being
designated ghost-spots, or ghost-pinches. It is
also supposed in some parts of Norway that certain
spirits cry like children, and entice people to them,
such being thought to derive their origin from
murdered infants. A similar belief exists in
Sweden, where the spirits of little children that
have been murdered are said to wander about
wailing, within an assigned time, so long as their
lives would have lasted on earth, had they been
allowed to live. As a terror for unnatural mothers
who destroy their offspring, their sad cry is said to
be ' Mama ! Mama ! ' If travellers at night pass
by them, they will hang on the vehicle, when the
most spirited horses will sweat as if they were
dragging too heavy a load, and at length come
to a dead stop. The peasant then knows that
a ghost or pysling has attached itself to his
vehicle.[1]

The nautical ghost is often a malevolent spirit, as
in Shelley's ' Revolt of Islam '; and Captain Marryat
tells a sailor story of a murdered man's ghost appearing every night, and calling hands to witness a

[1] Thorpe's *Northern Mythology*, ii. pp. 94, 95.

piratical scene of murder, formerly committed on board the ship in which he appeared. A celebrated ghost is that of the 'Shrieking Woman,' long supposed to haunt the shores of Oakum Bay, near Marblehead. She was a Spanish lady murdered by pirates in the eighteenth century, and the apparition is thus described by Whittier in his 'Legends of New England':

> 'Tis said that often when the moon,
>   Is struggling with the gloomy even,
> And over moon and star is drawn
>   The curtain of a clouded heaven,
> Strange sounds swell up the narrow glen,
>   As if that robber crew was there;
> The hellish laugh, the shouts of men
>   And woman's dying prayer.

Many West Indian quays were thought to be the haunts of ghosts of murdered men; and Sir Walter Scott tells how the Buccaneers occasionally killed a Spaniard or a slave, and buried him with their spirits, under the impression that his ghost would haunt the spot, and keep away treasure hunters. He quotes another incident of a captain who killed a man in a fit of anger, and, on his threatening to haunt him, he cooked his body in the stove kettle.

The crew believed that the murdered man took his place at the wheel, and on the yards. The captain, troubled by his conscience and the man's ghost, finally jumped overboard, when, as he sank, he threw up his arms and exclaimed, 'Bill is with me now!'

In most parts of the world similar tales are recorded, and are as readily believed as when they were first told centuries ago. A certain island on the Japanese coast is traditionally haunted by the ghosts of Japanese slain in a naval battle. Even ' to-day the Chousen peasant fancies he sees the ghostly armies baling out the sea with bottomless dippers, condemned thus to cleanse the ocean of the slain of centuries ago.' [1] According to an old Chinese legend the ghost of a captain of a man-of-war junk, who had been murdered, reappeared and directed how the ship was to be steered to avoid a nest of pirates.[2]

In this country, many an old mansion has its haunted room, in which the unhappy spirit of the

[1] Griffis, *The Mikado's Kingdom.*
[2] Denny's *Folk-lore of China*; see Bassett's *Legends and Superstitions of the Sea*, p. 296.

murdered person is supposed, on certain occasions, to appear. Generation after generation do such troubled spirits return to the scene of their life, and persistently wait till some one is bold enough to stay in the haunted room, and to question them as to the cause of their making such periodical visits. Accordingly, when a murder has been committed and not discovered, often, it is said, has the spirit of the murdered one continued to come back and torment the neighbourhood till a confession of the crime has been made, and justice satisfied. Mr. Walter Gregor,[1] detailing instances in Scotland of haunted houses, tells how ' in one room a lady had been murdered, and her body buried in a vault below it. Her spirit could find no rest till she had told who the murderer was, and pointed out where the body lay. In another, a baby heir had its little life stifled by the hand of an assassin hired by the next heir. The estate was obtained, but the deed followed the villain beyond the grave, and his spirit could find no peace. Night by night the ghost had to return at the hour of midnight to the room in which the murder was committed, and in agony

[1] *Folk-lore of North-East of Scotland*, 1881, p. 68.

spend in it the hours till cock-crowing, when everything of the supernatural had to disappear.'

The ghost of Lady Hamilton of Bothwellhaugh,
who always appears in white, carrying her child in
her arms, has long been, as Mr. Ingram says,[1] 'an
enduring monument of the bloodthirsty spirit of
the age in which she lived.'   Whilst her husband
was away from home, a favourite of the Regent
Murray seized his house, turned his wife, on a
cold night, naked, into the open fields, where, before
morning, she was found raving mad; her infant
perishing either by cold or murder.   The ruins of
the mansion of Woodhouslee, 'whence Lady Bothwell was expelled in the brutal manner which occasioned her insanity and death,' have long been
tenanted with the unfortunate lady's ghost; 'and
so tenacious is this spectre of its rights, that a part
of the stones belonging to the ancient edifice having
been employed in building or repairing the new
Woodhouslee, the apparition has deemed it one of
her privileges to haunt that house also.'

Samlesbury Hall, Lancashire, has its ghosts;
and it is said that 'on certain clear still evenings a

[1] *Haunted Homes of England*, 1884, p. 286.

lady in white can be seen passing along the gallery and the corridors, and then from the hall into the grounds; then she meets a handsome knight who receives her on bended knees, and he then accompanies her along the walks. On arriving at a certain spot, most probably the lover's grave, both the phantoms stand still, and, as they seem to utter lost wailings of despair, they embrace each other, and then melt away into the clear blue of the surrounding sky.' The story goes that one of the daughters of Sir John Southworth, a former owner, formed an attachment with the heir of a neighbouring house; but when Sir John said 'no daughter of his should ever be united to the son of a family which had deserted its ancestral faith,' an elopement was arranged. The day and place were overheard by the lady's brother, and, on the evening agreed upon, he rushed from his hiding-place and slew her lover. But soon afterwards her mind gave way, and she died a raving maniac.[1]

Mrs. Murray, a lady born and brought up in the borders, writes Mr. Henderson,[2] tells me of 'a

---

[1] *Haunted Homes of England*, 2nd S., pp. 222-225.
[2] *Folk-lore of Northern Counties*, p. 267.

cauld lad,' of whom she heard in her childhood
during a visit to Gilsland, in Cumberland. He
perished from cold, at the behest of some cruel
uncle or stepdame, and ever after his ghost haunted
the family, coming shivering to their bedsides
before anyone was stricken by illness, his teeth
audibly chattering; and if it were to be fatal, he
laid his icy hand upon the part which would be
the seat of the disease, saying:

> Cauld, cauld, aye cauld !
> An' ye see he cauld for evermair.

St. Donart's Castle, on the southern coast of
Glamorganshire, has its favourite ghost, that of
Lady Stradling, who is said to have been murdered
by one of her family. It appears, writes the late
Mr. Wirt Sikes,[1] 'when any mishap is about to befall a member of the house of Stradling, the direct
line, however, of which is extinct. She wears high-
heeled shoes, and a long trailing gown of the finest
silk.' While she wanders, the castle hounds refuse
to rest, but with their howling raise all the dogs in
the neighbourhood. The Little Shelsey people
long preserved a tradition that the court-house in

[1] *British Goblins*, pp. 143, 144.

that parish was haunted by the spirit of a Lady
Lightfoot, who was said to have been imprisoned
and murdered;[1] and Cumnor Hall has acquired a
romantic interest from the poetic glamour flung
over it by Mickle in his ballad of Cumnor Hall, and
by Sir Walter Scott in his ' Kenilworth.' Both refer
to it as the scene of Amy Robsart's murder, and
although the jury agreed to accept her death as
accidental, the country folk would not forego their
idea that it was the result of foul play. Ever
since the fatal event it was asserted that ' Madam
Dudley's ghost did use to walk in Cumnor Park, and
that it walked so obstinately, that it took no less
than nine parsons from Oxford to lay her.' According to Mickle—

> The village maids, with fearful glance,
>   Avoid the ancient moss-grown wall;
> Nor ever lead the merry dance
>   Among the groves of Cumnor Hall.

About half a mile to the east of Maxton, a small
rivulet runs across the old turnpike road, at a spot
called Bow-brig-syke. Near this bridge is a tri-
angular field, in which for nearly a century it was

[1] *Gentleman's Magazine*, 1855, part ii. p. 58.

averred that the forms of two ladies, dressed in
white, might be seen pacing up and down, walking
over precisely the same spot of ground till morning
light. But one day, while some workmen were
repairing the road, they took up the large flagstones
upon which foot-passengers crossed the burn, and
found beneath them the skeletons of two women
lying side by side. After this discovery the Bow-
brig ladies, as they were called, were never again
seen to walk in the three-corner field. The story
goes that these two ladies were sisters to a former
laird of Littledean, who is said to have killed them
in a fit of passion, because they interfered to protect from ill-usage a young lady whom he had met
at Bow-brig-syke. Some years later he met with
his own death near the same fatal spot.[1]

Mr. Sullivan, in his 'Cumberland and West-
moreland,' relates how, some years ago, a spectre
appeared to a man who lived at Henhow Cottage,
Martindale. Starting for his work at an early
hour one morning, he had not gone two hundred
yards from his house when his dog gave signs of
alarm, and, on looking round, he saw a woman

[1] See Henderson's *Folk-lore of Northern Counties*, pp. 324-325.

carrying a child in her arms. On being questioned as to what was troubling her, the ghost replied that she had been seduced, and that her seducer, to conceal his guilt and her frailty, had given her medicine, the effect of which was to kill both mother and child. Her doom was to wander for a hundred years, forty of which had expired. The occurrence is believed to have made a lasting impression on the old man, who, says Sullivan, 'was until lately a shepherd on the fells. There can be no moral doubt that he both saw and spoke with the apparition; but what share his imagination had therein, or how it had been excited, are mysteries, and so they are likely to remain.' But as Grose remarks, ghosts do not go about their business like living beings. In cases of murder, 'a ghost, instead of going to the next justice of the peace and laying its information, or to the nearest relation of the person murdered, it appears to some poor labourer who knows none of the parties, draws the curtains of some decrepit nurse or alms-woman, or hovers about the place where his body is deposited.' The same circuitous mode, he adds, 'is pursued with respect to redressing injured orphans or widows,

when it seems as if the shorter and more certain
would be to go to the person guilty of the injustice,
and haunt him continually till he be terrified into
a restitution.'

From early days the phantoms of the murdered
have occasionally appeared to the living, and made
known the guilty person or persons who committed
the deed.   Thus Cicero relates how ' two Arcadians
came to Megara together; one lodged at a friend's
house, the other at an inn. During the night, the
latter appeared to his fellow-traveller, imploring
his help, as the innkeeper was plotting his death;
the sleeper sprang up in alarm, but thinking the
vision of no importance, he went to sleep again.
A second time his companion appeared to him,
to entreat that, though he had failed to help, he
would at least avenge, for the innkeeper had killed
him, and hidden his body in a dung-cart, wherefore he charged his fellow-traveller to be early next
morning at the city gate before the cart passed out.
The traveller went as bidden, and there found the
cart; the body of the murdered man was in it, and
the innkeeper was brought to justice.' [1]

[1] Quoted in Tylor's *Primitive Culture*, i. p. 444.

Of the many curious cases recorded of a murder being discovered through the ghost of the murdered person, may be quoted one told in Aubrey's 'Miscellanies.' It appears that on Monday, April 14, 1690, William Barwick was walking with his wife close to Cawood Castle, when, from motives not divulged at the trial, he determined to murder her, and finding a pond conveniently at hand, threw her in. But on the following Tuesday, as his brother-in-law, Thomas Lofthouse, 'about half an hour after twelve of the clock in the daytime, was watering quickwood, as he was going for the second pail, there appeared walking before him an apparition in the shape of a woman, "her visage being like his wife's sister's." Soon after, she sat down over against the pond, on a green hill. He walked by her as he went to the pond, and, on his return, he observed that she was dangling " something like a white bag " on her lap, evidently suggestive of her unborn baby that was slain with her. The circumstance made such an impression on him, that he immediately suspected Barwick, especially as he had made false statements as to the whereabouts of his wife, and obtained a warrant for his arrest.

The culprit when arrested confessed his crime, and the body of the murdered woman being recovered, was found dressed in clothing similar, apparently, to that worn by the apparition. Ultimately Barwick was hanged for his crime.'[1]

A similar case, which occurred in the county of Durham in 1631, and is the subject of a critical historical inquiry in Surtees's 'History of Durham,' may be briefly summed up.[2] 'One Walker, a yeoman of good estate, a widower, living at Chester-le-Street, had in his service a young female relative named Anne Walker. The results of an amour which took place between them caused Walker to send away the girl under the care of one Mark Sharp, a collier, professedly that she might be taken care of as befitted her condition, but in reality that she might no more be troublesome to her lover. Nothing was heard of her till, one night in the ensuing winter, one James Graham, coming down from the upper to the lower floor of his mill, found a woman standing there with her hair hanging about her head, in which were five bloody wounds. According to the man's evidence, she

[1] See Ingram's *Haunted Homes*, 1884, pp. 33-36.
[2] See *Book of Days*, ii. p. 287.

gave an account of her fate ; having been killed by
Sharp on the moor in their journey, and thrown
into a coal pit close by, while the instrument of her
death, a pick, had been hid under a bank along
with his clothes, which were stained with her blood.
She demanded of Graham that he should expose
her murder, which he hesitated to do, until she
had twice reappeared to him, the last time with a
threatening aspect.

'The body, the pick, and the clothes having been
found as Graham had described, Walter and Sharp
were tried at Durham, before Judge Davenport, in
August 1631. The men were found guilty, condemned, and executed.'

In 'Ackerman's Repository' for November
1820, there is an account of a person being tried
on the pretended evidence of a ghost. A farmer,
on his return from the market at Southam, co.
Warwick, was murdered. The next morning a
man called upon the farmer's wife, and related
how on the previous night her husband's ghost
had appeared to him, and, after showing him
several stabs on his body, had told him that he
was murdered by a certain person, and his corpse

thrown into a marl-pit. A search was instituted, the body found in the pit, and the wounds on the body of the deceased were exactly in the parts described by the pretended dreamer; the person who was mentioned was committed for trial on the charge of murder, and the trial came on at Warwick before Lord Chief Justice Raymond. The jury would have convicted the prisoner as rashly as the magistrate had committed him, but for the interposition of the judge, who told them he did not put any credence in the pretended ghost story, since the prisoner was a man of unblemished reputation, and no ill-feeling had ever existed between himself and the deceased. He added that he knew of no law which admitted of the evidence of a ghost, and, if any did, the ghost had not appeared. The crier was then ordered to summon the ghost, which he did three times, and the judge then acquitted the prisoner, and caused the accuser to be detained and his house searched, when such strong proofs of guilt were discovered, that the man confessed the crime, and was executed for murder at the following assizes.

CHAPTER VII

PHANTOM BIRDS

ONE of the forms which the soul is said occasionally to assume at death is that of a bird—a pretty
belief which, under one form or another, exists all
over the world. An early legend tells how, when
St. Polycarp was burnt alive, there arose from his
ashes a white dove which flew towards heaven;
and a similar story is told of Joan of Arc. The
Russian peasantry affirm that the souls of the
departed haunt their old homes in the shape of
birds for six weeks, and watch the grief of the
bereft, after which time they fly away to the other
world. In certain districts bread-crumbs are
placed on a piece of white linen at a window
during those six weeks, when the soul is believed to
come and feed upon them in the form of a bird.
It is generally into pigeons or crows that the dead

are transformed. Thus, when the Deacon Theodore
and his three schismatic brethren were burnt in
the year 1682, writes Mr. Ralston,[1] 'the souls of
the martyrs appeared in the air as pigeons.' In
Volhynia dead children are believed to come back
in the spring to their native village under the
semblance of swallows and other small birds,
endeavouring, by soft twittering or song, to console
their sorrowing parents. The Bulgarians say that
after death the soul assumes the form of a bird;
and according to an old Bohemian fancy the soul
flies out of the dying in a similar shape. In the
'Chronicles of the Beatified Anthony'[2] we find
described fetid and black pools 'in regione Puteo-
lorum in Apulia,' whence the souls arise in the
form of monstrous birds in the evening hours of
the Sabbath, which neither eat nor let themselves
be caught, but wander till in the morning an
enormous lion compels them to submerge themselves in the water.

It is a German belief that the soul of one who

[1] *Songs of the Russian People*, p. 118.
[2] Quoted by Gubernatis, *Zoological Mythology*, 1872, ii. pp. 254,
255.

has died on shipboard passes into a bird, and when
seen at any time it is supposed to announce the
death of another person. The ghost of the
murdered mother comes swimming in the form of
a duck, or the soul sits in the likeness of a bird on
the grave. This piece of folk-lore has been introduced into many of the popular folk-tales, as in
the well-known story of the juniper tree. A little
boy is killed by his step-mother, who serves him
up as a dish of meat to his father. The father
eats in ignorance, and throws away the bones, which
are gathered up by the half-sister, who puts them
into a silk handkerchief and buries them under a
juniper tree. But presently a bird of gay plumage
perches on the tree, and whistles as it flits from
branch to branch :

> Min moder de mi slach't,
> Min fader de mi att,
> Min swester de Marleenken,
> Söcht alle mine Beeniken,
> Und bindt sie in een syden Dodk,
> Legst unner den Machandelboom ;
> Ky witt ! ky witt ! Ach watt en schön vogel bin ich !

—a rhyme which Goethe puts into the mouth of

Gretchen in prison.[1]   In Grimm's story of ' The
White and the Black Bride,' the mother and sister
push the true bride into the stream.   At the same
moment a snow-white swan is discovered swimming
down the stream.

Swedish folk-lore tells us that the ravens which
scream by night in forest swamps and wild moors
are the ghosts of murdered men whose bodies have
been hidden by their undetected murderers, and
not had Christian burial.   In Denmark the night-
raven is considered an exorcised spirit, and there
is said to be a hole in its left wing caused by the
stake driven into the earth.   Where a spirit has
been exorcised, it is only through the most frightful swamps and morasses that it ascends, first
beginning under the earth with the cry of 'Rok! rok!'
then ' Rok op ! rok op ! ' and when it has thus come
forth, it flies away screaming ' Hei ! hei ! he !—i ! '
When it has flown up it describes a cross, but one
must take care, it is said, not to look up when the
bird is flying overhead, for he who sees through
the hole in its wing will become a night-raven him-

[1] Countess Evelyn Martinengo-Cesaresco, *Study of Folk-songs*
p. 10; Thorpe's *Northern Mythology*, i. p. 289.

self, and the night-raven will be released. This
ominous bird is ever flying towards the east, in the
hope of reaching the Holy Sepulchre, for when it
arrives there it will find rest.[1]   Then there is the
romantic Breton ballad of 'Lord Nann and the
Korrigan,' wherein it is related how—

> It was a marvel to see, men say,
> The night that followed the day,
> The ledy in earth by her lord lay,
>
> To see two oak trees themselves rear,
> From the new made grave into the air ;
>
> And on their branches two doves white,
> Who there were hopping, gay and light,
>
> Which sang when rose the morning ray,
> And then towards heaven sped away.

In Mexico it is a popular belief that after death
the souls of nobles animate beautiful singing birds,
and certain North American Indian tribes maintain
that the souls of their chiefs take the form of
small woodbirds.[2]   Among the Abipones of Paraguay we are told of a peculiar kind of little ducks

[1] Henderson's *Folk-lore of Northern Counties*, p. 126; Thorpe's
Northern Mythology, ii. p. 211.
[2] See Dorman's *Primitive Superstitions*, pp. 48, 49.

which fly in flocks at night-time, uttering a mournful tone, and which the popular imagination associates with the souls of those who have died. Darwin mentions a South American Indian who would not eat land-birds because they were dead men; and the Californian tribes abstain from large game, believing that the souls of past generations have passed into their bodies. The Içannas of Brazil thought the souls of brave warriors passed into lovely birds that fed on pleasant fruits; and the Tapuyas think the souls of the good and the brave enter birds, while the cowardly become reptiles. Indeed, the primitive psychology of such rude tribes reminds us how the spirit freed at death—

> Fills with fresh energy another form,
> And towers an elephant, or glides a worm;
> Swims as an eagle in the eye of noon,
> Or wails a screech-owl to the deaf cold moon.

It was also a belief of the Aztecs that all good people, as a reward of merit, were metamorphosed at the close of life into feathered songsters of the grove, and in this form passed a certain term in the umbrageous bowers of Paradise; while certain African tribes think that the souls of wicked men become jackals. The Brazials imagined that the souls of the bad animated those birds that inhabited the cavern of Guacharo and made a mournful cry, which birds were religiously feared.

Tracing similar beliefs in our own country, may be compared the Lancashire dread of the so-called ' Seven Whistlers,' which are occasionally heard at night, and are supposed to contain the souls of those Jews who assisted at the Crucifixion, and in consequence of their wickedness were doomed to float for ever in the air. Numerous stories have been told, from time to time, of the appearance of these ' Seven Whistlers,' and of their being heard before some terrible catastrophe, such as a colliery explosion. A correspondent of 'Notes and Queries' relates how during a thunderstorm which passed over Kettering, in Yorkshire, on the evening of September 6, 1871, 'on which occasion the lightning was very vivid, an unusual spectacle was witnessed. Immense flocks of birds were flying about, uttering doleful affrighted cries as they passed over the locality, and for hours they kept up a continual whistling like that made by sea-birds. There must have been great numbers of them, as

they were also observed at the same time in the
counties of Northampton, Leicester, and Lincoln.
The next day, as my servant was driving me to a
neighbouring village, this phenomenon of the flight
of birds became the subject of conversation, and on
asking him what birds he thought they were, he
told me they were what were called the " Seven
Whistlers," and that whenever they were heard it
was considered a sign of some great calamity, and
that the last time he heard them was the night
before the great Hartley Colliery explosion. He had
also been told by soldiers, that if they heard them
they always expected a great slaughter would take
place soon. Curiously enough, on taking up the
newspaper the following morning, I saw headed
in large letters, " Terrible Colliery Explosion at
Wigan," &c.' Wordsworth speaks of the ' Seven
Whistlers ' in connection with the spectral hounds
of the wild huntsman :

> He the seven birds hath seen that never part—
>   Seen the seven whistlers on their nightly rounds,
> And counted them. And oftentimes will start,
>   For overhead are sweeping Gabriel's hounds,
> Doomed, with their impious lord, the flying hart
>   To chase for ever on ærial grounds.

A similar tradition prevails on the Bosphorus with reference to certain flocks of birds, about the size of a thrush, which fly up and down the Channel, and are never seen to rest on the land or water. These are supposed to be the souls of the damned, and condemned to perpetual motion. Among further instances of the same belief may be mentioned one current among the Manx herring fishermen, who, from time immemorial, have been afraid of going to sea without a dead wren, for fear of disasters and storms. The story goes that once upon a time 'a sea spirit hunted the herring track, always attended by storms, but at last assumed the form of a wren, and flew away.' Accordingly they believe that so long as they have a dead wren with them all is snug and safe. Similarly, in the English Channel a rustling, rushing sound is occasionally heard on the dark still nights of winter, and is called the herring spear, or herring piece, by the fishermen of Dover and Folkestone. But this strange sound is really caused by the flight of the little redwings as they cross the Channel on their way to warmer regions.

Stories of disembodied souls appearing as birds

are very numerous. An old well-known Cornish
legend tells how, in days of old, King Arthur was
transformed into a chough, 'its talons and beak all
red with blood,' denoting the violent end to which
the celebrated chieftain came. In the same way
a curious legend in Poland affirms that every
member of the Herburt family assumes the form
of an eagle after death, and that the eldest
daughters of the Pileck line take the shape of
doves if they die unmarried, of owls if they die
married, and that they give previous notice of their
death to every member of their race by pecking a
finger of each. A wild song sung by the boatmen
of the Molo, Venice, declares that the spirit of
Daniel Manin, the patriot, is flying about the
lagunes to this day in the shape of a beautiful
white dove.[1] There is the ancient Irish tradition
that the first father and mother of mankind exist
as eagles in the island of Innis Bofin, at the mouth
of Killery Bay, in Galway; indeed, survivals of
this old belief occur under all manner of forms.
There is the popular legend of the owl and the
baker's daughter which Shakespeare has immor-

[1] Jones' *Credulities, Past and Present*, p. 376.

talised in 'Hamlet' (iv. 5), where Ophelia exclaims,
'They say the owl was a baker's daughter; Lord,
we know what we are, but know not what we may
be.'¹ Gervase of Tilbury tells how the stork was
formerly regarded as both bird and man, on account of which superstition it is carefully protected
in Prussia from any kind of injury. The stork,
too, is still held in superstitious dread by the
Chinese, who, on the twenty-first day of the period
of mourning for the dead, place three large paper
birds resembling storks on high poles in front of
the house of mourning. The birds are supposed
to carry the soul of the deceased person to Elysium,
and during the next three days the Buddhist prays
to the ten kings of the Buddhist Hades, calling on
them to hasten the flight of the departed soul to
the Western Paradise.² The Virginian Indians had
great reverence for a small bird called Pawcorance,
that flies in the woods, and in its note continually
sounds that name. This bird flies alone, and is
heard only in twilight. It is said to be the son of
one of their priests, and on this account they

¹ See Dasent's *Tales of the Norse*, 1859, p. 230.
² Jones' *Credulities, Past and Present*, p. 373.

would not hurt it; but there was once a profane
Indian who was hired to shoot one of them, but
report says he paid dearly for his act of presump-
tion, for a few days afterwards he disappeared, and
was never heard of again.[1] The Indians dwelling
about the Falls of St. Anthony supposed that the
spirits of their dead warriors animated the eagles
which frequented the place, and these eagles were
objects of their worship. In the 'Sæmund Edda'
it is said that in the nether world souls as singed
birds fly about like swarms of flies—

> Of that is to be told
> What I just observed,
> When I had come into the land of torment:
> Singed birds,
> That had been souls,
> Flew as many as gnats.

The Finns and the Lithuanians speak of the
'Milky Way' as the Bird's Way—the way of
souls. According to Kuhn, the notion of the soul
assuming the form of a bird is closely allied with
the primitive tradition of birds as soul-bringers.
Thus, as it has been suggested, 'the soul and the

[1] Dorman's *Primitive Superstitions*, pp. 255, 256.

bird that brought it down to earth may have been supposed to become one, and to enter and quit the body together.' In the Egyptian hieroglyphics a bird signified the soul of man; and the German name for stork, writes Grimm, is literally child, or soul-bringer. Hence the belief that the advent of infants is presided over by this bird, which obtains so wide a credence in Denmark and Germany.[1]

The idea of the bird as a ' soul bringer ' probably gave rise to the popular belief that it is unlucky when a bird hovers near the window of a sick-room, a superstition to which Mrs. Hemans has prettily alluded :

> Say not 'tis vain ! I tell thee some
> Are warned by a meteor's light,
> Or a pale bird flitting calls them home,
> Or a voice on the winds by night.

There are various stories told of mysterious birds appearing at such a time in different localities. In Devonshire the appearance of a white breasted bird has long been considered a presage of death, a notion which is said to have originated

---

[1] Hardwick's *Traditions, Superstitions, and Folk-lore, Indo-* p. 243 ; Thorpe's *Northern Mythology,* i. p. 289. See Kelly's 1872, *European Folk-lore,* p. 103.

in a tragic occurrence that happened to one of the Oxenham family. A local ballad tells how on the bridal eve of Margaret, heiress of Sir James Oxenham, a silver-breasted bird flew over the wedding guests just as Sir James stood up to thank them for good wishes. The next day she was slain by a discarded lover, and the ballad records how—

> Round her hovering flies,
> The phantom-bird, for her last breath,
> To bear it to the skies.

In Yorkshire, Berry Well was supposed to be haunted by a bogie in the form of a white goose, and the Rev. S. Baring-Gould informs us how Lew Trenchard House is haunted by a white lady who goes by the name of Madame Gould, and is supposed to be the spirit of a lady who died there, April 10, 1795. 'A stone is shown on the "ramps" of Lew Slate Quarry, where seven parsons met to lay the old madame, and some say that the white owl, which nightly flits to and fro in front of Lew House, is the spirit of the lady conjured by the parsons into a bird.' [1]

---

[1] See Henderson's *Folk-lore of Northern Counties*, pp. 331–335.

Similarly, whenever the white owls are seen perched on the family mansion of the noble family of Arundel of Wardour, it is regarded as a certain indication that one of its members will shortly be summoned out of the world. In Count Montalembert's 'Vie de Ste. Elizabeth' it is related how 'Duke Louis of Thuringia, the husband of Ste. Elizabeth of Hungary, being on the point of expiring, said to those around him, "Do you see those doves more white than snow?" His attendants supposed him to be a prey to visions; but a little while afterwards he said to them, "I must fly away with those brilliant doves." Having said this he fell asleep in peace. Then his almoner, Berthold, perceived doves flying away to the east, and followed them along with his eyes.' We may compare a similar story told of the most beautiful woman of the Knistenaux, named 'Foot of the Fawn,' who died in her childbirth, and her babe with her. Soon afterwards two doves appeared, one full grown, and the other a little one. They were the spirits of the mother and child, and the Indians would gather about the tree on which they were perched with reverential love, and worship

them as the spirit of the woman and child.[1] There
is Lord Lyttelton's well-known ghost story, and the
belief of the Duchess of Kendal that George I.
flew into her window in the shape of a raven.
Another well-known case was that of the Duchess
of St. Albans, who, on her death-bed, remarked
to her step-daughter, Lady Guilford, ‘ I am so
happy to day because your father's spirit is
breathing upon me ; he has taken the shape of
a little bird singing at my window.’ Kelly relates
an anecdote of a credulous individual who believed
that the departing soul of his brother-in-law, in the
form of a bird, tapped at his window at the time
of his death ; [2] and in FitzPatrick's ‘ Life of Bishop
Doyle ’ it is related, in allusion to his death, that,
‘ considering the season was midsummer, and not
winter, the visit of two robin redbreasts to the
sick-room may be noticed as interesting. They
remained fluttering round, and sometimes perching
on the uncurtained bed. The priests, struck by
the novelty of the circumstance, made no effort to
expel the little visitors, and the robins hung

[1] Dorman's *Primitive Superstitions*, p. 255.
[2] *Indo-European Folk-lore*, pp. 104, 105.

lovingly over the bishop's head until death released him.' A singular instance of this belief was the extraordinary whim of a Worcester lady, who, imagining her daughter to exist in the shape of a singing-bird, literally furnished her pew in the Cathedral with cages full of the kind ; and we are told in Lord Oxford's letters that, as she was rich, and a benefactress in beautifying the church, no objection was made to her harmless folly.

CHAPTER VIII

ANIMAL GHOSTS

It is the rule rather than the exception for ghosts to take the form of animals. A striking feature of this form of animism is its universality, an argument, it is said, in favour of its having originally sprung from the old theory of metempsychosis which has pertinaciously existed in successive stages of the world's culture. 'Possibly,' it has been suggested, 'the animal form of ghosts is a mark of the once-supposed divinity of the dead. Ancestor worship is one of the oldest of the creeds, and in all mythologies we find that the gods could transform themselves into any shape at will, and frequently took those of beasts and birds.' [1] At the same time, one would scarcely expect to come across nowadays this fanciful belief in our

---

[1] *Shropshire Folk-lore*, p. 131.

own and other civilised countries, and yet instances
are of constant occurrence, being deeply rooted in
many a local tradition.. Acts of injustice done to a
person cause the soul to return in animal form by
way of retribution.   Thus, in Cornwall, it is a very
popular fancy that when a young woman who has
loved not wisely but too well dies forsaken and
broken-hearted, she comes back to haunt her de-
ceiver in the form of a white hare.[1]   This phantom
pursues the false one everywhere, being generally
invisible to everyone but himself.   It occasionally
rescues him from danger, but invariably causes his
death in the end.   A Shropshire story tells [2] how
'two or three generations back there was a lady
buried in her jewels at Fitz, and afterwards the
clerk robbed her; and she used to walk Cuthery
Hollow in the form of a colt.   They called it
Obrick's Colt, and one night the clerk met it, and
fell on his knees, saying, "Abide, Satan ! abide ! I am
a righteous man, and a psalm singer." ' [3]   The ghost
was known as Obrick's Colt from the name of the
thief, who, as the peasantry were wont to say, 'had

---

[1] Hunt's *Popular Romances of the West of England*, p. 377.
[2] *Shropshire Folk-lore*, pp. 105, 106.
[3] See *Ibid*. pp. 108–111.

niver no pace atter; a was sadly troubled in his
yed, and mithered.'[1]

Sometimes the spirit in animal form is that of
a wicked person doomed to wear that shape for some
offence. A man who hanged himself at Broom-
field, near Shrewsbury, 'came again in the form of
a large black dog;' and an amusing Shropshire story
is told of the laying of an animal ghost at Bagbury,
which took the form of a roaring bull, and caused
no small alarm. This bull, it appears, had been a
very bad man, but when his unexpected presence
as a bull-ghost terrified the neighbourhood, it was
deemed desirable by the twelve parsons whose help
had been invoked to run him to earth in Hyssington
Church, with candles and all the paraphernalia employed on such occasions. But the bull, becoming
infuriated, 'made such a bust that he cracked the
wall of the church from the top to the bottom.'
Their efforts were ultimately successful, for they
captured him, and as he was compressible, they
shut him up in a snuff-box, and laid him in the
Red Sea for a thousand years.

Lady Howard, a Devonshire notable of the time

---

[1] See Hartshorne's *Salopia Antiqua*, p. 522

of James I., in spite of her beauty and accomplishments, had many bad qualities, and amongst others was not only guilty of unnatural cruelty to her only daughter, but had a mysterious knack of getting rid of her husbands, having been married no less than four times. Her misdemeanours, however, did not escape with impunity, for, on her death, her spirit was transformed into a hound, and compelled to run every night, between midnight and cockcrow, from the gateway of Fitzford, her former residence, to Oakhampton Park, and bring back to the place from whence she started a blade of grass in her mouth, and this penance she is doomed to continue till every blade of grass is removed from the park, which she will not be able to effect till the end of the world.

Many spectral dogs, believed to be the souls of wicked persons, are said to haunt the sides of rivers and pools, and the story goes that there once lived in the hamlet of Dean Combe, Devon, a weaver of great fame and skill. After a prosperous life he died, but the next day he appeared sitting at the loom and working diligently as when he was alive. His sons applied to the parson, who, hearing the noise of the weaver's shuttle above, cried, 'Knowles! come down; this is no place for thee.' 'I will,' said the weaver, 'as soon as I have worked out my quill' (the quill is the shuttle-full of wool). 'Nay,' said the vicar, 'thou hast been long enough at thy work, come down at once!' So when the spirit came down, the vicar took a handful of earth from the churchyard, and threw it on its face, and instantly it became a black hound. Then the vicar took a nutshell with a hole in it, and led the hound to the pool below the waterfall. 'Take this shell,' he said, 'and when thou shalt have dipped out the pool with it, thou mayest rest, not before.'[1]   On the west coast of Ireland, fishermen have a strong prejudice against killing seals, owing to a popular tradition that they enshrined 'the souls of them that were drowned at the flood.' It was also said that such seals possessed the power of casting aside their external skins, and disporting themselves in human form on the sea-shore.

Within the parish of Tring, Hertford, a poor old woman was drowned in 1751 for suspected

[1] *Notes and Queries*, 1st S. ii. p. 515.

witchcraft. A chimney-sweeper, who was the
principal perpetrator of this deed, was hanged
and gibbeted near the place where the murder
was committed; and while the gibbet stood, and
long after it had disappeared, the spot was haunted
by a black dog. A correspondent of the 'Book of
Days' (ii. 433) says that he was told by the village
schoolmaster, who had been 'abroad,' that he
himself had seen this diabolical dog. 'I was
returning home,' said he, 'late at night in a gig
with the person who was driving. When we came
near the spot, where a portion of the gibbet had
lately stood, he saw on the bank of the roadside a
flame of fire as large as a man's hat. "What's
that?" I exclaimed. "Hush!" said my companion, and suddenly pulling in his horse, made
a dead stop. I then saw an immense black dog
just in front of our horse, the strangest looking
creature I ever beheld. He was as big as a
-Newfoundland, but very gaunt, shaggy, with long
ears and tail, eyes like balls of fire, and large, long
teeth, for he opened his mouth and seemed to grin
at us. In a few minutes the dog disappeared,
seeming to vanish like a shadow, or to sink into

the earth, and we drove on over the spot where he had lain.'

Occasionally, when loss of life has happened through an accident, a spectre animal of some kind has been afterwards seen. Some years ago an accident happened in a Cornish mine, whereby several men lost their lives. As soon as help could be procured, a party descended, but the remains of the poor fellows were discovered to be mutilated beyond recognition. On being brought up to the surface, the clothes and a mass of mangled flesh dropped from the bodies. A by-stander, anxious to spare the feelings of the relatives present, quickly cast the unsightly mass into the blazing furnace of an engine close at hand. But ever since that day the engineman positively asserted that troops of little black dogs continually haunted the locality. Then there is the pretty legend mentioned by Wordsworth in his poem entitled, 'The White Doe of Rylstone,' in which is embodied a Yorkshire tradition to the effect that the lady founder of Bolton Abbey revisited the ruins of the venerable structure in the form of a spotless white doe :

Which, though seemingly doomed in its breast to sustain
A softened remembrance of sorrow and pain,
Is spotless, and holy, and gentle, and bright,
And glides o'er the earth like an angel of light.

So common in France are human ghosts in
bestial form, 'that M. D'Assier has invented a
Darwinian way of accounting for the phenomena.
M. D'Assier, a positivist, is a believer in ghosts,
but not in the immortality of the soul. He
suggests that the human *revenants* in the guise of
sheep, cows, and shadowy creatures may be
accounted for by a kind of Atavism, or "throwing
back," on the side of the spirit to the lower animal
forms out of which humanity was developed!' [1]

According to a German piece of folk-lore, the
soul takes the form of a snake, a notion we find
shared by the Zulus, who revere a certain kind
of serpents as the ghosts of the dead; and the
Northern Indians speak of a serpent coming out
of the mouth of a woman at death. It is
further related that out of the mouth of a sleeping
person a snake creeps and goes a long distance,
and that whatever it sees, or suffers, on its way,

[1] *Nineteenth Century*, April 1885, p. 625.

the sleeper dreams of. If it is prevented from returning, the person dies.[1] Another belief tells us that the soul occasionally escapes from the mouth in the shape of a weasel or a mouse, a superstition to which Goethe alludes in 'Faust':

> Ah! in the midst of her song,
> A red mouseskin sprang out of her mouth.

Turning to similar beliefs current among distant nations, we are told that the Andaman Islanders had a notion that at death the soul vanished from the earth in the form of various animals and fishes; and in Guinea, monkeys found in the locality of a graveyard are supposed to be animated by the spirits of the dead. As Mr. Andrew Lang remarks:[2] 'Among savages who believe themselves to be descended from beasts, nothing can be more natural than the hypothesis that the souls revert to bestial shapes.' Certain of the North American Indian tribes believe that the spirits of their dead enter into bears; and some of the Papuans in New Guinea 'imagine they will reappear as certain of the animals in their own

---

[1] See Thorpe's *Northern Mythology*, ii. pp. 289, 290.
[2] *Nineteenth Century*, April 1885, p. 625.

island. The cassowary and the emu are the
most remarkable animals that they know of; they
have lodged in them the shades of their ancestors,
and hence the people abstain from eating them.' [1]
Spiritualism, we are told, is very widely spread
among the Esquimos, who maintain that all
animals have their spirits, and that the spirits of
men can enter into the bodies of animals.[2] In the
Ladrone Islands it was supposed that the spirits
of the dead animated the bodies of the fish, and
'therefore to make better use of these precious
spirits, they burnt the soft portions of the dead
body, and swallowed the cinders which they let
float on the top of their cocoa-nut wine.' [3]

In most parts of England there is a popular
belief in a spectral dog, which is generally described as 'large, shaggy, and black, with long
ears and tail. It does not belong to any species of
living dogs, but is severally said to represent a
hound, a setter, a terrier, or a shepherd dog,
though often larger than a Newfoundland.' [4] It is
commonly supposed to be a bad spirit, haunting

[1] Letourneau's *Sociology*, p. 250. [2] *Ibid.* p. 264.
[3] *Ibid.* p. 266. [4] *Book o Days*, ii. p. 433.

places where evil deeds have been done, or where
some calamity may be expected. In Lancashire,
this spectre-dog is known as 'Trash' and 'Striker,'[1]
its former name having been applied to it from
the peculiar noise made by its feet, which is supposed to resemble that of a person walking along a
miry, sloppy road, with heavy shoes; and its latter
appellation from its uttering a curious screech,
which is thought to warn certain persons of the
approaching death of some relative or friend. If
followed, it retreats with its eyes fronting its
pursuer, and either sinks into the ground with a
frightful shriek, or in some mysterious manner
disappears. When struck, the weapon passes
through it as if it were a mere shadow. In
Norfolk and Cambridgeshire this apparition is
known to the peasantry by the name of 'shuck'
—the provincial word for 'shag'—and is reported
to haunt churchyards and other lonely places. A
dreary lane in the parish of Overstrand is called
from this spectral animal 'Shuck's Lane,' and it
is said that if the spot where it has been seen
be examined after its disappearance, it will be

[1] See Harland and Wilkinson's *Lancashire Folk-lore*, p. 91.

found to be scorched, and strongly impregnated with the smell of brimstone. Mrs. Latham tells [1] how a man of notoriously bad character, who lived in a lonely spot at the foot of the South Downs, without any companion of either sex, was believed to be nightly haunted by evil spirits in the form of rats. Persons passing by his cottage late at night heard him cursing them, and desiring them to let him rest in peace. It was supposed they were sent to do judgment on him, and would carry him away some night. But he received his death-blow in a drunken brawl.

In the neighbourhood of Leeds there is the Padfoot, a weird apparition about the size of a small donkey, 'with shaggy hair and large eyes like saucers.' Mr. Baring-Gould relates [2] how a man in Horbury once saw 'the Padfooit,' which 'in this neighbourhood is a white dog like a "flay-craw."' It goes sometimes on two legs, sometimes it runs on three, and to see it is a prognostication of death. He was going home by Jenkin, and he saw a white dog in the hedge. He struck at it, and the stick

[1] 'West Sussex Superstitions,' *Folk-lore Record*, i. p. 23.
[2] Henderson's *Folk- ore of Northern Counties*, pp. 274, 275.

passed through it. Then the white dog looked at him, and it had ' great saucer e'en '; and he was so ' flayed,' that he ran home trembling and went to bed, when he fell ill and died. With this strange apparition may be compared the Barguest, Bahrgeist, or Boguest of Northumberland, Durham, and Yorkshire, and the Boggart of Lancashire; an uncanine creature, which generally assumes the form of a large black dog with flaming eyes, and is supposed to be a presage of death. The word 'barguest,' according to Sir Walter Scott, is from the German 'bahrgeist'—spirit of the bier; and, as it has been pointed out, the proverbial expression to ' war like a Barguest,' shows how deep a hold this apparition once had on the popular mind. There is a Barguest in a glen between Darlington and Houghton, near Throstlenest, and another haunted a piece of waste land above a spring called the Oxwells, between Wreghorn and Headingly Hill, near Leeds. On the death of any person of local importance in the neighbourhood the creature would come forth, followed by all the dogs barking and howling.[1] Another form of this

---

[1] Henderson's *Folk-lore of Northern Counties*, p. 275.

animal spectre is the Capelthwaite, which, according to common report, had the power of appearing in the form of any quadruped, but usually chose that of a large black dog. It does not seem to have appeared of late years, for tradition tells how a vicar of Beetham went out in his ecclesiastical vestments to lay this troublesome spirit in the River Bela.[1]

In Wales, there is the Gwyllgi, or ' dog of darkness,' a terrible spectre of a mastiff which, with a baleful breath and blazing red eyes, has often inspired terror even amongst the strong-minded Welsh peasantry. Many stories are told of its encountering unwary travellers, who have been so overcome by its unearthly howl, or by the glare of its fiery eyes, that they have fallen senseless on the ground. A certain lane, leading from Mowsiad to Lisworney-Crossways, is said to have been haunted by a Gwyllgi of the most terrible aspect. A farmer, living near there, was one night returning home from market on a young mare, when suddenly the animal shied, reared, tumbled the farmer off, and bolted for home. The farm-servants,

[1] See Henderson's *Folk-lore of Northern Counties*, pp. 274–278.

finding the mare trembling by the barn door, suspected she had seen the Gwyllgi, and going in
search of their master, they found him on his back
in the mud, who, being questioned, protested 'it
was the Gwyllgi, and nothing less, that had made
all this trouble.' [1]

It is a popular belief in Wales that horses have
the peculiar 'gift' of seeing spectres, and carriage
horses have been known to display every sign of
the utmost terror when the occupants of the
carriage could see no cause for alarm. Such an
apparition is an omen of death, and an indication
that a funeral will pass before long, bearing to the
grave some person not dead at the time of the
horses' fright. Another famous dog-fiend, in the
shape of a shaggy spaniel, was the 'Mauthe Doog,'
which was said to haunt Peel Castle, Isle of Man.
Its favourite place was the guard-chamber, where
it would lie down by the fireside. According to
Waldron, 'the soldiers lost much of their terror
by the frequency of the sight ; yet, as they believed
it to be an evil spirit waiting for an opportunity to
hinder them, the belief kept them so far in order

[1] See Wirt Sikes' *British Goblins*, pp. 167-169.

that they refrained from swearing in its presence. But, as the Mauthe Doog used to come out and return by the passage through the church, by which also somebody must go to deliver the keys every night to the captain, they continued to go together; he whose turn it was to do that duty being accompanied by the next in rotation. On a certain night, however, one of the soldiers, being the worse for liquor, would go with the key alone, though it really was not his turn. His comrades tried to dissuade him, but he said he wanted the Mauthe Doog's company, and would try whether he was dog or devil. Soon afterwards a great noise alarmed the soldiers; and when the adventurer returned, he was struck with horror and speechless, nor could he even make such signs as might give them to understand what had happened to him; but he died with distorted features in violent agony. After this the apparition was never seen again.'

Then there are the packs of spectral hounds, which some folk-lorists tell us are evil spirits that have assumed this form in order to mimic the sports of men, or to hunt their souls. They are variously named in different parts of the country—

being designated in the North, ' Gabriel's Hounds ';
in Devon, the ' Wisk', ' Yesk,' ' Yeth,' or ' Heath
Hounds '; in Wales, ' Cwn Annwn' or ' Cwn
y Wybr '; and in Cornwall, the ' Devil and his
Dandy-Dogs.'   Such spectral hounds are generally
described as ' monstrous human-headed dogs,' and
' black, with fiery eyes and teeth, and sprinkled all
over with blood.' They are often heard though
seldom seen, ' and seem to be passing along simply in
the air, as if in hot pursuit of their prey '; and when
they appear to hang over a house, then death or
misfortune may shortly be expected.   In the gorge
of Cliviger the spectre huntsman, under the name of
' Gabriel Ratchets,' with his hounds yelping through
the air, is believed to hunt a milk-white doe
round the Eagle's Crag, in the Vale of Todmorden,
on All Hallows Eve.[1]   Mr. Holland, of Sheffield,
has embodied the local belief in the subjoined
sonnet, and says: ' I never can forget the impression made upon my mind when once arrested
by the cry of these Gabriel hounds as I passed the
parish church of Sheffield one densely dark and

[1] See Roby's *Traditions of Lancashire*; Homerton's *Isles of
Loch Awe*; Hardwick's *Traditions, Superstitions, and Folk-lore*,
pp. 153-176.

very still night. The sound was exactly like the questing of a dozen beagles on the foot of a race, but not so loud, and highly suggestive of ideas of the supernatural.'

Oft have I heard my honoured mother say,
  How she has listened to the Gabriel hounds—
  Those strange, unearthly, and mysterious sounds
Which on the ear through murkiest darkness fell ;
And how, entranced by superstitious spell,
  The trembling villager nor seldom heard,
  In the quaint notes of the nocturnal bird,
Of death premonished, some sick neighbour's knell.
I, too, remember, once at midnight dark,
  How these sky-yelpers startled me, and stirred
  My fancy so, I could have then averred
A mimic pack of beagles low did bark.
Nor wondered I that rustic fear should trace
A spectral huntsman doomed to that long moonless chase.

In the neighbourhood of Leeds these hounds are known as 'Gabble Retchets,' and are supposed, as in other places, to be the souls of unbaptized children who flit restlessly about their parents' abode. The Yeth hounds were heard some few years ago in the parish of St. Mary Tavy by an old man named Roger Burn. He was walking in the fields, when he suddenly heard the baying of the hounds, the shouts and horn of the huntsman, and the smacking of his whip. The last point the old man quoted as at once settling the question, 'How could I be mistaken? Why, I heard the very smacking of his whip.'

But, as Mr. Yarrell has long ago explained, this mysterious noise is caused by bean-geese, which, coming southwards in large flocks on the approach of winter—partly from Scotland and its islands, but chiefly from Scandinavia—choose dark nights for their migration, and utter a loud and very peculiar cry. The sound of these birds has been observed in every part of England, and as far west as Cornwall. One day a man was riding alone near Land's End on a still dark night, when the yelping cry broke out above his head so suddenly, and to appearance so near, that he instinctively pulled up the horse as if to allow the pack to pass, the animal trembling violently at the unexpected sounds.

An amusing account of the devil and his dandy-dogs is given by Mr. J. Q. Couch, in his 'Folk-lore of a Cornish Village,' from which it appears that 'a poor herdsman was journeying homeward across the moors one windy night, when he heard at a distance among the Tors the baying of hounds, which he soon recognised as the dismal chorus of the dandy-dogs. It was three or four miles to his house, and, very much alarmed, he hurried onward as fast as the treacherous nature of the soil and the uncertainty of the path would allow; but, alas! the melancholy yelping of the hounds, and the dismal holloa of the hunter, came nearer and nearer. After a considerable run they had so gained upon him that on looking back—oh, horror! he could distinctly see hunter and dogs. The former was terrible to look at, and had the usual complement of *saucer-eyes*, horns, and tail accorded by common consent to the legendary devil. He was black, of course, and carried in his hand a long hunting pole. The dogs, a numerous pack, blackened the small patch of moor that was visible, each snorting fire, and uttering a yelp of indescribably frightful tone. No cottage, rock, or tree was near to give the herdsman shelter, and nothing apparently remained to him but to abandon himself to their fury, when a happy thought suddenly flashed upon him and suggested a resource. Just as they were about to rush upon him, he fell on his knees in prayer.

There was a strange power in the holy words he
uttered, for immediately, as if resistance had been
offered, the hell hounds stood at bay, howling more
dismally than ever, and the hunter shouted, "Bo
Shrove," which means "The boy prays," at which
they all drew off on some other pursuit and
disappeared.'

Gervase of Tilbury informs us that in the
thirteenth century the wild hunt was often seen by
full moon in England traversing forest and down.
In the twelfth century it was known as the Herle-
thing, the banks of the Wye having been the scene
of the most frequent chases.

In Wales, the Cwn Annwn, or Dogs of Hell, or,
as they are sometimes called, 'Dogs of the Sky,' howl
through the air 'with a voice frightfully dispro-
portionate to their size, full of a wild sort of
lamentation,' but, although terrible to hear, they are
harmless, and have never been known to commit
any mischief. One curious peculiarity is that the
nearer these spectral hounds are to a man, the less
loud their voices sound; and the farther off they
are, the louder is their cry. According to one popular tradition, they are supposed to be hunting

through the air the soul of the wicked man the instant it quits the body.

This superstition occupies, too, a conspicuous place in the folk-lore of Germany and Norway. Mr. Baring-Gould, in his 'Iceland, its Scenes and Sages,' describes it as he heard it from his guide Jon, who related it to him under the title of the 'Yule Host.' He tells us how 'Odin, or Wodin, is the wild huntsman who nightly tears on his white horse over the German and Norwegian forests and moor-sweeps, with his legion of hell hounds. Some luckless woodcutter, on a still night, is returning through the pine-woods when suddenly his ear catches a distant wail; a moan rolls through the interlacing branches; nearer and nearer comes the sound. There is the winding of a long horn waxing louder and louder, the baying of hounds, the rattle of hoofs and paws on the pine-tree tops.' This spectral chase goes by different names. In Thuringia and elsewhere it is 'Hakelnberg' or 'Hackeln-bärend,' and the story goes that Hakelnberg was a knight passionately fond of the chase, who, on his death-bed, would not listen to the priest, but said, 'I care not for heaven, I care only for the chase.'

Then 'hunt until the last day,' exclaimed the
priest.   And now, through storm and sunshine, he
fleets, a faint barking or yelping in the air announcing his approach.   Thorpe quotes a similar story
as current in the Netherlands,[1] and in Denmark it
occurs under various forms.[2]   In Schleswig it is
Duke Abel, who slew his brother in 1252. Tradition
says that in an expedition against the Frieslanders,
he sank into a deep morass as he was fording the
Eyder, where, being encumbered with the weight
of his armour, he was slain.   His body was buried
in the Cathedral, but his spirit found no rest.
The canons dug up the corpse, and buried it in a
morass near Gottorp, but in the neighbourhood of
the place where he is buried all kinds of shrieks
and strange sounds have been heard, and 'many
persons worthy of credit affirm that they have
heard sounds so resembling a huntsman's horn,
that anyone would say that a hunter was hunting
there.   It is, indeed, the general rumour that
Abel has appeared to many, black of aspect, riding
on a small horse, and accompanied by three hounds,

[1] *Northern Mythology*, iii. p. 219.
[2] *Ibid.* ii. pp. 195–202.

which appear to be burning like fire.'[1] In Sweden, when a noise like that of carriage and horses is heard at night, the people say, ' Odin is passing by,' and in Norway this spectral hunt is known as the ' Chase of the inhabitants of Asgarth.' In Danzig, the leader of the hounds is Dyterbjernat, *i.e.* Diedrick of Bern. Near Fontainebleau, Hugh Capet is supposed to ride, having, it is said, rushed over the palace with his hounds before the assassination of Henry IV.; and at Blois, the hunt is called the ' Chasse Macabee.' In some parts of France the wild huntsman is known as Harlequin, or Henequin, and in the Franche Comté he is ' Herod in pursuit of the Holy Innocents.' This piece of folk-lore is widespread, and it may be added that in Normandy, the Pyrenees, and in Scotland, King Arthur has the reputation of making nightly rides.

Another form of spectre animal is the kirk-grim, which is believed to haunt many churches. Sometimes it is a dog, sometimes a pig, sometimes a horse, the haunting spectre being the spirit of an animal buried alive in the churchyard for the purpose of scaring away the sacrilegious. Swedish

[1] *Northern Mythology*, ii. pp. 198, 199.

tradition tells how it was customary for the early founders of Christian churches to bury a lamb under the altar. It is said that when anyone enters a church out of service time he may chance to see a little lamb spring across the choir and vanish. This is the church lamb, and its appearance in the churchyard, especially to the grave-digger, is said to betoken the death of a child.[1] According to a Danish form of this superstition, the kirk-grim dwells either in the tower or wherever it can find a place of concealment, and is thought to protect the sacred building; and it is said that in the streets of Kroskjoberg, a grave-sow, or as it is also called, a 'gray-sow,' has frequently been seen. It is thought to be the apparition of a sow formerly buried alive, and to forebode death and calamity.

[1] See Thorpe's *Northern Mythology*, ii. pp. 102, 166, 167.

CHAPTER IX

PHANTOM LIGHTS

STORIES of mysterious lights suddenly illuminating
the nocturnal darkness of unfrequented spots have
long been current throughout the world. In the
'Odyssey,' when Athene was mystically present as
Odysseus and Telemachus were moving the weapons
out of the hall (xix. 21–50), Telemachus exclaims,
'Father, surely a great marvel is this I behold!
Meseemeth that the walls of the hall, and the fair
spaces between the pillars, and the beams of pine,
and the columns that run aloft, are bright as it
were with flaming fire. Verily some god is within
of them that hold the wide heaven.' Odysseus
answers, 'Lo, this is the wont of the gods that
possess Olympus.' In Theocritus, when Hera
sends the snakes to attack the infant Heracles,
a mysterious flame shines forth. The same

phenomenon occurs in the Sagas of Burut Njas, when Gunnar sings within his tomb. The brilliance of the light which attends the presence of the supernatural is indeed widely diffused, and, as Mr. Andrew Lang writes,[1] 'Philosophers may dispute whether any objective fact lies at the bottom of this belief, or whether a savage superstition has survived into Greek epic and idyll and into modern ghost stories.'

Although science has years ago explained many such phosphoric appearances as governed by certain atmospheric laws, superstitious fancy has not only attributed to them supernatural causes, but associated them with all kinds of weird and romantic tales. According to one popular notion, strange lights of this kind are the spirits of persons who, for some reason, cannot remain quiet. Thus a spectre known as the ' Lady and the Lantern,' has long been said to haunt the beach at St. Ives, Cornwall, in stormy weather. The story goes that a lady and her child had been saved from a wreck, but the child was swept away and drowned, and

[1] The *Nineteenth Century*, 'Comparative Study of Ghost Stories,' 1885, xvii. pp. 629, 630.

she is supposed to be hunting for its body. Similar tales are told elsewhere, but the object of search is not always the same. A light, for instance, hovers about a stone on the Cornish coast, locally designated ' Madge Figg's Chair,' which is supposed to be the ghost of a wrecked lady whom Madge stripped of her jewels. In Scotland the appearance of a spectral ' lady of the golden casket' was attended by a phantom light, and it is also related how the ghost of a murdered woman is seen by her lover at sea, approaching in the shape of a bright light, which assumes the human form as it draws nearer. She finally calls him, and he springs into her arms, and disappears in a flash of fire.[1]

There is the popular legend of the ' Radiant Boy '—a strange boy with a shining face, who has been seen in certain Lincolnshire houses and elsewhere. This ghost was described to Mr. Baring-Gould [2] by a Yorkshire farmer, who, as he was riding one night to Thirsk, suddenly saw pass

[1] Rev. W. Gregor, *Folk-lore of North-East of Scotland*, 1881, p. 69.
[2] *Yorkshire Oddities*, ii. p. 105.

K

by him a 'radiant boy' on a white horse. To
quote his own words, 'there was no sound of
footfall as the boy drew nigh. He was first aware
of the approach of the mysterious rider by seeing
the shadow of himself and his horse flung before
him on the high road. Thinking there might be a
carriage with lamps, he was not alarmed till, by
the shortening of the shadow, he knew that the light
must be near him, and then he was surprised to
hear no sound. He thereupon turned in his saddle,
and at the same moment the "radiant boy" passed
him. He was a child of about eleven, with a fresh
bright face. "Had he any clothes on? and if so,
what were they like?" I asked. But the old man
could not tell. His astonishment was so great that
he took no notice of particulars. The boy rode on
till he came to a gate which led into a field; he
stooped as if to open the gate, rode through, and
all was instantly dark.'

At the commencement of the present century
the little village of Black Heddon, near Stam-
fordham, in Northumberland, was greatly disturbed by an apparition known as 'Silky,' from
the nature of her dress. She suddenly appeared

to benighted travellers, breaking forth upon them in dazzling splendour, in the darkest and most lonely parts of the road. This spirit exercised a marvellous power over the brute creation, and once, it is said, waylaid a waggon bringing coals to a farm near Black Heddon, and fixed the team upon a bridge, since called, after her, 'Silky's Brig.' Do what he could, the driver could not make the horses move a step, and there they would have stayed all night had not another farm servant come up with some mountain ash about him. It was generally supposed that Silky, who suddenly disappeared, was the troubled phantom of some person who had died miserable because she owned treasure, and was overtaken by death before she had disclosed its hiding-place.

An old barn situated near Birchen Tower, Hollinwood, which was noted for the apparition of Madame Beswick on dark and wintry nights, at times, it is said, appears to be on fire, a red glare of glowing heat being observable through the loopholes and crevices of the building. Sometimes the sight is so threatening that the neighbours will raise an alarm that the barn is in flames. But when the

premises are searched, everything is in order, and
nothing found wrong.[1]   And a Welsh romance
tells how, after Howel Sele slew his cousin Glendower, and buried him in ' a broad and blasted oak,
scorched by the lightning's vivid glare,'

> Pale lights on Cader's rocks were seen,
> And midnight voices heard to moan.

Such phantom lights are not confined to land, and
most of the tales of spectre ships speak of their
being seen by the affrighted crews.   In the ' Salem
Spectre Ship ' we are told how

> The night grew thick, but a phantom light
> Around her path was shed.

They are generally dreaded as foreboding a catastrophe, and have given rise to a host of curious
stories.   A light is said to hover about in Sennen
Cove, which is thought to be an ill-omened apparition; and a Welsh story speaks of a ghost,
the ' Cyhyraeth,' that appears on the beach, in a
light, with groanings and cries.[2]   Flames are reported to issue from the Eider River, and from
several lakes in Germany.   Where ships have been

---

[1] See Ingram's *Haunted Homes*, 2nd S. pp. 29, 30.
[2] See Wirt Sikes' *British Goblins*, pp. 219–221.

wrecked, blue lights are supposed to faintly glimmer, occasionally accompanied by the spirits of
wrecked or injured persons. A notable instance is
told of Sable Island,[1] where, with the leaping flames,
is seen the 'Lady of Copeland' wrecked and murdered by pirates from the Amelie transport. She
has one finger missing on her hand.

Sometimes weird lights flickering in solitary
places are thought to be the unhappy spirits of
wicked persons who have no rest in the grave.
Milton refers to this fancy in his 'Paradise Lost'
(ix. 634) :

> A wandering fire,
> Compact of unctuous vapour, which the night
> Condenses, and the cold environs round,
> Kindled through agitation to a flame,
> Which oft, they say, some evil spirit attends,
> Hovering and blazing with delusive light,
> Misleads the amazed night wanderer from his way
> To bogs and mires ; and oft through pond or pool
> There swallowed up and lost from succour far.

Hence they were doomed to wander backwards and
forwards carrying a light. A tradition current in
Normandy says that a pale light occasionally seen
by travellers is the unquiet spirit of some unfortu-

[1] 'Secrets of Sable Island,' *Harper's Magazine.*

hate woman who, as a punishment for her intrigues
with a minister of the Church, is doomed to this
existence.   There are various versions of this story,
and one formerly current in this country tells
how the hovering flame—the cause of terror to
many—is the soul of a priest who has been condemned to expiate his vows of perpetual chastity
by thus haunting the scenes of his disobedience.
Brand, quoting from an old work on 'Lights that
Lead People out of their Ways in the Night,' informs
us that the lights which are seen in churchyards
and Moorish places were represented by the Popish
clergy to be 'souls come out of purgatory all in
flame, to move the people to pray for their entire
deliverance, by which they gulled them of much
money to say mass for them, everyone thinking it
might be the soul of his or her deceased relations.'

According to another explanation, it is believed
on the Continent that the ghosts of those who in
their lifetime were guilty of removing their neighbours' landmarks are fated to rcam hither and
thither, lantern in hand, 'sometimes impelled to
replace the old boundary mark, then to move it
again, constantly changing their course with their

changing purpose.' A Swedish tradition adds that such a spirit may be heard saying in a harsh, hoarse voice, ' It is right! it is right! it is right!' But the next moment qualms of conscience and anguish seize him, and he then exclaims, ' It is wrong! it is wrong! it is wrong!'[1] It is also said that these lights are the souls of land-measurers, who, having acted dishonestly in their business, are trying to remedy the wrong measurements they made. A German legend tells how, at the partition of the land, there arose between the villages of Alversdorf and Röst, in South Ditmarschen, great disputes. One man gave fraudulent measurements, but after his death he wandered about as a fire sprite. A flame, the height of a man, was seen dancing about till the moor dried up. Whenever it flared up higher than usual, the people would cry out, ' Dat is de Scheelvalgt '—that is the land-divider. There is a tale told of a certain land-measurer near Farsum, in the Netherlands, who had in his lifetime acted dishonestly when he had a piece of land to measure. He suffered himself ' to

---

[1] See Thorpe's *Northern Mythology*, ii. pp. 97, 202, 211; iii. pp. 11, 158, 268.

be bribed by one or other, and then allotted to the
party more than was just, for which offence he
was condemned after death to wander as a burning
man with a burning measuring-staff.'

Popular fancy, too, has long identified phantom
lights as being the souls of unbaptized children.
Because such souls cannot enter heaven, they make
their abodes in forests, and in dark and lonely places,
where they mourn over their hard lot.   If at night
they chance to meet anyone, they run up to him, and
walk on before to show him the way to some water
where they may be baptized.   The mysterious lady,
Frau Bertha, is ever attended by troops of unbaptized
children, whom she takes with her when she joins
the wild huntsman.   One tradition relates how a
Dutch parson, happening to return home later
than usual, was confronted with no less than
three of these fiery phenomena.   Remembering
them to be the souls of unbaptized children, he
thoughtfully stretched out his hand, and pronounced
the words of baptism over them.   But, much to his
unexpected surprise, in the same instant hundreds of
these moving lights made their appearance, which so
frightened him that, forgetting his good intentions,

he ran home as fast as he could. In Ireland unbaptized children have been represented as sitting blindfolded within fairy moats, the peasantry supposing such souls 'go into nought.' A somewhat similar idea may be found in Longfellow's 'Evangeline,' where we have introduced among the *contes* of an Arcadian village notary allusion to

> The white Létiche, the ghost of a child unchristened,
> Died, and was doomed to haunt unseen the chambers of children.

Closely allied with the notion of phantom lights are the strange phosphoric appearances said occasionally to be seen about the dying. In Russia, the soul under certain circumstances is believed to assume the form of a flame, and such a ghostly apparition cannot be banished till the necessary prayers have been offered up.[1] According to a Sussex death-omen, lights of a circular form seen in the air are significant, and it is supposed that the death of sick persons is shown by the prognostic of 'shell-fire.' This is a sort of lambent flame, which seems to rise from the bodies of those who are ill, and to envelope the bed. On one occasion, con-

[1] *Songs of the Russian People*, 1872, p. 116.

siderable alarm was created in a Sussex village by
a pale light being observed to move over the bed of
a sick person, and after flickering for some time in
different parts of the room, to vanish through the
window. But the difficulty was eventually explained, for the light was found to proceed from a
luminous insect—the small glow-worm.[1] Marsh [2]
relates how a pale moonlight-coloured glimmer was
once seen playing round the head of a dying girl
about an hour and a half before her last breath.
The light proceeded from her head, and was faint and
tremulous like the reflection of summer lightning,
which at first those watching her mistook it to be.
Another case, reported by a medical man in Ireland,
was that of a consumptive patient, in whose cabin
strange lights had been seen, filling the neighbourhood with alarm. To quote a further instance,
from the mouth of a patient in a London hospital,
some time since, the nurses observed issuing a pale
bluish flame, and soon after the man died. The
frightened nurses were at a loss to account for this
unusual sight, but a scientific explanation of the

[1] *Folk-lore Record*, 1878, i. p. 54.
[2] *Evolution of Light from the Living Subject.*

phenomenon ascribed it to phosphoretted hydrogen,
a result of incipient decomposition.[1]

Dante Rossetti, in his 'Blessed Damozel,' when
he describes her as looking down from heaven
towards the earth that 'spins like a fretful image,'
whence she awaits the coming of her lover, depicts
the souls mounting up to God as passing by her
'like thin flames.'

Another form of this superstitious fancy is the
corpse-candle, or 'tomb-fire,' which is invariably a
death-warning. It sometimes appears 'as a stately
flambeau, stalking along unsupported, burning with
a ghastly blue flame. Sometimes it is a plain tallow
"dip" in the hand of a ghost; and when the ghost
is seen distinctly, it is recognised as that of some
person still living, who will now soon die [2]—in fact,
a wraith.' Occasionally the light issues from the
person's mouth, or nostrils. The size of the candle
indicates the age of the person who is about to die,
being large when it is a full-grown person whose
death is foretold, small when it is a child, still
smaller when an infant. When two candles to-

[1] *Transactions Cardiff Natural Society*, iv. p. 5.
[2] Wirt Sikes, *British Goblins*, p. 239.

gether are seen, one of which is large and the other
small, it is a mother and child who are to die.
When the flame is white the doomed person is a
woman, when red a man. A Carmarthenshire
tradition relates how one evening, when the coach
which runs between Llandilo and Carmarthen was
passing by Golden Grove, the property of the Earl
of Cawdor, three corpse-candles were observed
on the surface of the water gliding down the
stream which runs near the road. A few days
afterwards, just as many men were drowned there.
Such a light, too, has long been thought to hover
near the grave of the drowned, reminding us of
Moore's lines—

Where lights, like charnel meteors, burned the distant wave,
Bluely as o'er some seaman's grave,

and stories of such uncanny appearances have been
told of nearly every village churchyard.

It should be added that, according to a popular
idea, the presence of ghosts was announced, in bygone years, by an alteration in the tint of the lights
which happened to be burning—an item of folk-lore
alluded to in 'Richard III.' (Act v. sc. 3), where
the tyrant exclaims as he awakens—

The lights burn blue. It is now dead midnight,
Cold fearful drops stand on my trembling flesh.

. . . .

Methought the souls of all that I had murder'd
Came to my tent.

So in 'Julius Cæsar,' (Act iv. sc. 3), Brutus, on
seeing the ghost of Cæsar, exclaims:

How ill this taper burns! Ha! Who comes here?

Phantom lights have also been associated with
buildings, as in the case of the ancient chapel of
Roslin, founded in the year 1446 by William St.
Clair, Prince of Orkney. It is believed that
whenever any of the founder's descendants are
about to depart this life, the chapel appears to be
on fire, a weird and terrible occurrence graphically
portrayed by Harold's song in 'The Lay of the
Last Minstrel':

O'er Roslin all that dreary night,
    A wondrous blaze was seen to gleam;
'Twas broader than the watch-fire light,
    And redder than the bright moonbeam.

It glared on Roslin's castled rock,
    It ruddied all the copse-wood glen;
'Twas seen from Dryden's groves of oak,
    And seen from cavern'd Hawthornden.

Seem'd all on fire that chapel proud,
  Where Roslin's chiefs uncoffin'd lie ;
Each Baron, for a sable shroud,
  Sheathed in his iron panoply.

Seem'd all on fire, within, around,
  Deep sacristy and altar's pale ;
Shone every pillar foliage-bound,
  And glimmer'd all the dead men's mail.

Blazed battlement and pinnet high,
  Blazed every rose-carved buttress fair ;
So still they blaze when fate is nigh,
  The lordly line of Hugh St. Clair.

But notwithstanding the fact that the last
'Roslin,' as he was called, died in 1778, and the
estates passed into the possession of the Erskines,
Earls of Rosslyn, the old tradition has not yet
been extinguished.[1] Sir Walter Scott also tells us
that the death of the head of a Highland family
is sometimes announced by a chain of lights, of
different colours, called Dr'eug, or death of the
Druid. The direction which it takes is supposed to
mark the place of the funeral.[2] A correspondent of
'Notes and Queries' gives a curious account of a

---

[1] See Ingram's *Haunted Homes*, 2nd S. pp. 219–221.
[2] See ' Essay on Fairy Superstitions ' in the *Border Minstrelsy*.

house at Taunton which possessed 'a luminous chamber,' for, as common report said, 'the room had a light of its own.' As an eye-witness observed, 'A central window was generally illuminated.' All the other windows were dark, but from this was a wan, dreary light visible; and as the owners had deserted the place, and it had no occupant, the lighted window became a puzzle.

With the North American tribes one form of spiritual manifestation is fire; and among the Hurons, a female spirit, who was supposed to cause much of their sickness, appeared like a flame of fire. Of the New England Indians it is related that 'they have a remarkable observation of a flame that appears before the death of an Indian, upon their wigwams, in the dead of night. Whenever this appears, there will be a death.'[1] The Eskimos believe that the Inue, or powerful spirits, 'generally have the appearance of a fire or bright light, and to see them is very dangerous, particularly as foreshadowing the death of a relation.'[2]

[1] Rink's *Tales and Traditions of the Eskimos*, p. 43.
[2] Josselyn's *Two Voyages*, p. 133.

CHAPTER X

THE HEADLESS GHOST

LOCALITIES where any fatal accident has happened, or murder been committed, are frequently supposed to be haunted by that uncanny apparition known as 'the headless ghost.' Many curious tales are still told by the peasantry of this mysterious spectre, whose weird movements have long been the subject of comment. Sir Walter Scott, it may be remembered, speaking of the Irish dullahan, writes: ' It puts me in mind of a spectre at Drumlanrick Castle, of no less a person than the Duchess of Queensberry—"Fair Kitty, blooming, young, and gay"—who, instead of setting fire to the world in mama's chariot, amuses herself with wheeling her own head in a wheelbarrow through the great gallery.'

But it has often puzzled the folk-lorist why

ghosts should assume this form, although the idea is by no means a modern one, for, as Dr. Tylor has pointed out,[1] a people of wide celebrity are Pliny's Blemmyæ, said 'to be headless, and accordingly to have their mouths and eyes in their breasts—creatures over whom Prester John reigned in Asia, and who dwelt far and wide in South America.' Stories, too, like that of St. Denis, who is said to have walked from Paris, *sans tête*, to the place which bears his name, show that the living, as well as the dead, occasionally managed to do without their heads—a strange peculiarity which Kornmann, in his 'De Miraculis Vivorum,' would attempt to account for philosophically. Princess Marie Lichtenstein, in her 'History of Holland House,' tells us that one room of this splendid old mansion is believed to be haunted by Lord Holland, the first of his name, and the chief builder of Holland House. To quote her words, 'The gilt room is said to be tenanted by the solitary ghost of its just lord, who, according to tradition, issues forth at midnight from behind a secret door, and walks slowly through the scenes of former triumphs with his

---

[1] *Primitive Culture*, i. p. 390.

head in his hand.   To add to this mystery, there is
a tale of three spots of blood on one side of the
recess whence he issues—three spots which can
never be effaced.'   Such a strange act, on the part
of the dead, is generally regarded as a very bad
omen.   The time of the headless ghost's appearance
is always midnight, and in Crofton Croker's 'Fairy
Legends of Ireland' it is thus described :

> 'Tis midnight ; how gloomy and dark !
>   By Jupiter, there's not a star !
> 'Tis fearful ! 'tis awful ! and hark !
>   What sound is that comes from afar ?
>
> A coach ! but the coach has no head ;
>   And the horses are headless as it,
> Of the driver the same may be said,
>   And the passengers inside who sit.

According to the popular opinion, there is no
authority to prove that headless people are unable
to speak; on the contrary, a variation of the story
of 'The Golden Mountain,' given in a note to the
'Kindermärchen,' relates how a servant without a
head informed the fisherman (who was to achieve
the adventure) of the enchantment of the king's
daughter, and of the mode of liberating her.   There

is the Belludo, a Spanish ghost mentioned by
Washington Irving in his ' Tales of the Alhambra.'
It issues forth in the dead of night, and scours
the avenues of the Alhambra, and the streets of
Granada, in the shape of a headless horse, pursued
by six hounds, with terrible yellings and howlings.
It is said to be the spirit of a Moorish king, who
killed his six sons, who, in revenge, hunt him in
the shape of hounds at night-time.

In some cases, as it has been humorously
observed, the headless ghosts of well-known persons
have continued to set up their carriage after death.
Thus, for years past, it has been firmly believed
that Lady Anne Boleyn rides down the avenue of
Blickling Park once a year, with her bloody head
in her lap, sitting in a hearse-like coach drawn by
four headless horses, and attended by coachmen
and attendants, who have, out of compliment to
their mistress, also left their heads behind them.
Nor, if tradition is to be believed, is her father
more at rest than she, for Sir Thomas Boleyn is
said to be obliged to cross forty bridges to avoid
the torments of the furies. Like his daughter, he
is reported to drive about in a coach and four with

headless horses, carrying his head under his arm.[1]
Young Lord Dacre, who is said to have been
murdered at Thetford, through the contrivance of
his guardian, Sir Richard Fulmerston, in 1569, by
the falling of a wooden horse, purposely rendered
insecure, used to prance up and down on the ghost
of a headless rocking-horse.

Another romantic story is told [2] of a large field
at Great Melton, divided from the Yare by a
plantation, along which the old Norwich road ran.
'Close to the edge of where the road is said to have
run is a deep pit or hole of water, locally reputed
to be fathomless. Every night at midnight, and
every day at noon, a carriage drawn by four horses,
driven by headless coachmen and footmen, and
containing four headless ladies in white, rises
silently and dripping wet from the pool, flits stately
and silently round the field, and sinks as silently
into the pool again.' The story goes that long,
long ago, a bridal party driving along the old
Norwich Road were accidentally upset into the deep
hole, and were never seen again. Strangely

---

[1] See *The Norfolk Antiquarian Miscellany*, 1877, i. pp. 288,
289.   [2] *Eastern Counties Collectanea*, . 3.

enough the same story is told of fields near Bury
St. Edmunds, and at Leigh, Dorsetshire.[1]   Another
Norfolk story, amusingly told by the late Cuthbert
Bede,[2] informs us how, ' on the anniversary of the
death of the gentleman whose spectre he is supposed to be, his ghostship drives up to his old family
mansion. He drives through the wall, carriage
and horses and all, and is not seen again for a
twelvemonth. He leaves, however, the traces of
his visit behind him ; for, in the morning, the
stones of the wall through which he had ridden
over-night are found to be loosened and fallen ;
and though the wall is constantly repaired, yet the
stones are as constantly loosened.'   In the little
village of Acton, Suffolk, it was currently reported
not many years ago that on certain occasions the
park gates were wont to fly open at midnight
' withouten hands,' and that a carriage drawn by
four spectral horses, and accompanied by headless
grooms and outriders, proceeded with great rapidity
from the park to a spot called ' the nursery corner,'

[1] See *Notes and Queries*, 1st S. xii. p. 486, for another hole or
pit story.

[2] *The Curate of Cranston, and other Stories*, 1862, ' Carriage
and Four Ghosts.'

a spot where tradition affirms a very bloody
engagement took place in olden times, when the
Romans were governors of England.[1] A similar
tale is related of Caistor Castle, the seat of
the Falstofs, where the headless apparition drives
round the courtyard, and carries away some
unearthly visitors.

At Beverley, in Yorkshire, the headless ghost of
Sir Joceline Percy drives four headless horses at
night, above its streets, passing over a certain
house which was said to contain a chest with one
hundred nails in it, one of which dropped out every
year. The reason assigned for this nocturnal disturbance is attributed to the fact that Sir Joceline
once rode on horseback into Beverley Minster. It
has long been considered dangerous to meet such
spectral teams, for fear of being carried off by them,
so violent and threatening are their movements.
In ' Rambles in Northumberland ' we are told how,
' when the death-hearse, drawn by headless horses,
and driven by a headless driver, is seen about midnight proceeding rapidly, but without noise, towards the churchyard, the death of some consider-

[1] *Notes and Queries*, 1st S. v. p. 295.

able personage in the parish is sure to happen at no distant period.'

Night after night, too, when it is sufficiently dark, the headless coach whirls along the rough approach to Langley Hall, near Durham, drawn by black and fiery steeds; and many years ago a headless boggart was supposed to haunt Preston streets and neighbouring lanes. Its presence was often accompanied by the rattling of chains. It presently changed its form, and whether it appeared as a woman or a black dog, it was always headless. The story went that this uncanny apparition was at length 'laid' by some magical or religious ceremony in Walton churchyard.[1]

Many spots where suicides have been buried are supposed to be haunted by headless ghosts attired in white grave-clothes. Some few years ago, as a peasant was passing in a waggon with three horses a 'four-lane-end' in Lyneal Lane, Ellesmere, Shropshire, where a man was buried with a forked stake run through the body to keep it down, a woman was seen without a head. The horses took fright, and started off, overturning the waggon, and

[1] Hardwick's *Traditions, Superstitions, and Folk-lore*, p. 130.

pitching the man into the Drumby Hole, where
the waggon and shaft-horse fell upon him. The
other horses broke loose and galloped home, where
they arrived covered with foam, and on a search
being made, the dead body of the waggoner was
found in the hole.[1] Exactly twelve months afterwards, his son, it is said, was killed by the same
horses on the same spot. As Miss Jackson points
out, the headless ghost in this story is of a different
sex from the person whose death is supposed to
cause its restlessness. The same, she adds, is the
case 'with the ghost of the Mary Way, a now
almost forgotten spectre of more than a hundred
years ago. The figure of a woman in white was
supposed to haunt the spot where a murderer was
buried—more probably a suicide—at the cross
roads about two miles from Wenlock, on the Bridg-
north road, which is known as the "Mary Way,"
no doubt from some chapel, or processional route,
in honour of the Virgin.' Another story is told of
the Baschurch neighbourhood, where the ghost of
a man who hanged himself at Nesscliff is to be seen
'riding about in his trap at night without a head.'

[1] *Shropshire Folk-lore*, p. 112.

A tragic case is recorded by Crofton Croker, who tells how, many years ago, a clergyman belonging to St. Catharine's Church, Dublin, resided at the old Castle of Donore, in the vicinity of that city. From melancholy, or some other cause, he put an end to his existence by hanging himself out of a window near the top of the castle. After his death, a coach, sometimes driven by a coachman without a head, and occasionally drawn by headless horses, was observed at night driving furiously by Roper's Rest.

Referring to spots where murders have taken place, a Shropshire tradition informs us how, at a certain house at Hampton's Wood, near Ellesmere, six illegitimate children were murdered by their parents, and buried in a garden. But, soon after this unnatural event, a ghost in the form of a man, sometimes headless, at other times not so, haunted the stables, rode the horses to water, and talked to the waggoner. Once it appeared to a young lady who was passing on horseback, and rode before her on her horse. Eventually, after much difficulty, this troublesome ghost was laid, but 'the poor minister was so exhausted by the task that he died.' [1]

[1] *Shropshire Folk-lore*, pp. 113, 114.

There is a haunted room at Walton Abbey frequented by a spectre known as 'The Headless Nun of Walton.' The popular belief is that this is the unquiet spirit of a transgressing nun of the twelfth century, but some affirm it to be that of a lady brutally beheaded in the seventeenth century.[1] Another instance is that of Calverley Hall, in the same county. In 'The Yorkshireman' for January 5, 1884, the particulars of this strange apparition are given, from which it appears that Walter Calverley, on April 23, 1604, went into a fit of insane frenzy of jealousy, or pretended to do so. Money-lenders were pressing him hard, and he had become desperate. Rushing madly into the house, he plunged a dagger into one and then into another of his children, and then tried to take the life of their mother, a crime for which he was pressed to death at York Castle. But his spirit could not rest, and he was often seen galloping about the district at night on a headless horse, being generally accompanied by a number of followers similarly

[1] A full account will be found in a paper by Mr. F. Ross, in the *Leeds Mercury*, 1884, entitled 'Yorkshire Legends and Traditions.'

mounted, who attempted to run down any poor
benighted folks whom they chanced to meet. These
spectral horsemen nearly always disappeared in
a cave in the wood, but this cave has now been
quarried away.[1]

It would seem that in years gone by one of the
punishments assigned to evil doers guilty of a lesser
crime than that of murder, was their ceaselessly
frequenting those very spots where in their lifetime
they had committed their wicked acts, carrying
their heads under their arms. Numerous tales of
this kind have been long current on the Continent,
and at the present day are told by the simple-
minded peasantry of many a German village with
the most implicit faith. It is much the same in
this country, and Mr. Henderson [2] has given several
amusing anecdotes. At Dalton, near Thirsk, there
was an old barn, said to be haunted by a headless
woman. One night a tramp went into it to sleep; at
midnight he was awakened by a light, and, sitting
up, he saw a woman coming towards him from the
end of the barn, holding her head in her hands

[1] See Ingram's *Haunted Homes*, 2nd S. pp. 72-78.
[2] *Folk-lore of the Northern Counties*, pp. 326-328.

like a lantern, with light streaming out of the eyes,
nostrils, and mouth. Hunt, too, in his 'Popular
Romances,' notices this superstition as existing in
the West of England ; and Mrs. Latham, in her
' Sussex Superstitions,' tells us how spirits are
reported to walk about without their heads ;
others carry them under their arms ; and one
haunting a dark lane is said to have ' a ball of fire
upon its shoulders in lieu of the natural finial.'
At Haddington, Worcestershire, there is an avenue
of trees locally known as 'Lady Winter's Walk,'
where, it is said, the lady of Thomas Winter, who was
obliged to conceal himself on account of his share in
the Gunpowder Plot, was in the habit of awaiting
her husband's further visits, and here the headless
spectre of her ladyship used to be seen occasionally
pacing up and down beneath the sombre shade of
the aged trees.

Lady Wilde [1] has given a laughable specimen of
the headless ghost as believed in by the Irish
peasantry. One Denis Molony, a cow-jobber, was
on his way to the great fair at Navan when he was
overtaken by night. He laid down under a hedge,

---

[1] *Ancient Cures, Charms, and Usages of Ireland*, pp. 163, 164.

but 'at that moment a loud moaning and screaming came to his ear, and a woman rushed past him
all in white, as if a winding sheet were round her,
and her cries of despair were terrible to hear.
Then, after her, a great black coach came thundering along the road, drawn by two black horses.
But when Denis looked close at them he saw that the
horses had no heads, and the coachman had no head;
and out sprang two men from the coach, and they
had no heads either; and they seized the woman and
carried her by force into the carriage and drove off.'

It appears that the woman Denis saw was ' an
evil liver and a wicked sinner, and no doubt the
devils were carrying her off from the churchyard,
for she had been buried that morning. To make
sure, they went next morning to the churchyard to
examine the grave, and there, sure enough, was the
coffin, but it was open, and not a trace of the dead
woman was to be seen. So they knew that an evil
fate had come on her, and that her soul was gone
to eternal tortures.' [1]

[1] See notes to Crofton Croker's *Fairy Legends and Traditions
of the South of Ireland*, where much curious information will be
found on this subject.

Connected also with the legend of the headless ghost is the old belief that persons prior to their death occasionally appear to their friends without their heads. Dr. Ferrier, in his 'Theory of Apparitions,' tells of an old Northern chieftain who informed a relative of his 'that the door of the room in which they and some ladies were sitting had appeared to open, and that a little woman without a head had entered the room; and that the apparition indicated the sudden death of some person of his acquaintance.' The 'Glasgow Chronicle' (January, 1826) records how, on the occasion of some silk-weavers being out of work, mourning-coaches drawn by headless horses were seen about the town; and some years ago a very unpleasant kind of headless ghost used to drive every Saturday night through the town of Doneraile, Ireland, and to stop at the doors of different houses, when, if anyone were so foolhardy as to open the door, a basin of blood was instantly flung in his face.

CHAPTER XI

PHANTOM BUTTERFLIES

DEPARTED souls, according to a Cornish piece of
folk-lore, are occasionally said to take the form of
moths, and in Yorkshire, writes a correspondent
of 'Notes and Queries,' 'the country people used,
and perhaps do still, call night-flying white moths,
especially the *Hepialus humuli*, which feeds while
in the grub state on the roots of docks and other
coarse plants, " souls." ' By the Slavonians the
butterfly seems to have been universally accepted
as an emblem of the soul. Mr. Ralston, in his
'Songs of the Russian People' (p. 117), says that
in the Government of Yaroslaw one of its names
is *dushichka*, a caressing diminutive of *dusha*, the
soul. In that of Kherson it is believed that if the
usual alms are not distributed at a funeral, the
dead man's soul will reveal itself to its relatives in

the form of a moth flying about the flame of a candle. The day after receiving such a warning visit they call together the poor and distribute food among them. In Bohemia there is a popular tradition that if the first butterfly a man sees in the spring-time is a white one, he is destined to die within the year. According to a Servian belief, the soul of a witch often leaves her body while she is asleep, and flies abroad in the shape of a butter-fly. If, during its absence, her body be turned round, so that her feet are placed where her head was before, the soul will not be able to find her mouth, and so will be shut out from her body. Thereupon the witch will die. The Bulgarians believe that at death the soul assumes the form of a butterfly, and flits about on the nearest tree till the funeral is over. The Karens of Burma 'will run about pretending to catch a sick man's wandering soul, or, as they say with the ancient Greeks, his " butterfly," and at last drop it down upon his head.' [1] The idea is an old one, and, as Gubernatis remarks in his ' Zoological Mythology ' (ii. 213), ' the butterfly was both a phallic symbol and a

[1] Tylor's *Primitive Culture*, i. p. 437.

funereal one, with promises of resurrection and
transformation ; the souls of the departed were
represented in the forms of butterflies carried
towards Elysium by the dolphin.' According to
another belief, the soul was supposed to take
the form of a bee, an old tradition telling us
that 'the bees alone of all animals descended
from Paradise.' In the Engadine, in Switzerland, it is believed that the souls of men emigrate
from the world and return to it in the forms of
bees. In this district bees are considered mes-
sengers of death. When someone dies, the bee is invoked as follows, 'almost as if requesting the soul
of the departed,' says De Gubernatis, 'to watch for
ever over the living' : [1]

> Bienchen, unser Herr ist todt,
> Verlass mich nicht in meiner Noth.

In Russia gnats and flies are often looked upon
as equally spiritual creatures. 'In Little Russia,'
says Mr. Ralston,[2] 'the old women of a family will
often, after returning from a funeral, sit up all
night watching a dish in which water and honey

---

[1] *Zoological Mythology*, ii. p. 218.
[2] *Folk-songs of the Russian People*, p. 118.

M

in it have been placed, in the belief that the spirit
of their dead relative will come in the form of a
fly, and sip the proffered liquid.'

Among North American tribes we are told how
the Ojibways believe that innumerable spirits
appear in the varied forms of insect life,[1] while
some tribes supposed that 'most souls went to a
common resort near their living habitat, but returned in the daytime in the shape of flies in
order to get something to eat.'[2]

[1] Dorman's *Primitive Superstitions*, p. 23.
[2] *Ibid.* p. 42.

CHAPTER XII

RAISING GHOSTS

THE trade of raising spirits has probably existed at all times in which superstition has been sufficiently prevalent to make such a practice a source of power or of profit, and nations—the most polished as well as the most barbarous—have admitted the claims of persons who professed to be able to control spirits. One of the most graphic illustrations of an incantation for evoking spirits is in connection with the appearance of the shade of Darius in the 'Persæ' of Æschylus, which is very nobly given. After receiving news of the great defeat of her son Xerxes at Salamis, Atossa has prepared the requisite offerings to the dead— milk from a white cow, honey, water from a pure fountain, unadulterated wine, olives, and flowers— and she instructs the ancient counsellors of the

M 2

deceased king to evoke his shade. They who form
the tragic chorus commence an incantation from
which we quote the following :

> Royal lady, Persia's pride,
> Thine offerings in earth's chamber hide ;
> We, meanwhile, with hymns will sue
> The powers who guard hell's shadowy crew,
> Till they to our wish incline.
> Gods below, ye choir divine,
> Earth, Hermes, and thou King of night,
> Send his spirit forth to light !
> If he knows worse ills impending,
> He alone can teach their ending.
> &c., &c., &c.

The incantation is successful, but Darius
assures his friends that exit from below is far
from easy, and that the subterranean gods are far
more willing to take than to let go. Indeed, the
raising of spirits was a trick of magic much in
use in ancient times, and the scene that took
place at Endor when Saul had recourse to a
professor of the art is familiar to all. The
Egyptian magicians, Simon Magus, and Elymas
the sorcerer, all, it is said, exhibited such corporeal
deceptions. Tertullian, in his tract 'De Anima,'
inquires whether a departed soul, either at his

own will, or in obedience to the command of
another, can return from the 'Inferi'? After
discussing the subject, he sums up thus: 'If
certain souls have been recalled into their bodies
by the power of God, as manifest proof of His
prerogative, that is no argument that a similar
power should be conferred on audacious magicians,
fallacious dreamers, and licentious poets.'

Among certain Australian tribes the necro-
mants are called Birraark. It is said that a
Birraark was supposed to be initiated by the
'mrarts' (ghosts) when they met him wandering
in the bush. It was from the ghosts that he
obtained replies to questions concerning events
passing at a distance, or yet to happen, which
might be of interest or moment to his tribe. An
account of a spiritual séance in the bush is given
in 'Kamilaroi and Kurnai' (p. 254) : 'The fires
were let down; the Birraark uttered the cry
"Coo-ee" at intervals. At length a distant reply
was heard, and shortly afterwards the sound as of
persons jumping on the ground in succession. A
voice was then heard in the gloom asking in a
strange intonation, "What is wanted?" At the

termination of the séance, the spirit voice said, "We are going." Finally, the Birraark was found in the top of an almost inaccessible tree, apparently asleep.'

In Japan, ghosts can be raised in various ways. One mode is to 'put into an andon' (a paper lantern in a frame) 'a hundred rushlights, and repeat an incantation of a hundred lines. One of these rushlights is taken out at the end of each line, and the would-be ghost-seer then goes out in the dark with one light still burning, and blows it out, when the ghost ought to appear. Girls who have lost their lovers by death often try that sorcery.' [1]

Shakespeare has several allusions to the popular belief of certain persons being able to exorcise, or raise, spirits, and he represents Ligarius, in 'Julius Cæsar' (iv. 2) as saying :

> Soul of Rome !
> Brave son, derived from honourable loins !
> Thou, like an exorcist, has conjured up
> My mortified spirit.   Now bid me run,
> And I will strive with things impossible ;
> Yea, get the better of them.

---

[1] Miss Bird's *Unbeaten Tracks in Japan*, i. p. 380.

In days gone by, it would seem, numerous for-
malities were observed by the person whose object
was to ' constrain ' some spirit to appear before
him. It was necessary to fix upon a spot proper
for such a purpose, ' which had to be either in a
subterranean vault hung round with black, and
lighted by a magical torch, or else in the centre of
some thick wood or desert, or upon some extensive unfrequented plain, where several roads met,
or amidst the ruins of ancient castles, abbeys,
monasteries, &c., or amongst the rocks on the
sea-shore, in some private detached churchyard,
or any other solemn melancholy place, between the
hours of twelve and one in the morning, either
when the moon shone very bright, or else when
the elements were disturbed with storms of thunder,
lightning, wind, and rain, for in these places, times,
and seasons it was contended that spirits could with
less difficulty manifest themselves to mortal eyes,
and continue visible with the least pain in this
elemental external world.' [1]   Great importance was
attached to the magic circle in the invocation of
spirits, the mode of procedure being thus : ' A piece

[1] *Occult Sciences*, 1855, Elihu Rich, p. 188.

of ground was usually chosen, nine feet square,
at the full extent of which parallel lines were
drawn, one within the other, having sundry crosses
and triangles described between them, close to
which was formed the first or outer circle; then,
about half a foot within the same, a second circle was
described, and within that another square correspondent to the first, the centre of which was the spot
where the master and associate were to be placed.
The vacancies formed by the various lines and
angles of the figure were filled up by the holy names
of God, having crosses and triangles described
between them. . . . The reason assigned for the use of
circles was, that so much ground being blessed and
consecrated by such holy words and ceremonies as
they made use of in forming it, had a secret force
to expel all evil spirits from the bounds thereof, and
being sprinkled with pure sanctified water, the
ground was purified from all uncleanness; besides,
the holy names of God being written over every
part of it, its force became so powerful that no
evil spirits had ability to break through it, or to get
at the magician and his companion, by reason of
the antipathy in nature they bore to these sacred

names. And the reason given for the triangles was, that if the spirit was not easily brought to speak the truth, they might by the exorcist be conjured to enter the same, where, by virtue of the names of the essence and divinity of God, they could speak nothing but what was true and right.'[1] We are further informed, that if the ghost of a deceased person was to be raised, the grave had to be resorted to at midnight, when a special form of conjuration was deemed necessary; and there was another for 'any corpse that hath hanged, drowned, or otherwise made away with itself.' And in this case, it is added, 'the conjurations are performed over the body, which will at last arise, and, standing upright, answer with a faint and hollow voice the questions that are put to it.'

The mode of procedure as practised in Scotland was thus. The haunted room was made ready. He 'who was to do the daring deed, about nightfall entered the room, bearing with him a table, a chair,

[1] For works on this subject may be consulted, Colin de Plancy's *Dictionnaire Infernal*; the *Malleus Maleficarum* of the Germans; Del Rio's *Disquisitiones Magicæ*; and *Occult Sciences*, paper by Elihu Rich, pp. 189-191.

a candle, a compass, a crucifix if one could be got, and a Bible. With the compass he cast a circle on the middle of the floor, large enough to hold the chair and the table. He placed within the circle the chair and the table, and on the table he laid the Bible and the crucifix beside the lighted candle. If he had not a crucifix, then he drew the figure of a cross on the floor within the circle. When all this was done, he seated himself on the chair, opened the Bible, and waited for the coming of the spirit. Exactly at midnight the spirit came. Sometimes the door opened slowly, and there glided in noiselessly a lady sheeted in white, with a face of woe, and told her story to the man on his asking her in the name of God what she wanted. What she wanted was done in the morning, and the spirit rested ever after. Sometimes the spirit rose from the floor, and sometimes came forth from the wall. One there was who burst into the room with a strong bound, danced wildly round the circle, and flourished a long whip round the man's head, but never dared to step within the circle. During a pause in his frantic dance he was asked, in God's name, what he wanted. He ceased his dance and told his wishes. His wishes were carried out, and the spirit was in peace.' [1]

In Wraxall's 'Memoirs of the Courts of Berlin, Dresden, Warsaw, and Vienna' [2] there is an amusing account of the raising of the ghost of the Chevalier de Saxe. Reports had been circulated that at his palace at Dresden there was secreted a large sum of money, and it was urged that if his spirit could be compelled to appear, that interesting secret might be extorted from him. Curiosity, combined with avarice, accordingly prompted his principal heir, Prince Charles, to try the experiment, and on the appointed night, Schrepfer was the operator in raising the apparition. He commenced his proceedings by retiring into a corner of the gallery, where, kneeling down with many mysterious ceremonies, he invoked the spirit to appear. At length a loud clatter was heard at all the windows on the outside, resembling more the effect produced by a number of wet fingers drawn over the edge of glasses than anything else to which it could well be compared. This sound announced the arrival

Gregor, *Folk-lore of North-East of Scotland*, pp. 68, 69.
1799, i. p. 281.

of the good spirits, and was shortly followed by a
yell of a frightful and unusual nature, which indicated the presence of malignant spirits. Schrepfer
continued his invocations, when 'the door suddenly
opened with violence, and something that resembled
a black ball or globe rolled into the room. It was
enveloped in smoke or cloud, in the midst of
which appeared a human face, like the countenance
of the Chevalier de Saxe, from which issued a loud
and angry voice, exclaiming in German, " Carl, was
wollte du mit mich ? "—Charles, what would thou
do with me ? ' By reiterated exorcisms Schrepfer
finally dismissed the apparition, and the terrified spectators dispersed, fully convinced of his
magical powers.[1] Roscoe has given an interesting
account[2] of Benvenuto Cellini's experiences of
raising spirits by incantation, but the Sicilian priest
who acquainted him with the mysteries of his art
of necromancy, as it has been remarked, had far
greater knowledge of 'chemistry and pharmacy
than he required for his thurible or incense pot.'
His accomplices, of course, could see and report

---

[1] See ' Ghosts and Ghost-lore,' *Leisure Hour*, 1871, pp. 334–
766.   [2] *Life of Benvenuto Cellini.*

sights of any wonderful kind. Those who penetrate into 'magic circles may expect startling sights, overpowering smells, strange sounds, and even demoniacal dreams.' Instances, it is stated, are recorded of many who perished by raising up spirits, particularly 'Chiancungi,' the famous Egyptian fortune-teller, who was so famous in England in the seventeenth century. He undertook for a wager to raise up the spirit 'Bokim,' and having described the circle, he seated his sister Napula by him as his associate. 'After frequently repeating the form of exorcism, and calling upon the spirit to appear, and nothing as yet answering his demand, they grew impatient of the business, and quitted the circle; but it cost them their lives, for they were instantaneously seized and crushed to death by that infernal spirit, who happened not to be sufficiently constrained till that moment to manifest himself to human eyes.'

Among the many curious stories told of ghost-raising may be mentioned a somewhat whimsical one related by a correspondent of a Bradford paper, who tells how, in his youthful days, he assisted in an attempt to raise the ghost of the wicked old squire of Calverley Hall. 'About a dozen scholars,' to quote his words, 'used to assemble close to the venerable church of Calverley, and then put their hats and caps on the ground, in a pyramidal form. Then taking hold of each other's hands, they formed a "magic circle," holding firmly together, and making use of an old refrain :

> Old Calverley, old Calverley, I have thee by the ears,
> I'll cut thee into collops, unless thee appears.

Whilst this incantation was going on, crumbs of bread mixed with pins were strewn on the ground, the lads meanwhile tramping round in the circle with a heavy tread. Some of the more venturesome boys had to go round to each of the church doors, and whistle aloud through the keyholes, repeating the magic couplet which their comrades in the circle were chanting. But, at this critical point, a pale and ghostly figure was expected to appear, and, on one occasion, some kind of apparition is said to have issued forth from the church, the lads in their terrified haste making their escape as quickly as they could.'

In the search after the philosopher's stone, and

elixir of life, the most revolting ingredients were turned to use, such as blood and dead men's bones, but occasionally with unexpected results. On one occasion, for instance, three alchemists obtained some earth mould from St. Innocent's Church, Paris, thinking that from it might be extracted the philosopher's stone. But, after subjecting it to distillation, they perceived in their receivers forms of men produced which caused them to desist from their labours. The Paris Institute took up the matter, and the result of their inquiries appears in the 'Miscellanea Curiosa.' An abstract of one of these French documents was published by Dr. Ferrier in the 'Manchester Philosophical Transactions,' which we quote below :

'A malefactor was executed, of whose body a grave physician got possession for the purpose of dissection. After disposing of the other parts of the body, he ordered his assistant to pulverise a part of the cranium, which was a remedy at that time administered in dispensaries. The powder was left in a paper on the table in the museum, where the assistant slept. About midnight he was awakened by a noise in the room, which obliged him to rise immediately. The noise continued about the table without any visible agent, and at length he traced it to the powder, in the midst of which he now beheld, to his unspeakable dismay, a small head, with large eyes, staring at him. Presently two branches appeared, which formed into arms and hands. Next the ribs became visible, which were soon clothed with muscles and integuments. Next the lower extremities sprouted out, and, when they appeared perfect, the puppet (for his size was small) reared himself on his feet; instantly his clothes came upon him, and he appeared in the very cloak he wore at his execution. The affrighted spectator, who stood hitherto mumbling his prayers with great application, was simply awe-struck ; but still greater was his bewilderment when the apparition planted himself in his way, and after divers fierce looks and threatening gestures, opened the door and went out. No doubt the powder was missing next day.'

A similar strange experience is recorded by Dr. Webster in his book on witchcraft, on the authority of Dr. Flud, the facts of which were thus:

'A certain chemical operator, named La Pierre, received blood from the hands of a certain bishop

to operate upon, which he, setting to work upon
the Saturday, did continue it for a week, with divers
degrees of fire. But about midnight the Friday
following, this artificer, lying in a chamber next to
his laboratory, betwixt sleeping and waking, heard
a horrible noise like unto the lowing of kine or the
roaring of a lion; and continuing quiet, after the
ceasing of the sound in the laboratory, the moon
being at the full, and by shining enlightening the
chamber, suddenly, betwixt himself and the window
he saw a thick little cloud condensed into an oval
form, which after, by little and little, did seem
completely to put on the shape of a man, and
making another and sharp clamour did suddenly
vanish. And not only some noble persons in the
next chambers, but also the host and his wife, lying
in a lower room of the house, and also the neighbours dwelling on the opposite side of the street,
did distinctly hear the bellowing as well as the
voice, and some of them were awakened with the
vehemence thereof. But the artificer said that in
this he found solace, because the bishop from
whom he had it did admonish him that if any
of them from whom the blood was extracted
should die in the time of its putrefaction, his spirit

N

was wont often to appear to the sight of the artificer with perturbation. Also forthwith, upon the Saturday following, he took the retort from the furnace and broke it with the slight stroke of a little key, and there, in the remaining blood, found the perfect representation of a human head, agreeable in face, eyes, nostrils, mouth, and hairs, that were somewhat thin and of a golden colour.' Webster adds : 'There were many ocular witnesses, as the noble person Lord of Bourdalone, the chief secretary to the Duke of Guise, and he (Flud) had this relation from the Lord of Menanton, living in that house at the same time, from a certain doctor of physic, from the owner of the house, and many others.'

In recent years the so-called spiritualism has attracted much attention, and ' as of old, men live now in habitual intercourse with the spirits of the dead. . . . The spirits of the living as well as of the dead, the souls of Strauss and Carl Vogt as well as of Augustine and Jerome, are summoned by mediums to distant spirit-circles.' [1] But for further information on this subject reports of the Psychical Research Society should be consulted.[2]

[1] Tylor's *Primitive Culture*, i. p. 143.
[2] See also *Real Ghost Stories*. Edited by W. T. Stead.

CHAPTER XIII

GHOST LAYING

In his amusing account of the art of 'laying' ghosts,
published in the last century, Grose tells us 'a
ghost may be laid for any term less than a hundred
years, and in any place or body, full or empty; as
a solid oak, the pommel of a sword, a barrel of beer,
if a yeoman or simple gentleman; or a pipe of
wine, if an esquire or a justice.' But this, as Dr.
Tylor writes,[1] 'is one of the many good instances
of articles of serious savage belief surviving as jests
among civilised men.' However whimsical the
idea of laying a ghost may seem to the prosaic
mind, an inquiry into the history of human belief
shows how widely this expedient has been resorted
to in times past, although St. Chrysostom is said

[1] *Primitive Culture*, ii. p. 153.

to have insulted some African conjurors of old with this quaint and humiliating observation : ' Miserable and woful creatures that we are, we cannot so much as expel fleas, much less devils.'

It was not so very long ago that, at the trial of Laurie for the murder of Mr. Rose,[1] Sergeant Munro, on being asked by the Dean of Faculty a question as to the disappearance of the murdered man's boots, replied that he believed they had been buried on the beach at Corne, below high-water mark. This curious ceremony seems to have been adopted by the Highland police, with the intention of laying Mr. Rose's ghost—an object which, according to tradition, might be attained by burying his boots under water. The expedient resorted to by the Highland police was founded not upon any inadequate estimate of the powers of ghosts, but upon an intimate knowledge of their likes and dislikes. They are known to entertain a strong objection to water, an antipathy which is sufficiently strong to make them shun a spot on which water

[1] See *Daily Telegraph*, Nov. 17, 1890. Article on ' Ghost Laying.' Burns's ' Tam o' Shanter ' turns on this point, and it is noticed by Sir Walter Scott in ' The Lay of the Last Minstrel ' (Canto III. Stanza 13) : ' The running stream dissolv'd the spell.'

is to be found; in fact, as Mr. Hunt writes,[1] spirits
are supposed to be unable to cross water.

A story is told of 'Dary Pit,' Shropshire, a dismal pool, which was a much dreaded spot, because
it was said spirits were laid under the water, and
might, it seems, in spite of being so laid, walk abroad.

This belief may be traced in various parts of
the world, and 'one of the most striking ways,'
writes Mr. James G. Frazer,[2] 'of keeping down
the dead man is to divert the course of a river,
bury him in its bed, and then allow the river to
resume its course. It was thus that Alaric was
buried, and Commander Cameron found the same
mode of burial in vogue amongst a tribe in Central
Africa.'

Among the Tipperahs of Chittagong, if a man
dies away from home, his friends stretch a thread
over all the intermediate streams, so that the spirit
of the dead man may return to his own village;
'it being supposed that,[3] without assistance, spirits
are unable to cross running water,' and hence streams
are occasionally bridged over in the manner afore-

[1] *Romances of West of England*, p. 470.
[2] *Contemporary Review*, xlviii. p. 107.
[3] Lewin, *Hill Tracts of Chittagong*, p. 84.

said.[1] A somewhat similar idea prevails among the
Fijians, and we are told how those who have reason
to suspect others of plotting against them occasionally ' build themselves a small house, and surround
it with a moat, believing that a little water will
neutralise the charms which are directed ' to hurt
them.[2]

The idea of water as a barrier against ghosts
has given rise to many strange customs, some of
which Mr. Frazer quotes in his paper on ' The
Primitive Ghost.'[3] Among the Metamba negroes,
a woman is bound hand and foot by the priest, who
flings her into the water several times over with
the intention of drowning her husband's ghost, who
may be supposed to be clinging to his unfeeling
spouse. A similar practice exists in Angola, and
in New Zealand those who have attended a funeral
plunge several times into the nearest stream. In
Tahiti, all who assisted at a burial plunged into the
sea; and in some parts of West Africa, after the
corpse has been deposited in the grave, ' all the

[1] See Sir John Lubbock, *Origin of Civilisation and Primitive Condition of Man*, 1870, p. 145.
[2] *Fiji and the Fijians*, i. p. 248.
[3] *Contemporary Review* xlviii. p. 113.

bearers rush to the waterside and undergo a thorough ablution before they are permitted to return to the town.'

According to Mr. Ralston, the Lusatian Wends place water between themselves and the dead as they return from a burial, even, if necessary, breaking ice for the purpose. And 'in many parts of Germany, in modern Greece, and in Cyprus, water is poured out behind the corpse when it is carried from the house, in the belief that if the ghost returns he will not be able to cross it.' [1] A Danish tradition says, 'If a person dies who, it is feared, will reappear, as a preventive let a basinful of water be thrown after the corpse when it is carried out' [2] and there will be no further cause of alarm. In Bohemia, after a death, the water-butt is turned upside down, for if the ghost bathe in it, and anyone should happen to drink of it afterwards, he would be a dead man within the year. In Pomerania, after a funeral, no washing is done for some time, lest the dead man should be wet in his grave.

Drake, in his legends of New England, alludes

[1] *Folk-songs of Russia*, p. 320.
[2] Thorpe's *Northern Mythology*, ii. p. 275.

to a story of a wreck at Ipswich, and says that,
when the storms come, the howling of the wind is
'Harry Main'—a legend which has thus been
versified by A. Morgan :

> He blasphemed God, so they put him down,
> With his iron shovel at Ipswich Bar,
> They chained him there for a thousand years,
> And the sea rolls up, to shovel it back.
> So when the sea cries, the good wives say,
> 'Harry Main growls at his work to-day.'

Similarly the Chibchas in their mythology had
a great river that souls had to pass over on floats
made of cobwebs.   On this account they never
killed spiders.   The Araucanian soul is borne across
the Stygian flood by a whale, and the Potawatomis
think 'the souls of the dead cross a large stream
over a log, which rolls so that many slip off into the
water.   One of their ancestors went to the edge of
the stream, but, not liking to venture on the log,
he came back two days after his death.   He reported that he heard the sounds of the drum on
the other side of the river, to the beat of which the
souls of the dead were dancing.'[1]   The Ojibways

---

[1] Dorman's *Primitive Superstitions*, p. 37.

speak of a similar stream, across which lies a serpent, over whose body the soul must cross.

A favourite mode of capturing a ghost in days gone by was to entice it into something small, such as a bottle, and as a decoy, to doubt its power to do so—a mode of exorcism which would seem to have suggested our 'bottle-imps.' An amusing story of laying a ghost by this means, and which illustrates the popular belief, is recorded in the 'Folk-lore Record' (ii. 176), on the authority of the late Thomas Wright. 'There lived in the town of ——————, in that part of England which lies towards the borders of Wales, a very curious simple kind of a man, though all said he knew a good deal more than other people did not know. There was in the same town a very old house, one of the rooms of which was haunted by a ghost, which prevented people making use of it. The man above mentioned was reported to be very clever at dealing with ghosts, and so the owner of the haunted house sent for him, and asked him if he could undertake to make the ghost quit the house. Tommy, for that was the name he generally went by, agreed to do this, on condition that three things were provided him—an empty bottle, a bottle of brandy with a tumbler, and a pitcher of water. So Tommy locked the door safely inside, and sat down to pass the night drinking brandy and water.

'Just as the clock struck twelve, he was roused by a slight noise, and lo! there was the ghost standing before him. Says the ghost, "Well, Tommy, how are ye?" "Pretty well, thank ye," says he, "but pray, how do you know my name?" "Oh, very well indeed," said the ghost. "And how did you get in?" "Oh, very easily." "Not through the door, I'm sure." "No, not at all, but through the keyhole." "D'ye say so? None of your tricks upon me; I won't believe you came through the keyhole." "Won't ye? but I did." "Well, then," says Tommy, pointing to the empty bottle, which he pretended to have emptied, "if you can come through the keyhole you can get into this bottle, but I won't believe you can do either." Now the ghost began to be very angry that Tommy should doubt his power of getting into the bottle, so he asserted most confidently that the thing was easy to be done. "No," said Tommy, "I won't believe it till I have seen you get in." "Here goes then," said the ghost, and sure enough

into the bottle he went, and Tommy corked him up
quite tight, so that he could not get out, and he
took the bottle to the bridge where the river was
wide and deep, and he threw the bottle exactly over
the keystone of the middle arch into the river, and
the ghost was never heard after.'

This cunning mode of laying a ghost is very old,
and reminds us of the amusing story of the fisherman and the genie in the Arabian Nights. The
tale tells how, one day, a fisherman drew a brazen
bottle out of the sea, sealed with the magic seal of
Suleyman Ben Daood, out of which there issued an
enormous genie, who threatened the fisherman with
death. The latter, feeling his life was at stake,
bethought him of doubting the genie's ability to
enter so small a vessel, whereupon the affronted
genie returned thither to vindicate his character,
and so placed himself in the fisherman's power.
In the same way a Bulgarian sorcerer armed with
a saint's picture will hunt a vampire into a bottle
containing some of the food that the demon loves ;
as soon as he is fairly inside, he is corked down,
the bottle is thrown into the fire, and the vampire
disappears for ever.

Miss Jackson [1] quotes a story from Montgomery-shire, of how the spirit of Lady Jeffreys, who for some reason could not rest in peace, and 'troubled people dreadfully,' was 'persuaded to contract her dimensions and enter a bottle. She did so, after appearing in a good many hideous forms; but when once in the bottle it was corked down securely, and the bottle was thrown into the pool underneath the Short Bridge, over the Severn, in Llanidloes; and in the bottle she was to remain until the ivy that crept along the buttresses overgrew the sides of the bridge and reached the top of the parapet; then when this took place she should be released from her bottle prison.' In the 'Collectanea Archæologica' (vol. i. part 1) we are told on the authority of one Sarah Mason, of Baschurch, that 'there was a woman hanged on a tree at Cutberry, and she came again so badly that nine clergymen had to be fetched to lay her. So they read and read until they got her into a bottle, and they buried it under a flat sandstone in the road. We used to go past the stone every time we went to church, and I've often wondered if she was still there, and what would

[1] *Shropshire Folk-lore*, pp. 140, 141.

happen if anyone was to pull the stone up.' And as a further safeguard a correspondent of ' Notes and Queries,' writing from Ecclesfield, says it is best in laying ghosts to cheat them to consent to being laid while hollies are green, for hollies being evergreen, the ghost can reappear no more.

In Wales, the objectionable spectre must be conjured in the name of Heaven to depart, and return no more, the strength of the exorcism being doubled by employing the Latin language to deliver it, which, to be perfectly effectual, must be done by three clergymen. The exorcism is usually for a stated time, seven years is the favourite period, and one hundred years the limit. Instances are recorded where a ghost which had been laid a hundred years returned at the end of the time to its old haunts. According to Mr. Wirt Sikes,[1] 'in all cases it is necessary the ghost should agree to be exorcised; no power can lay it if it be possessed of an evil demon. In such cases the terrors of Heaven must be rigorously invoked, but the result is only temporary. Properly constituted family ghosts, however, will lend a reasonable ear to entreaty backed by prayer.'

[1] *British Goblins*, p. 165.

Candles have generally played an important part in the ceremony of ghost laying, one popular idea being that ghosts have no power by candle-light. Thus, in many tales, the ghost is cheated into a promise not to return till the candle is burnt out, whereupon the crafty parson immediately blows it out, throwing it into a pond, or burying it in the earth. The belief is an old one, for, in one of the Sagas quoted by Mr. Baring-Gould,[1] the tomb-breaking hero finds an old Viking sitting in his dragon-ship, with his five hundred comrades motionless about him. He is about to depart, after possessing himself of the dead man's treasures, when the taper goes out, whereupon they all rise and attack the intruder, who barely escapes by invoking St. Olaf's aid. In all Shropshire stories, we are told that the great point is to keep the candles lighted in spite of the ghost's utmost efforts to blow them out; an amusing instance being that of the Bagbury ghost, which appeared in the shape of a bull, and was so troublesome that twelve parsons were required to lay it. The story goes that they got him into Hyssington Church; 'they

---

[1] *Shropshire Folk-lore*, pp. 138, 139.

all had candles, and one blind old parson, who knowed him, and knowed what a rush he would make, he carried his candle in his top-boot. And he made a great rush, and all the candles went out, all but the blind parson's, and he said, "You light your candles by mine." '

Miss Jackson also tells [1] how 'Squire Blount's ghost' long haunted Kinlet Hall, because his daughter had married a page-boy. At last it was found necessary to pull down Kinlet Old Hall, and to build it again on a fresh site, 'for he would even come into the room where they were at dinner, and drive his coach and four white horses across the dinner table.' But 'at last they got a number of parsons together and lighted candles, and read and read till all the candles were burnt out but one; and so they quieted him, and laid him in the sea. There was, it is reported, a little bottle under his monument in Kinlet Church, and if that were broken he would come again. It is a little flat bottle seven or eight inches long, with a glass stopper in it, which nobody could get out; and if anyone got hold of it, the remark was made, "Take

[1] *Shropshire Folk-lore*, pp. 122, 123.

care as you dunna let that fall, for if it breaks, old
Blount will come again." '

According to Mr. Henderson[1] there was a house
in a village of Arkingarthdale which had long been
haunted by a bogle. At last the owner adopted the
following plan for expelling it. Opening the Bible,
he placed it on a table with a lighted candle, and
said aloud to the bogle, ' Noo thoo can read or
dance, or dea as ta likes.' He then turned round
and walked upstairs, when the bogle, in the form
of a grey cat, flew past and vanished in the air.
Years passed without its being seen again, but one
day he met it on the stairs, and he was that day
killed in the mines.

At Leigh, Worcestershire, a spectre known as
' Old Coles ' formerly appeared, and would drive a
coach and four over the great barn at Leigh Court,
and then cool the fiery nostrils of his steeds in the
waters of the Teme. This perturbed spirit was at
length laid in a neighbouring pool by twelve parsons
at midnight, by the light of an inch of candle; and
as he was not to rise again until the candle was

---

[1] *Folk-lore of Northern Counties*, p. 247.

quite burnt out, it was thrown into the pool, and
to make all sure, the pool was filled up,

> And peaceful ever after slept
> Old Coles's shade.[1]

But sometimes, when the candles burn out their
time, it is an indication that none of the party can
lay the ghost, as happened in the case of a certain
Dartmoor vicar's unquiet spirit described by Mr.
Henderson.[2] 'A jury of seven parsons was convoked
to lay it, and each sat for half an hour with a candle
in his hand, but it burned out its time with each.
The spirit could afford to defy them; it was not
worth his while to blow their candles out. But the
seventh parson was a stranger and a scholar fresh
from Oxford. In his hand the light went out at
once. He was clearly the man to lay the ghost; he
laid it at once, and in a beer-barrel.'

According to another way of ejecting or laying
ghosts, there must be two or three clergymen, and
the ceremony must be performed in the Latin
language, which, it is said, will strike the most
audacious ghost with terror. Allan Ramsay men-

[1] Jabez Allies, Worcestershire.
[2] *Folk-lore of Northern Counties*, p. 337.

tions, as common in Scotland, the vulgar notion
that a ghost cannot be laid till some priest speaks
to it, and ascertains what prevents it from resting.

> For well we wat it is his ghaist
> Wow, wad some folk that can do't best,
> Speak tol't, and hear what it confest.
> To send a wand'ring saul to rest
>   'Tis a good deed
>   Amang the dead.

And in the ' Statistical Account of Scotland' (xiii.
557) the writer, speaking of the parish of Locharron,
county of Ross, alludes to the same idea: 'There
is one opinion which many of them entertain, and
which, indeed, is not peculiar to this parish alone,
that a Popish priest can cast out devils and cure
madness, and that the Presbyterian clergy have
no such power. A person might as well advise
a mob to pay no attention to a merry Andrew, as
to desire many ignorant people to stay from the
priest.'

On a small island off Scotland, called Ledge's
Holm, writes Mr. Bassett, there is a quarry called
' The Crier of Claife.' According to a local tradition,
a ferryman was hailed on a dark night from the
island, and went over. After a long absence he

returned, having witnessed many horrible sights
which he refused to relate. Soon afterwards he
became a monk. After a time the same cry was
heard, and he went over and succeeded in laying
the ghost where it now rests. But Bourne, who
has preserved a form for exorcising a haunted house,
ridicules the fancy that 'none can lay spirits but
Popish priests,' and says that ' our own clergy know
just as much of the black art as the others do '—
a statement which is amply confirmed. Thus,
a ghost known as 'Benjie Gear' long troubled
the good people of Okehampton to such an extent
that, ' at last,' writes Mr. James Spry, in ' The
Western Antiquary,' 'the aid of the archdeacon was
called in, and the clergy were assembled in order
that the troubled spirit might be laid and cease to
trouble them. There were twenty-three of the
clergy who invoked him in various classic languages,
but the insubordinate spirit refused to listen to
their request. At length, one more learned than
the rest addressed him in Arabic, to which he was
forced to succumb, saying, " Now thou art come, I
must be gone ! " He was then compelled to take
the form of a colt ; a new bridle and bit, which had

never been used, were produced, with a rider, to whom the Sacrament was administered. The man was directed to ride the colt to Cranmere Pool, on Dartmoor, the following instructions being given him. He was to prevent the colt from turning its head towards the town until they were out of the park, and then make straight for the pool, and when he got to the slope, to slip from the colt's back, pull the bridle off, and let him go. All this was dexterously performed, and the impetus thus gained by the animal with the intention of throwing the rider over its head into the Pool, accomplished its own fate.'

Another curious account of laying a ghost is connected with Spedlin's Tower, which stands on the south-west bank of the Annan. The story goes, that one of its owners, Sir Alexander Jardine, confined, in the dungeon of his tower, a miller named Porteous, on suspicion of having wilfully set fire to his own premises. Being suddenly called away to Edinburgh, he forgot the existence of his captive until he had died of hunger. But no sooner was the man dead, than his ghost began so persistently to disturb Spedlin's Tower, that Sir Alexander Jardine summoned 'a whole legion of ministers to his aid,

and by their efforts Porteous was at length confined
to the scene of his mortal agonies, where, at times,
he was heard screaming, "Let me out, let me out,
for I'm deein' o' hunger!"' The spell which compelled his spirit to remain in bondage was attached
to a large black-lettered Bible used by the exorcists,
and afterwards deposited in a stone niche, which still
remains in the wall of the staircase. On one occasion the Bible, requiring to be re-bound, was sent to
Edinburgh, whereupon the ghost of Porteous re-
commenced its annoyances, so that the Bible was
recalled before reaching Edinburgh, and was re-
placed in its former situation. But, it would seem,
the ghost is at last at rest, for the Bible is now kept
at Jardine Hall.

Then there is the ghost of 'Madam Pigott,'
once the terror of Chetwynd and Edgmond.
Twelve of the neighbouring clergy were summoned
to lay her by incessantly reading psalms till they
had succeeded in making her obedient to their
power. 'Mr. Foy, curate of Edgmond,' says
Miss Jackson,[1] 'has the credit of having accomplished this, for he continued reading after all the
others were exhausted.' But, 'ten or twelve years

[1] *Shropshire Folk-lore*, p. 125.

after his death, some fresh alarm of Madam Pigott
arose, and a party went in haste to beg a neighbouring rector to come and lay the ghost ; and to this day
Chetwynd Hall has the reputation of being haunted.'
It is evident that 'laying a ghost' was far from an
easy task. A humorous anecdote is told [1] of a
haunted house at Homersfield, in Suffolk, where an
unquiet spirit so worried and harassed the inmates
that they sent for a parson. On his arrival he commenced reading a prayer, but instantly the ghost got
a line ahead of him. Happily one of the family hit
on this device: the next time, as soon as the parson
began his exorcism, two pigeons were let loose; the
spirit stopped to look at them, the priest got before
him in his prayer, and the ghost was laid.

Clegg Hall, Lancashire, was the scene of a
terrible tragedy, for tradition tells how a wicked
uncle destroyed the lawful heirs—two orphans that
were left to his care—by throwing them over a
balcony into the moat, in order that he might seize
on their inheritance. Ever afterwards the house
was the reputed haunt of a troubled and angry
spirit, until means were taken for its expulsion.

[1] Henderson's *Folk-lore of Northern Counties*, p. 338.

Mr. William Nuttall, in a ballad entitled ' Sir Roland and Clegg Hall Boggart,' makes Sir Roland murder the children in bed with a dagger. Remorse eventually drove him mad, and he died raving during a violent storm. The hall was ever after haunted by the children's ghosts, and also by demons, till St. Anthony, with a relic from the Virgin's shrine, exorcised and laid the evil spirits. According to Mr. Nuttall there were two boggarts of Clegg Hall, and it is related how the country people ' importuned a pious monk to exorcise or lay the ghost.' Having provided himself with a variety of charms and spells, he quickly brought the ghosts to a parley. They demanded as a condition of future quiet the sacrifice of a body and a soul. Thereupon the cunning monk said, ' Bring me the body of a cock and the sole of a shoe.' This being done, the spirits were forbidden to appear till the whole of the sacrifice was consumed, and so ended the laying of the Clegg Hall boggarts. But, for some reason or other, the plan of this wily priest did not prove successful, and these two ghosts have continued to walk.[1]

[1] See Harland and Wilkinson's *Lancashire Legends*, pp. 10-12.

With this idea of sacrifice as necessary for laying ghosts may be mentioned the apparition of a servant at Waddow Hall, known as 'Peg o' Nell.' On one occasion, the story goes, she had a quarrel with the lord or lady of Waddow Hall, who, in a fit of anger, wished that she ' might fall and break her neck.' In some way or other Peggy did fall and break her neck, and to be revenged on her evil wisher she haunted the Hall, and made things very uncomfortable. In addition to these perpetual annoyances, ' every seven years Peg required a life, and it is said that " Peg's night," as the time of sacrifice at each anniversary was called, was duly observed; and if no living animal were ready as a septennial offering to her manes, a human being became inexorably the victim. Consequently, it grew to be the custom on " Peg's night " to drown a bird, or a cat, or a dog in the river; and a life being thus given, Peg was appeased for another seven years.' [1]

At Beoley, Worcestershire, at the commencement of the present century, the ghost of a reputed murderer managed to keep undisputed possession of a certain house, until a conclave of clergymen

[1] Ingram's *Haunted Homes*, 2nd S. p. 265.

chained him to the Red Sea for fifty years. At the
expiration of this term of imprisonment, the released ghost reappeared, and more than ever
frightened the inmates of the said house, slamming
the doors, and racing through the ceilings. At
last, however, they took heart and chased the restless spirit, by stamping on the floor from one room
to another, under the impression that could they
once drive him to a trap door opening in the cheese-
room, he would disappear for a season.[1]

A curious case of laying a ghost occurs in ' An
account of an apparition attested by the Rev. W.
Ruddell, minister at Launceston, in Cornwall,' 1665,
quoted in Gilbert's ' Historical Survey of Cornwall.'
A schoolboy was haunted by Dorothy Dingley, and
he pined. He was thought to be in love, and when,
at the wishes of his friends, the parson questioned
him, he told him of his ghostly visitor, and showed
him the spectral Dorothy. Then comes the story
of the ghost-laying.

' The next morning being Thursday, I went out
very early by myself, and walked for about an hour's
space in meditation and prayer in the field adjoining

[1] See *Gentleman's Magazine*, 1855, part ii. pp. 58, 59.

to the Quartills.   Soon after five I stepped over the
stile into the disturbed field, and had not gone
above thirty or forty paces when the ghost appeared
at the further stile.   I spoke to it with a loud voice
in some such sentences as the way of these deal-
ings directed me; thereupon it approached, but
slowly, and when I came near it, it moved not.   I
spoke again, and it answered again in a voice which
was neither very audible nor intelligible.   I was
not the least terrified, therefore I persisted till it
spoke again, and gave me satisfaction.   But the
work could not be finished this time, wherefore the
same evening, an hour after sunset, it met me again
near the same place, and after a few words on each
side it quietly vanished, and neither doth appear
since, nor ever will more to any man's disturbance.'

Local tradition still tells us that ' Madam Dudley's ghost did use to walk in Cumnor Park, and
that it walked so obstinately, that it took no less
than nine parsons from Oxford "to lay her." That
they at last laid her in a pond, called " Madam
Dudley's Pond," and, moreover, wonderful to relate,
the water in that pond was never known to freeze
afterwards.'   Heath Old Hall, near Wakefield, is

haunted by the ghost of Lady Bolles, who is commonly reported to have been conjured down into a hole of the river, locally known as ' Bolles Pit.' But, as in many other cases of ghost-laying, ' the spell was not so powerful, but that she still rises, and makes a fuss now and then.' Various reasons have been assigned for her ' walking,' such as the non-observance by her executors of certain clauses in her will, whilst a story current in the neighbourhood tells us that a certain room in the Hall which had been walled up for a certain period, owing to large sums of money having been gambled away in it, was opened before the stipulated time had expired. Others assert that her unhappy condition is on account of her father's mysterious death, which was ascribed to demoniacal agency.[1]

But of all places the most common, in years gone by, for laying ghosts was the Red Sea, and hence, in one of Addison's plays, we read, ' There must be a power of spirits in that sea.' ' This is a locality,' says Grose, ' which ghosts least like, it being related in many instances that ghosts have most earnestly besought the exorcists not to confine them

[1] See Ingram's *Haunted Homes*, 2nd S. pp. 155–159.

in that place. It is, nevertheless, considered as an indisputable fact that there are an infinite number laid there, perhaps from its being a safer prison than any other nearer at hand.' But when such exiled ghosts did happen to re-appear, they were thought more audacious, being seen by day instead of at night.

In an amusing poem entitled 'The Ghost of a Boiled Scrag of Mutton,' which appeared in the 'Flowers of Literature' many years ago, the following verse occurs embodying the idea :

> The scholar was versed in all magical lore,
>   Most famous was he throughout college;
> To the Red Sea full many an unquiet ghost,
> To repose with King Pharaoh and his mighty host,
>   He had sent through his proverbial knowledge.

Addison tells us in the 'Spectator,' alluding to his London lodgings at a good-natured widow's house one winter, how on one occasion he entered the room unexpectedly, where several young ladies, visitors, were telling stories of spirits and apparitions, when, on being told that it was only *the gentleman*, the broken conversation was resumed, and 'I seated myself by the candle that stood at one end of the table, and, pretending to read a book that I took out of my pocket, heard several stories of ghosts that, pale as ashes, had stood at the bed's foot, or walked over a churchyard by moonlight; and others that had been conjured into the Red Sea for disturbing people's rest.' As it has been humorously remarked, it is not surprising that many a strange ghost story has been told by the sea-faring community, when we remember how many spirits have been banished to the Red Sea.

CHAPTER XIV

GHOSTS OF THE DROWNED

On the coast of Brittany there is the 'Bay of the Departed,' where, it is said, in the dead hour of night the boatmen are summoned by some unseen power to launch their boats and to ferry to a sacred island the souls of men who have been drowned. On such occasions the boat is so crowded with invisible passengers as to sink quite low in the water, while the wails and cries of the shipwrecked are clearly heard as the melancholy voyage progresses. On reaching the island of Sein, the invisible passengers are numbered by unseen hands, after which the wondering, awestruck sailors return to await in readiness the next supernatural summons. At Guildo, on the same coast, small phantom skiffs are reported to dart out from under the castle cliffs, manned by spectral figures, ferrying over the treacherous sands the souls of those unfortunate persons whose bodies lie engulfed in the neighbourhood. So strong is the antipathy to this weird spot that, after nightfall, none of the seafaring community will approach near it.[1] Similar superstitions are found elsewhere, and in Cornwall, sailors dislike walking at night near those parts of the shore where there have been wrecks, as they are supposed to be haunted by the ghosts of drowned sailors, and the ' calling of the dead has frequently been heard.' ' I have been told,' writes Mr. Hunt,[2] ' that, under certain circumstances, especially before the coming of storms, but always at night, these callings are common. Many a fisherman has declared he has heard the voices of dead sailors " hailing their own names." ' He further tells how a fisherman, or a pilot, was walking one night on the sands at Porth-Towan, when all was still save the monotonous fall of the light waves upon the sand. Suddenly, he distinctly heard a voice from the sea exclaiming: ' The hour is come, but not the man.'

This was repeated three times, when a black figure, like that of a man, appeared on the top of

[1] Jones : *Credulities Past and Present*, p. 92.
[2] *Romances of West of England*, p. 366.

the hill. It paused for a moment, then rushed impetuously down the steep incline, over the sands, and was lost in the sea. In different forms the story is current all round the Cornish shores, and on the Norfolk coast, when any person is drowned, a voice is said to be heard from the water, ominous of a squall.

On the Continent the same belief, with certain variations, is found. Lord Teignmouth, in his 'Reminiscences of Many Years,' speaking of Ullesvang, in Norway, writes : 'A very natural belief that the voice of a person drowned is heard wailing amidst the storm is, apparently, the only acknowledged remnant of ancient superstition still lingering along the shores of the fiords.' In Germany, it is said that whenever a man is drowned at sea, he announces his death to his relations, and haunts the sea-shore. Such ghosts are supposed to make their appearance at evening twilight, in the clothes in which they were drowned.[1] According to a Schleswig version of this belief, the spirits of the drowned do not enter the house, but linger about the threshold to announce their sad errand. A story is told of a

[1] Thorpe's *Northern Mythology*, pp. 10, 11.

young lad who was forced by his father to go to sea
against his will.   Before starting, he bid farewell to
his mother, and said, 'As you sit on the shore by
the lake think of me.' Shortly his ghost appeared to
her there, and she only knew too well afterwards
that he had perished.

Among Maine fishermen there are similar stories
of the ghost of the drowned being seen.   Mr. W. H.
Bishop, in 'Harper's Magazine' (Sept. 1880) tells
us ' there was particularly the story of the Hascall.
She broke loose from her moorings during a gale on
George's banks, and ran into and sank the Andrew
Johnson, and all on board.   For years afterwards the
spectres of the drowned men were reported to come
on board the Hascall at midnight, and go through the
dumb show of fishing over the side, so that no one
in Gloucester could be got to sail her, and she would
not have brought sixpence in the market.'   A Block
Island tradition affirms that the ghosts of certain
refugees, drowned in the surf during the revolution,
are often seen struggling to reach the shore, and
occasionally their cries are distinctly heard.[1]

---

[1] Quoted in Bassett's 'Legends of the Sea,' from Livermore's
History of Block Island.

There is the well-known anecdote which Lord
Byron, says Moore,[1] used sometimes to mention,
and which Captain Kidd related to him on the
passage. 'This officer stated that, being asleep
one night in his berth, he was awakened by the
pressure of something heavy on his limbs, and
there being a faint light in the room, could see, as he
thought, distinctly the figure of his brother, who was
at that time in the same service in the East Indies,
dressed in his uniform, and stretched across the
bed. Concluding it to be an illusion, he shut his
eyes, and made an effort to sleep. But still the
same pressure continued ; and as often as he
ventured to take another look, he saw the figure
lying across him in the same position. To add to
the wonder, on putting his hand forth to touch this
form, he found the uniform in which he appeared
dripping wet. On the entrance of one of his brother
officers, to whom he called out in alarm, the
apparition vanished, but, in a few months afterwards, he received the startling intelligence that
on that night his brother had been drowned in the
Indian Seas. Of the supernatural character of this

[1] *Life of Byron.*

appearance, Captain Kidd himself did not appear to have the slightest doubt.'

A strange antipathy has long existed against rescuing a drowning man, one reason being that the person saved would at some time or other do injury to the man who rescued him. In China, however, this reluctance to give help to a drowning man arises from another form of the same superstitious dread, the idea being that the spirit of a person who has been drowned continues to flit along the surface of the water, until it has caused by drowning the death of a fellow creature. A person, therefore, who is bold enough to attempt to rescue another from drowning is believed to incur the hatred of the unquiet spirit, which is supposed to be desirous, even at the expense of a man's life, of escaping from its unceasing wandering. The Bohemian fisherman shrinks from snatching a drowning man from the water, fearing that the water-demons would take away his luck in fishing, and drown him at the first opportunity. This, as Dr. Tylor points out,[1] is a lingering survival of the ancient significance of this superstition, the explanation being that the water spirit

[1] See Tylor's *Primitive Culture*, i. p. 109.

is naturally angry at being despoiled of his victim,
and henceforth bears a special grudge against the
unlucky person who has dared to frustrate him.
Thus, when a person is drowned in Germany
the remark is often made, 'The river spirit
claims his yearly sacrifice,' or 'The Nix has taken
him.'

Similarly the Siamese dreads the Pnük, or
water spirit, that seizes unwary bathers, and
drags them underneath the water; and the Sioux
Indians tell how men have been drowned by Unk-
tahe, the water demon. Speaking of the ghosts of
the drowned among savage tribes, Herbert Spenser
says:[1] 'An eddy in the river, where floating sticks
are whirled round and engulfed, is not far from the
place where one of the tribe was drowned and never
seen again. What more manifest, then, than that
the double of this drowned man, malicious as the
unburied dead ever are, dwells thereabouts, and
pulls these things under the surface—nay, in
revenge, seizes and drags down persons who
venture near? When those who knew the drowned
man are all dead, when, after generations, the

[1] *Principles of Sociology*, p. 219.

details of the story, thrust aside by more recent
stories, have been lost, there survives only the
belief in a water demon haunting the place.' We
may compare the practice of the Kamchadals, who,
instead of helping a man out of the water, would
drown him by force. If rescued by any chance,
no one would receive such a man into his house, or
give him food, but he was reckoned as dead.

CHAPTER XV

GHOST SEERS

ACCORDING to the popular creed, some persons have
the peculiar faculty of seeing ghosts, a privilege
which, it would seem, is denied to others. It has
been urged, however, that under certain conditions
of health there are those who are endowed with
special powers of perception, whereby they are
enabled to see objects not visible at other times.
Thus, as Sir William Hamilton has observed, 'however astonishing, it is now proved, beyond all
rational doubt, that in certain abnormal states of the
nervous organism, perceptions are possible through
other than the ordinary channels of the senses.'
But, without entering into this metaphysical
question, folk-lore holds that persons born at a
particular time of the day have the power of seeing
ghosts. Thus it is said in Lancashire, that

children born during twilight are supposed to have
this peculiarity, and to know who of their acquaintance will next die. Some say that this property
belongs also to those who happen to be born
exactly at twelve o'clock at night, or, as the
peasantry say in Somersetshire, 'a child born in
chime-hours will have the power to see spirits.'
The same belief prevails in Yorkshire, where it is
commonly supposed that children born during the
hour after midnight have the privilege through life
of seeing the spirits of the departed.   Mr. Henderson says [1] that 'a Yorkshire lady informed him
she was very near being thus distinguished, but the
clock had not struck twelve when she was born.
When a child she mentioned this circumstance to
an old servant, adding that mamma was sure her
birthday was the 23rd, not the 24th, for she had
inquired at the time. "Ay, ay," said the old woman,
turning to the child's nurse, "mistress would be
very anxious about *that*, for bairns born after midnight see more things than other folk." '

This superstition prevails on the Continent, and,
in Denmark, Sunday children have prerogatives

[1] *Folk-lore of Northern Counties*, p. 11.

far from enviable.   Thorpe[1] tells how 'in Fyer
there was a woman who was born on a Sunday,
and, like other Sunday children, had the faculty
of seeing much that was hidden from others.   But,
because of this property, she could not pass by the
church at night without seeing a hearse or a spectre.
The gift became a perfect burden to her; she therefore sought the advice of a man skilled in such
matters, who directed her, whenever she saw a spectre, to say, "Go to Heaven!" but when she met a
hearse, "Hang on!" Happening some time after to
meet a hearse, she, through lapse of memory, cried
out, "Go to Heaven!" and straightway the hearse
rose in the air and vanished.   Afterwards meeting
a spectre, she said to it, "Hang on!" when the
spectre clung round her neck, hung on her back,
and drove her down into the earth before it.   For
three days her shrieks were heard before the spectre
would put an end to her wretched life.'

It is a popular article of faith in Scotland that
those who are born on Christmas Day or Good
Friday have the power of seeing spirits, and even
of commanding them, a superstition to which Sir

[1] *Northern Mythology*, ii. p. 203.

Walter Scott alludes in his 'Marmion' (stanza xxii.). The Spaniards imputed the haggard and downcast looks of their Philip II. to the disagreeable visions to which this privilege subjected him.

Among uncultured tribes it is supposed that spirits are visible to some persons and not to others. The 'natives of the Antilles believed that the dead appeared on the roads when one went alone, but not when many went together; and among the Finns the ghosts of the dead were to be seen by the Shamans, but not by men generally unless in dreams.'[1] It is, too, as already noticed,[2] a popular theory with savage races that the soul appears in dreams to visit the sleeper, and hence it has been customary for rude tribes to drink various intoxicating substances, under the impression that when thrown into a state of ecstasy they would have pleasing visions. On this account certain tribes on the Amazon use certain narcotic plants, producing an intoxication lasting twenty-four hours. During this period they are said to be subject to extraordinary visions, in the course of which they acquire information on any subject they

[1] Tylor's *Primitive Culture*, i. p. 446.   [2] Chap. II.

may specially require. For a similar reason the inhabitants of North Brazil, when anxious to discover some guilty person, were in the habit of administering narcotic drinks to seers, in whose dreams the criminal made his appearance. The Californian Indians would give children certain intoxicants, in order to gain from the ensuing vision information about their enemies. And the Darien Indians used the seeds of the *Datura sanguinea* to produce in children prophetic delirium, during which they revealed the whereabouts of hidden treasure.

In our own country various charms have been practised from time immemorial for invoking spirits, and, as we shall show in a succeeding chapter, it is still a widespread belief that, by having recourse to certain spells at special seasons in the year, one, if so desirous, may be favoured with a view of the spirits of departed friends.

CHAPTER XVI

GHOSTLY DEATH-WARNINGS

THE belief in death-omens peculiar to certain
families has long been a fruitful source of superstition, and has been embodied in many a strange
legendary romance. Such family forewarnings of
death are of a most varied description, and are
still said to be of frequent occurrence. An ancient
Roman Catholic family in Yorkshire, of the name
of Middleton, is supposed to be apprised of the
death of any one of its members by the apparition
of a Benedictine nun; and Sir Walter Scott, in his
' Peveril of the Peak,' tells us how a certain spirit
is commonly believed to attend on the Stanley
family, warning them by uttering a loud shriek of
some approaching calamity, and especially ' weeping and bemoaning herself before the death of any
person of distinction belonging to the family.' In

his 'Waverley,' too, towards the end of Fergus
MacIvor's history, he alludes to the Bodach Glas,
or dark grey man. Mr. Henderson says,[1] 'Its
appearance foretold death in the Clan of ——, and
I have been informed on the most credible testimony of its appearance in our own day. The Earl
of E——, a nobleman alike beloved and respected
in Scotland, was playing on the day of his decease
on the links of St. Andrews at golf. Suddenly he
stopped in the middle of the game, saying, " I can
play no longer, there is the Bodach Glas. I have
seen it for the third time ; something fearful is
going to befall me." He died that night as he was
handing a candlestick to a lady who was retiring
to her room.' According to Pennant, most of the
great families in Scotland had their death-omens.
Thus it is reported 'the family of Grant Rothiemurcus had the "Bodach au Dun," or the Ghost of
the Hill ; and the Kinchardines the " Lham-dearg,"
or the Spectre of the Bloody Hand, of whom Sir
Walter Scott has given the subjoined account from
Macfarlane's MSS.: "There is much talk of a spirit
called ' Ly-erg,' who frequents the Glenmore. He

---

[1] *Folk-lore of Northern Counties*, p. 344.

appears with a red hand, in the habit of a soldier, and challenges men to fight with him. As lately as the year 1669 he fought with three brothers, one after another, who immediately died therefrom." '

The family of Gurlinbeg was haunted by Garlin Bodacher, and Tulloch Gorms by May Moulach, or the Girl with the Hairy Left Hand.[1] The Synod gave frequent orders that inquiry should be made into the truth of this apparition, and one or two declared that they had seen one that answered the description. An ancestor of the family of McClean, of Lochburg, was commonly reported, before the death of any of his race, to gallop along the sea-beach announcing the death by dismal lamentations; and the Banshee of Loch Nigdal used to be arrayed in a silk dress of greenish hue.

Reference is made elsewhere to the apparition of the Black Friar, the evil genius of the Byrons, supposed to forebode misfortune to the member of the family to whom it appeared, and Mr. Hunt has described the death-token of the Vingoes. It seems that above the deep caverns in a certain part

[1] See *Sir Walter Scott's Poetical Works*, 1853, viii. p. 126.

of their estate rises a cairn. On this, it is asserted, chains of fire were formerly seen ascending
and descending, which were frequently accompanied
by loud and frightful noises. But it is affirmed
that these warnings have not been heard since the
last male of the family came to a violent end.[1]
Whenever two owls are seen perched on the family
mansion of the family of Arundel of Wardour, it is
said that one of its members will shortly die. The
strange appearance of a white-breasted bird [2] was
long thought to be a warning of death to a family
of the name of Oxenham, in Devonshire.

Equally strange is the omen with which the old
baronet's family of Clifton, of Clifton Hall, in Not-
tinghamshire, is forewarned when death is about to
visit one of its members. It seems that, in this case,
the omen takes the form of a sturgeon, which is
seen forcing itself up the River Trent, on whose
bank the mansion of the Clifton family is situated.
With this curious tradition may be compared one
connected with the Edgewell Oak, which is commonly reported to indicate the coming death of an

[1] *Popular Romances of West of England*, p. 372.
[2] See Chapter on 'Phantom Birds.'

inmate of Castle Dalhousie by the fall of one of its branches. Burke, in his 'Anecdotes of the Aristocracy' (1849, i. 122), says that 'opposite the dining-room at Gordon Castle is a large and massive willow-tree, the history of which is somewhat singular. Duke Alexander, when four years of age, planted this willow in a tub filled with earth; the tub floated about in a marshy piece of land, till the shrub, expanding, burst its cerements, and struck root in the earth below; here it grew and prospered, till it attained the present goodly size. The Duke regarded the tree with a sort of fatherly and even superstitious regard, half believing there was some mysterious affinity between its fortunes and his own. If an accident happened to the one by storm or lightning, some misfortune was not long in befalling the other.'

It may be remembered, too, how in the Park of Chartley, near Lichfield, has long been preserved the breed of the indigenous Staffordshire cow, of sand white colour. In the battle of Burton Bridge a black calf was born, and the year of the downfall of the House of Ferrers happening about the same time,

gave rise to the tradition that the birth of a parti-
coloured calf from the wild herd in Chartley Park is
a sure omen of death within the same year to a
member of the family. Thus, ' by a noticeable coincidence,' says the ' Staffordshire Chronicle ' (July
1835), 'a calf of this description has been born whenever a death has happened to the family of late years.'
It appears that the death of the seventh Earl Ferrers,
and of his Countess, and of his son, Viscount Tam-
worth, and of his daughter, Mrs. William Joliffe,
as well as the deaths of the son and heir of the
eighth Earl and of his daughter, Lady Francis
Shirley, were each preceded by the ominous birth of
the fatal-hued calf. This tradition has been made
the subject of a romantic story entitled ' Chartley,
or the Fatalist.'

Walsingham, in his ' Ypodigma Neustriæ ' (1574,
p. 153), informs us how, on January 1, 1399, just
before the civil wars broke out between the houses
of York and Lancaster, the River Ouse suddenly
stood still at a place called Harewood, about five
miles from Bedford, so that below this place the
bed of the river was left dry for three miles
together, and above it the waters swelled to a great

height. The same thing is said to have happened at the same place in January 1648, which was just before the death of Charles I., and many superstitious persons 'have supposed both these stagnations of the Ouse to be supernatural and portentous; others suppose them to be the effect of natural causes, though a probable natural cause has not yet been assigned.' [1]

The following curious anecdote, styled 'An Irish Water-fiend,' said to be perfectly well authenticated, is related in Burke's 'Anecdotes of the Aristocracy' (i. 329). The hero of the tale was the Rev. James Crawford, rector of the parish of Killina, co. Leitrim. In the autumn of 1777, Mr. Crawford had occasion to cross the estuary called 'The Rosses,' on the coast of Donegal, and on a pillion behind him sat his sister-in-law, Miss Hannah Wilson. They had advanced some distance, until the water reached the saddle-laps, when Miss Wilson became so alarmed that she implored Mr. Crawford to get back as fast as possible to land. 'I do not think there can be danger,' replied Crawford, 'for I see a horseman crossing the ford not twenty yards

[1] *Gentleman's Magazine*, 1764, p. 59.

Q

before us.' Miss Wilson also saw the horseman.
'You had better hail him,' said she, 'and inquire
the depth of the intervening water.' Crawford
checked his horse, and hallooed to the other horseman to stop. He did stop, and turning round,
displayed a ghastly face grinning fiendishly at
Crawford, who waited for no further parley, but
returned as fast as he could. On reaching home
he told his wife of the spectral rencontre. The
popular belief was that whenever any luckless
person was foredoomed to be drowned in that
estuary, the fatal event was foreshown to the
doomed person by some such apparition as Crawford had seen. Despite this monitory warning,
Mr. Crawford again attempted to cross the ford of
the Rosses upon September 27, 1777, and was
drowned in the attempt.

A correspondent of the 'Gentleman's Magazine' speaks of a superstition prevalent among the
peasantry in Worcestershire, that when storms,
heavy rains, or other elemental strifes take place
at the death of a great man, the spirit of the storm
will not be appeased till the moment of burial.
'This superstition,' he adds, 'gained great strength

on the occasion of the Duke of Wellington's funeral, when, after some weeks of heavy rain, and one of the highest floods ever known in this country, the skies began to clear, and both rain and flood abated. It was a common observation in this part of the country, in the week before the interment of his Grace, " Oh, the rain won't give over till the Duke is buried."

In Germany several princes have their warnings of death. In some instances it is the roaring of a lion, and in others the howling of a dog. Occasionally a similar announcement was made by the tolling of a bell, or the striking of a clock at an unusual time. Then there is the time-honoured White Lady, whose mysterious appearance has from time immemorial been supposed to indicate some event of importance. According to a popular legend, the White Lady is seen in many of the castles of German princes and nobles, by night as well as by day, especially when the death of any member of the family is imminent. She is regarded as the ancestress of the race, ' shows herself always in snow white garments, carries a bunch of keys at her side, and sometimes rocks and watches over the children

at night when their nurses sleep.' The earliest
instance of this apparition was in the sixteenth
century, and is famous under the name of 'Bertha of
Rosenberg,' in Bohemia. The white lady of other
princely castles was identified with Bertha, and the
identity was accounted for by the intermarriages
of other princely houses with members of the
house of Rosenberg,[1] in whose train the White Lady
passed into their castles. According to Mrs.
Crowe[2] the White Lady was long supposed to be a
Countess Agnes of Orlamunde; but a picture of a
princess called Bertha, or Perchta von Rosenberg,
discovered some time since, was thought so to
resemble the apparition, that it is a disputed point
which of the two ladies it is, or whether it is or is
not the same apparition that is seen at different
places. The opinion of its being the Princess
Bertha, who lived in the fifteenth century, was
somewhat countenanced by the circumstance that,
at a period when, in consequence of the war, an
annual benefit which she had bequeathed to the
poor was neglected, the apparition appeared more

[1] See Moncure Conway's *Demonology and Devil Lore.*
[2] *Night Side of Nature*, 1854, p. 315.

frequently, and seemed to be unusually disturbed. The 'Archæologia' (xxxiii.) gives an extract from Brereton's 'Travels' (i. 33), which sets forth how the Queen of Bohemia told William Brereton 'that at Berlin—the Elector of Brandenburg's house— before the death of any related in blood to that house, there appears and walks up and down that house like unto a ghost in a white sheet, which walks during the time of their sickness and until their death.[1]

Cardan and Henningius Grosius relate a similar marvel of some of the ancient families of Italy, the following being recorded by the latter authority: 'Jacopo Donati, one of the most important families in Venice, had a child, the heir to the family, very ill. At night, when in bed, Donati saw the door of his chamber opened and the head of a man thrust in. Knowing that it was not one of his servants, he roused the house, drew his sword, went over the whole palace, all the servants declaring that they had seen such a head thrust in at the doors of their several chambers at the same hour ; the fastenings were found all secure, so that no one could have come in from without. The next day the child died.'

[1] See *Notes and Queries*, 5th S. xi. p. 334.

Burton, in his 'Anatomy of Melancholy,' says that near Rufus Nova, in Finland, Sweden, 'there is a lake in which, when the governor of the castle dies, a spectrum is seen, in the habit of Arion, with a harp, and makes excellent music, like those clocks in Cheshire which (they say) presage death to the master of the family; or that oak in Lanthadran Park, in Cornwall, which foreshows as much.'

One of the most celebrated ghosts of this kind in Britain is the White Lady of Avenel, the creation of Sir Walter Scott. In the Highlands it was long a common belief that many of the chiefs had some kind spirit to watch over the fortunes of their house. Popular tradition has many well-known legends about white ladies, who generally dwell in forts and mountains as enchanted maidens waiting for deliverance. They delight to appear in warm sunshine to poor shepherds, or herd boys. They are either combing their long hair or washing themselves, drying wheat or spinning, they also point out treasures, &c. They wear snow-white or half-white black garments, yellow or green shoes, and a bunch of keys at their side. All these and many other traits that appear in individual legends may be traced back to a

goddess of German mythology who influences birth
and death, and presides over the ordering of the
household.[1]

An interesting instance of a death-warning
among uncultured tribes is told by Mr. Lang,[2] on
the authority of Mr. J. J. Atkinson, late of Noumea,
New Caledonia, which is curious because it offers
among the Kanekas an example of a belief current
in Breton folk-lore. Mr. Atkinson relates how one
day a Kaneka of his acquaintance paid a visit and
seemed loth to go away. After some hesitation he
explained that he was about to die, and would never
see his English friend again, as his fate was sealed.
He had lately met in the wood one whom he took
for the Kaneka girl of his heart, but he became
aware too late that she was no mortal woman, but
a wood-spirit in the guise of his beloved. As he
said, so it happened, for the unlucky man shortly
afterwards died. ‘This is the ground-work,’ adds
Mr. Lang, ‘of the old Breton ballad of “Le Sieur
Nann,” who died after his intrigue with the forest
spectre !’ A version of the ballad is printed by De la

[1] Chambers's *Encyclopædia*, 1886, x. p. 179.
[2] The *Nineteenth Century*, April 1865, p. 628; *Myth, Ritual, and Religion*, 1887, i. p. 104.

Villemarque, Barzaz-Breiz (i. 41), and variants exist
in Swedish, French, and even in a Lowland Scotch
version, sung by children in a kind of dancing game.[1]
Another story quoted by Mr. Lang tells how, in
1860, a Maneroo black fellow died in the service of
Mr. Du Ve. 'The day before he died, having been
ill some time, he said that in the night his father,
his father's friend, and a female spirit he could not
recognise, had come to him, and said that he would
die next day, and that they would wait for him.'
Mr. Du Ve adds that, ' though previously the Christian belief had been explained to this man, it had
entirely failed, and that he had gone back to the
belief of his childhood.' But cases of this kind, it
would appear, are not uncommon among rude races,
and have a special value to the student of comparative folk-lore.

[1] Fison's *Kamilaroi and Kurnai*, p. 253.

CHAPTER XVII

'SECOND SIGHT'

THE power of seeing things invisible to others is commonly known as ' second sight,' a peculiarity which the ancient Gaels called ' shadow sight.' The subject has, for many years past, excited popular interest, and demanded the attention even f our learned men. Dr. Johnson was so favourably impressed with the notion of 'second sight,' that after, in the course of his travels, giving the subject full inquiry, he confessed that he never could 'advance his curiosity to conviction, but came away at last only willing to believe.' Sir Walter Scott, too, went so far as to say that ' if force of evidence could authorise us to believe facts inconsistent with the general laws of nature, enough might be produced in favour of the existence of " second sight." ' When we recollect how all history

and tradition abound in instances of this belief,
oftentimes apparently resting on evidence beyond
impeachment, it is not surprising that it has
numbered among its adherents advocates of most
schools of thought. Although, too, of late years
the theory of 'second sight' has not been so widely
preached as formerly, yet it must not be supposed
that the stories urged in support of it are less
numerous, or that it has ceased to be regarded as
great a mystery as in days gone by.

In defining 'second sight' as a singular faculty
'of seeing an otherwise invisible object without any
previous means used by the person that beholds
it for that end,' we are at once confronted with the
well-known axiom that 'a man cannot be in two
places at once,' a rule with which it is difficult to
reconcile such statements as those recorded by
Pennant of a gentleman of the Hebrides said to
have had the gift of foreseeing visitors in time to get
ready for them, or the anecdote which tells how St.
Ambrose fell into a comatose state while celebrating
the mass at Milan, and on his recovery asserted that
he had been present at St. Martin's funeral at
Tours, where it was afterwards declared he had been

seen. But it must be remembered that believers in 'second sight' base their faith not so much on metaphysical definitions as on the evidence of daily experience, it being of immaterial importance to them how impossible a certain doctrine may seem, provided it only has the testimony of actual witnesses in its favour. Hence, in spite of all arguments against the so-called 'second sight,' it is urged, on the other hand, that visions coinciding with real facts and events occurring at a distance— oftentimes thousands of miles away—are beheld by persons possessing this remarkable faculty. Thus Collins, in his ode on the 'Popular Super- stitions of the Highlands,' alludes to this belief :

> To monarchs dear, some hundred miles astray
> Oft have they seen Fate give the fatal blow.
> The seer, in Sky, shrieked as the blood did flow
> When headless Charles warm on the scaffold lay.

Accounts differ largely respecting the faculty of 'second sight.' Some make it hereditary, and according to an account communicated to Aubrey from a gentleman at Strathspey, some of the seers acknowledged the possibility of teaching it. A corre- spondent of the 'Gentleman's Magazine'[1] says 'the

[1] 1822, Part ii. pp. 598, 599.

visions attendant on "second sight" are not confined
to solemn or important events. The future visit of
a mountebank or piper, the arrival of common
travellers, or, if possible, still more trifling matters
than these, are foreseen by the seers. Not only
aged men and women have the " second sight," but
also children, horses, and cows. Children endowed with that faculty manifest it by crying aloud
at the very time a corpse appears to a seer. That
horses possess it is likewise plain, from their violent
and sudden starting when their rider, or a seer in
company with him, sees a vision of any kind, by night
or by day. It is observable of a horse, that he will
not go forwards towards the apparition but must
be led round, at some distance from the common
road ; his terror is evident, from his becoming all
over in a profuse sweat, although quite cool a
moment before. Balaam's ass seems to have
possessed this power or faculty ; and, perhaps, what
we improperly style a startlish horse may be one who
has the gift of the " second sight." That cows have
the " second sight " is proved by the following circumstance. If a woman, whilst milking a cow,
happen to have a vision of that kind, the cow runs

away in a great fright at the same instant, and cannot, for some time, be brought to stand quietly.' It is further added, that persons who have not long been gifted with ' second sight,' after seeing a vision without doors, on coming into a house, and approaching the fire, will immediately fall into a swoon. All those, too, who have the ' second sight ' do not see these appearances at the same time, but if one having this faculty designedly touches his fellow seer at the instant that a vision appears to him, in that case it will be seen by both.

Goethe relates that as he was once riding along a footpath towards Drusenheim, he saw, ' not with the eyes of his body, but with those of his spirit, himself on horseback coming towards him, in a dress that he then did not possess. It was grey, and trimmed with gold. Eight years afterwards he found himself, quite accidentally, on that spot, on horseback, and in precisely that attire.' [1]

In 1652 a Scottish lawyer, Sir George Mackenzie, afterwards Lord Tarbat, when driven to the Highlands by fear of the Government of Cromwell, made very extensive inquiries concerning this sup-

[1] Quoted in Mrs. Crowe's *Night Side of Nature*, 1854, p. 181.

posed supernatural faculty, and wrote an elaborate account of its manifestations to the celebrated Robert Boyle, published in the correspondence of Samuel Pepys. Aubrey, too, devoted considerable attention to the subject, and in the year 1683 appeared the treatise of ' Theophilus Insularum,' with about one hundred cases gathered from various sources.

It was, however, in Scotland that this belief gained a specially strong footing. In the year 1799, a traveller writing of the peasants of Kirkcudbrightshire relates : ' It is common among them to fancy that they see the wraiths of persons dying which will be visible to one and not to others present with him. Within these last twenty years it was hardly possible to meet with any person who had not seen many wraiths and ghosts in the course of his experience.' Indeed, we are told that many of the Highlanders gained a lucrative livelihood by enlightening their neighbours on matters revealed to them through ' second sight ; ' and Mr. Jamieson writes : ' Whether this belief was communicated to the Scotch by the northern nations who so long had possession of it, I shall not pretend to determine, but traces of the same wonderful faculty may be found among the Scandinavians.' One of the best illustrations of this superstition as it prevailed in the Highlands is that given by Dr. Johnson in his 'Journey to the Hebrides' : 'A man on a journey far from home falls from a horse ; another, who is perhaps at work about the house, sees him bleeding on the ground, commonly with a landscape of the place where the accident befalls him. Another seer, driving home his cattle, or wandering in idleness, or musing in the sunshine, is suddenly surprised by the appearance of a bridal ceremony, or funeral procession, and counts the mourners or attendants, of whom, if he knows them, he relates the names ; if he knows them not, he can describe the dresses. Things distant are seen at the instant when they happen.' 'At the Literary Club,' says Boswell, 'before Johnson came in, we talked of his "Journey to the Western Islands," and of his coming away "willing to believe the 'second sight,'" which seemed to excite some ridicule. I was then so impressed with many of the stories which I had been told, that I avowed my conviction, saying, "He is only willing to believe—I do believe ; the evidence is enough for me, though not for his great mind. What will not fill a quart bottle will fill a pint bottle; I am filled with belief." "Are you?" said George Colman; "then cork it up."' It is not many years ago since a man lived at Blackpool who was possessed, as he pretended, by this faculty, and was visited by persons from all parts anxious to gain information about absent friends. This belief, it may be added, is not confined to our own country, curious traces of it being found among savage tribes. Thus Captain Jonathan Carver obtained from a Cree medicine man a correct prophesy of the arrival of a canoe with news the following day at noon; and we are told how, when Mr. Mason Brown was travelling with the *voyageurs* on the Coppermine river, he was met by Indians of the very band he was seeking, these having been despatched by their medicine-man, who, on being interrogated, affirmed that 'he saw them coming, and heard them talk on their journey.'

Again, persons gifted with 'second sight' are said not only to know particular events at a distance precisely at the same moment as they happen, but also to have a foreknowledge of them before they take place, for—

As the sun,
Ere it is risen, sometimes paints its image
In the atmosphere, so often do the spirits
Of great events stride on before the events,
And in to-day already walks to-morrow.

Dr. Tylor, in his ' Primitive Culture,' relates the
case of a Shetland lady who affirmed how, some
years ago, she and a girl leading her pony recognised the familiar figure of one Peter Sutherland,
whom they knew to be at the time in Edinburgh.
He turned a corner, and they saw him no more, but
next week came the news of his sudden death.

A curious old story illustrative of ' second sight,'
of which there are several versions, is that of
' Booty's Ghost,' an account of which occurs in
Kirby's ' Wonderful and Eccentric Museum' (ii.
247). It was an action for slander of a deceased
husband brought by the widow, and the following
extract, which contains an outline of the strange
tale, is from the journal of Mr. Spinks:

' *Friday, May* 15, 1687.—We had the observation of Mr. Booty this day. Captain Barrisby,
Captain Bristowe, Captain Brown, I, and Mr. Ball,
merchant, went on shore in Captain Barnaby's boat
to shoot rabbits upon Stromboli; and when we had

R

done, we called our men together by us, and about
half an hour and fourteen minutes after three in
the afternoon, to our great surprise, we all of us saw
two men come running towards us with such swift-
ness that no living man could run half so fast as they
did run, when all of us heard Captain Barnaby say,
"Lord, bless me! the foremost is old Booty, my next
door neighbour," but he said he did not know the
other that run behind; he was in black clothes, and
the foremost was in grey.   Then Captain Barnaby
desired all of us to take an account of the time, and
put it down in our pocket-books, and when we got
on board we wrote it in our journals; for we saw
them into the flames of fire, and there was a great
noise which greatly affrighted us all, for we none
of us ever saw or heard the like before.   Captain
Barnaby said he was certain it was old Booty, which
he saw running over Stromboli and into the flames
of hell.   It is stated that Captain Barnaby told his
wife, and she told somebody else, and that it was
afterwards told to Mrs. Booty, who arrested Captain
Barnaby in a thousand pound action for what he
had said of her husband.   Captain Barnaby gave
bail to it, and it came on to a trial in the Court of

King's Bench, and they had Mr. Booty's wearing apparel brought into Court, and the sexton of the parish, and the people that were with him when he died; and we swore to our journals, and it came to the same time within two minutes. Ten of our men swore to the buttons on his coat, and that they were covered with the same sort of cloth his coat was made of, and so it proved. The jury asked Mr. Spinks if he knew Mr. Booty. He answered, " I never saw him till he ran by me on the burning mountain." '

The Chief Justice from April 1687 to February 1689 was Sir Robert Wright. His name is not given in the report, but the judge said: 'Lord, have mercy on me, and grant that I may never see what you have seen. One, two, or three may be mistaken, but thirty can never be mistaken.' So the widow lost her suit.[1]

It appears, also, that coming events are mostly forecasted by various symbolic omens which generally take the form of spectral exhibitions. Thus, a phantom shroud seen in the morning on a living person is said to betoken his death in the course of

---

[1] See *Notes and Queries*, 1st S. iii. 170.

the day; but if seen late in the evening, no particular time is indicated, further than that it will take place within the year. If, too, the shroud does not cover the whole body, the fulfilment of the vision may be expected at some distant period.

But these kind of omens vary largely in different countries; and, on the Continent, where much misplaced faith is attached to them, they are frequently the source of much needless dread.

CHAPTER XVIII

COMPACTS BETWEEN THE LIVING AND DEAD

SOMETIMES ghosts appear in consequence of an agreement made before death with some particular friend, that he or she who first died should appear to the survivor. Numerous tales are told illustrative of this belief, one of the best authenticated being that recorded by Lord Brougham,[1] who, speaking of his intimate friend at the University, writes: ' There was no divinity class, but we frequently in our walks discussed and speculated upon many grave subjects, among others, on the immortality of the soul and on a future state. This question and the possibility, I will not say of ghosts walking, but of the dead appearing to the living, were subjects of much speculation ; and we actually committed the

[1] *Life and Times of Lord Brougham*, written by himself, 1871.

folly of drawing up an agreement written with our
blood, to the effect that whichever of us died first
should appear to the other, and thus solve any
doubts we had entertained of the "life after
death."' Years afterwards—on December 19, 1799
—when Lord Brougham had almost forgotten
the existence of his friend, as he was taking a
warm bath, he appeared to him; but, as he adds,
'No doubt I had fallen asleep, and the appearance
presented to my eyes was a dream. I recollected
quickly enough our old discussion, and the bargain
we had made. I could not discharge from my
mind the impression that my friend must have
died, and that his appearance to me was to be received by me as a proof of his future state.' In
October 1862 Lord Brougham made this postscript:
'I have just been copying out from my journal the
account of this strange dream—*certissima mortis
imago*. And now to finish the story begun about
sixty years since. Soon after my return to Edinburgh, there arrived a letter from India, announcing G——'s death, and stating that he had died
on the 19th of December.'

A curious story is told by John Darley,

Carthusian monk, who relates that, as he was attending upon the death bed of Father Raby, in 1534, he said to the expiring man, 'Good Father Raby, if the dead can visit the living, I beseech you to pay a visit to me by-and-by;' and Raby answered, 'Yes;' immediately after which he drew his last breath. But on the same afternoon, about five o'clock, as Darley was meditating in his cell, the departed man suddenly appeared to him in a monk's habit, and said to him, 'Why do you not follow our father?' And I replied, 'Why?' He said, 'Because he is a martyr in heaven next to the angels.' Then I said, 'Where are all our fathers who did like to him?' He answered and said, 'They are all pretty well, but not so well as he is.' And then I asked him how he was, and he said 'Pretty well.' And I said, 'Father, shall I pray for you?' To which he replied, 'I am as well as need be, but prayer is at all times good,' and with these words he vanished.[1]

There is the well-known Beresford ghost tale, about which so many accounts have been given. It appears that Lord Tyrone and Miss Blank were orphans, educated in the same house 'in the

[1] See Brand's *Popular Antiquities*, 1870, iii. p. 117.

principles of Deism.' When they were about fourteen years old their preceptor died, and their new guardian tried to persuade them to embrace revealed religion. The boy and girl stuck to Deism. But they made a compact, that he or she who died first should appear to the survivor, 'to declare what religion was most approved by the Supreme Being.' Miss Blank married St. Martin Beresford, and one day she appeared at breakfast with a pale face, and a black band round her wrist. On her death-bed she explained how the ghost of Lord Tyrone had appeared to her at the hour of his death, and had correctly prophesied her future: 'He struck my wrist; his hand was as cold as marble; in a moment the sinews shrank up, every nerve withered. . . . I bound a piece of black ribbon round my wrist.' The black ribbon was formerly in the possession of Lady Betty Cobb, who, during her long life, was ever ready to attest the truth of this narration, as are, to the present hour, the whole of the Tyrone and Beresford families.[1]

As Mr. Andrew Lang points out in the

[1] Dr. F. G. Lee: *Glimpses of the Supernatural*; the subject has been discussed in *Notes and Queries*.

'Nineteenth Century,'[1] Lord Tyrone merely did
what many ghosts had done before in the matter of
touching Lady Beresford's wrist. Thus, as he says,
according to Henry More, ' one' (bogie) ' took a relation of Melanchthon's by the hand, and so scorched
her that she bore the mark of it to her dying day.'
Before Melanchthon the anecdote was improved by
Eudes de Shirton, in a sermon, who tells how a
certain clerk, Serlon, made with a friend the
covenant which Miss Blank made with Lord Tyrone.
The friend died, and appeared to Serlon ' in a parchment cloak, covered with the finest writing in the
world.'   Being asked how he fared, he said that
this cloak, a punishment for his love of logic,
weighed heavier than lead, and scorched like the
shirt of Nessus.   Then he held out his hand, and
let fall a drop which burned Serlon to the bone—

> And evermore that master wore
> A covering on his wrist.

Before Eudes de Shirton, William of Malmesbury
knew this anecdote. His characters are two clerks,
an Epicurean and a Platonist, who made the usual
compact that the first to die should appear to the

[1] *Comparative Study of Ghost Stories*, April 1885, pp. 630, 631.

survivor, and state whether Plato's ideas, or
Epicurus in his atoms, were the correct reply to the
conundrum of the universe. The visit was to be
paid within thirty days of the death. One of the
philosophical pair was killed, and appeared to the
other, but after the time arranged, explaining that
he had been unable to keep his appointment earlier,
and, stretching out his hand, let fall three burning
drops of blood, which branded the brow of the
psychical inquirer.

Mrs. Grant, in her 'Superstitions of the Highlands,' tells how a widow, returning home through
a wood at dusk, was met by her husband's ghost,
'who led her carefully along a difficult bridge, but
left a blue mark on her wrist which the neighbours
had opportunities of seeing during the week; she
survived the adventure.' A similar circumstance
is related by Richard Baxter,[1] in connection with a
lady, soon after the Restoration, when Parliament
was passing Acts which pressed sore on the dis-
senters. While praying for the deliverance of the
faithful from the evils which threatened them, 'it
was suddenly given her, that there should be a

_____
[1] *Certainty of a World of Spirits*, p. 181.

speedy deliverance, even in a very short time. She
desired to know which way, and it being set strongly
on her as a revelation, she prayed earnestly that
if this were a true divine impulse and revelation,
God would certify her by some sign, and she
ventured to choose the sign herself, and laid her
hand on the outside of the upper part of her leg,
begging of God, that if it were a true answer, He
would make on that place some visible mark.
There was presently the mark of black spots, like
as if a hand had burnt it, which her sister witnessed,
there being no such sign before.'

In Scott's well-known ballad, the phantom
knight impresses an indelible mark on the lady who
has been his paramour, and in the Tartan stories,
written by a Frenchman, a ghost appears to Prince
Faruk in a dream, and touches him on the arm.
The Prince finds the mark of the burn when he
awakes.[1] There are numerous stories of this kind
scattered here and there in the traditionary lore of
this and other countries, and such indelible marks,
left by ghosts of their visits, have been held as a
mysterious proof of their materialistic power.

[1] Yardley's *Supernatural in Fiction*, p. 94.

A correspondent of 'Notes and Queries' (2nd S. v. 343) vouches for the authenticity of the following 'incontrovertible facts,' which, he says, ' occurred to a friend of my own, and to the companion of his early youth, who, having obtained a cadetship, went to India.' The story runs thus. 'The former was towards evening driving across a long barren heath. Suddenly, by his side in the vehicle, was seen the figure of his playmate. Happening to turn his head from him to the horse, and on looking again, the apparition had vanished. Remembering the conversation that they had held together at parting, he doubted not but that his friend was at that moment dead, and that in his appearing to him, he was come in the fulfilment of their mutual promise, in order to remove all pre-existing doubts as to the possibility of a denizen of a higher sphere appearing to its friend on earth. By the next Indian Mail was received intelligence of his death, showing the exact coincidence as to the time of the two events.'

In the biography of William Smellie is the history of a compact he made with his friend William Greenlaw, whereby it was mutually agreed that whoever died first should return and give the other an account of his condition after death. Shortly after the anniversary of his death, the ghost of Greenlaw is reported to have appeared to Smellie, and in a solemn tone informed him 'that he had experienced great difficulties in procuring permission to return to this earth, according to their agreement; that he was now in a much better world than the one he had left,' but added ' that the hopes and wishes of its inhabitants were by no means satisfied, as, like those of the lower world, they still looked forward in the hope of eventually reaching a still happier state of existence.' Another case of a similar kind is that of the appearance of the Rev. Theodore Alois Buckley, formerly one of the chaplains of Christ Church, Oxford, to his friend Mr. Kenneth Mackenzie. The story, as narrated in Newton Crosland's ' Theory of Apparitions,' is, that about the year 1850 the two friends, when at Oxford, entered into a compact of the kind already described, the signal of appearance arranged between them being the laying of a ghostly hand on the forehead of the surviving friend. On January 30, 1856, Mr. Buckley died, and on February 2, it

is said, kept the agreement, for as Mr. Mackenzie
'was lying in bed, watching the candle expiring, he
felt placed over one eye and his forehead a cool,
damp hand, and on looking up saw Buckley in his
ordinary apparel, with his portfolio under his arm
standing by his bedside.'

The Duchess of Mazarin is said to have
appeared to Madame de Beauclair, in accordance
with a solemn compact made in life, that whoever
died first should return, if it were possible, and
inform the other of the existence of the future
state. But it was some years after her death that
the Duchess kept her promise, and when she did,
it was to make this announcement: 'Beauclair,
between the hours of twelve and one this night you
will be with me.' The non-appearance of her friend's
spirit for so long had caused Madame de Beauclair
to doubt the non-existence of a future life.[1]

But in some cases such compacts have not been
kept. Dr. Chance tells us in 'Notes and Queries'
(6th S. ii. 501) that in 1846–1847, as a young man,
he made such a compact, but when his friend died
in 1878 he did not appear, neither has he ever

[1] T. M. Jarvis: *Accredited Ghost Stories*, 1823

done so. To quote Dr. Chance's words : ' It is true my friend died about noon, and that I knew of his death the same evening, so that if he had appeared to me I should have learnt nothing new, whilst in most, if not all, of the recorded cases the apparition has been the first to convey the intelligence of the death. But this did not exonerate my friend from his promise ; and if he did not keep it, I must take it that he could not come, for nothing but inability would have kept me from fulfilling my share of the compact if I had been called upon to do so.'

In Mather's ' Remarkable Providences ' the failure of a spirit to keep a promise of appearing after its separation from the body is referred to, the author being of opinion that there is great hazard attending such covenants. To quote his words : ' It may be after men have made such agreements, devils may appear to them pretending to be their deceased friends, and thereby their souls may be drawn in woful snares. Who knoweth whether God will permit the persons, who have thus confederated, to appear in the world again after their death ? And if not, then the survivor will be under great temptation unto Atheism,

as it fell out with the late Earl of Rochester,
who (as is reported in his life by Dr. Burnet)
did in the year 1665 enter into a formal engagement with another gentleman, not without ceremonies of religion, that if either of them died,
he should appear, and give the other notice of the
future state if there were any.   After this the other
gentleman was killed, but did never appear after
his death to the Earl of Rochester, which was a
great snare to him during the rest of his life.
Though, when God awakened the Earl's conscience
upon his death-bed, he could not but acknowledge
that one who had so corrupted the natural principles of truth as he had done, had no reason to
expect that such an extraordinary thing should be
done for his conviction.   Or if such agreement
should necessitate an apparition, how would the
world be confounded with spectres; how many
would probably be scared out of their wits; or what
curious questions would vain men be proposing
about things which are (and it is meet they should
be) hid from mortals?'

CHAPTER XIX

MINERS' GHOSTS

MINES have long been supposed to be haunted, a
fact which is no cause of wonderment, considering
the many unearthly sounds—such as ' the dripping
of water down the shafts, the tunnelling of distant
passages, the rumbling of trains from some freshly-
exploded lode '—constantly to be heard there.   In
early times it was thought that all mines of gold,
&c. were guarded by evil spirits, a belief to which Falstaff alludes to in 2 Henry IV. (Act iv. sc. 3), where
he speaks of ' learning a mere hoard of gold kept
by a devil.'   The Peruvian Indians affirm that the
treasures in emerald mines are guarded by evil
spirits, and Stevenson, speaking of the emerald
mine in the neighbourhood of Los Esmeraldos,
writes: 'I never visited it, owing to the superstitious dread of the natives, who assured me it was

s

enchanted, and guarded by a dragon, which poured
forth thunder and lightning on those who dared to
ascend the river.'   The spirits that haunt mines are
considered to be unfriendly, because, as an old writer
quoted by Reginald Scot remarks, 'they do exceedingly envy every man's benefit in the discovery of hidden treasure, ever haunting such places where money
is concealed, and diffusing malevolent and poisonous
influences to blast the lives and limbs of those that
dare attempt the discovery thereof.' And 'modern
authors,' adds Fuller, 'avouch that malignant
spirits haunt the places where precious metals
are found, as if the devil did there sit abroad to
hatch them, cunningly pretending an unwillingness
to part with them; whereas, indeed, he gains more
by one mine minted out into money than by a
thousand concealed in the earth.'

It is supposed by the people who live in the
neighbourhood of Largo Law, in Fife, that there is
a very rich mine of gold under and near the mountain, which has never yet been properly searched
for.   So convinced are they that this is so, that,
whenever they see the wool of a sheep's side tinged
with yellow, they think it has acquired that colour

from having lain above the gold of the mine.
Many years ago a ghost made its appearance upon
the spot, supposed to be acquainted with the
secret of the mine, but, as it required to be spoken
to before it would condescend to speak, the question
arose as to who should accost it.   At length a shepherd volunteered to ask the ghost the cause of its
haunting this locality, and to his surprise it proved
very affable, promising to appear on a particular
night at eight o'clock, when, said the spirit,

> If Auchindownie cock disna craw,
> And Balmain horn disna blaw,
> I'll tell ye where the gowd mine is in Largo Law.

True to its promise, the ghost came ready to
divulge the secret, when Tammie Norrie, the cow-
herd of Balmain, either through obstinacy or
forgetfulness, ' blew a blast both loud and dread,' at
which the ghost vanished, after exclaiming—

> Woe to the man that blew the horn
> For out of the spot he shall ne'er be borne.

The unfortunate horn-blower was struck dead
on the spot, and as it was found impossible to
remove his body, which seemed, as it were, pinned

to the earth, a cairn of stones was raised over it, known still as Norrie's Law, and which is regarded as uncanny by the peasantry.[1]

Again, frequent accidents in mines were thought to be a proof of the potency ' of the metallic spirits, which so tormented the workmen in German mines, and in those of other countries, by blindness, giddiness, and sudden sickness, that they were obliged frequently to abandon mines well known to be rich in metals.' [2]

Strange noises are oftentimes a puzzle to the miner, and suggest a supernatural agency. In the mine at Wheal Vor, where there appears to have been a general belief in 'tokens' and supernatural appearances, a man one morning, on being relieved from his turn as watcher, reported that during the night he had heard a sound like the emptying of a cartload of rubbish in front of the account house where he was staying. On going out nothing was to be seen. The man, considering the strange sound as a warning, pined away and died within a few weeks.

[1] Chambers's *Popular Rhymes of Scotland*, pp. 238, 239.
[2] Jones's *Credulities Past and Present*, p. 123.

The Cornish miner too has long been a firm believer in the existence of a mysterious being known
as the ' Knocker.' The late Charles Kingsley, in his
' Yeast,' asks, ' Who are the knockers ? ' To which
question Tregarra answers : ' They are the ghosts,
the miners hold, of the old Jews that crucified Our
Lord, and were sent for slaves by the Roman
Emperors to work the mines. . . . We used to break
into the old shafts and adits which they had made,
and find fine old stag's horn pickaxes, that crumbled
to pieces when we brought them to grass. And
they say that if a man will listen on a still night
about these shafts, he may hear the ghosts of
them at work, knocking and picking, as clear as if
there was a man at work in the next level.'   In
some districts the knockers are designated ' the
buccas,' and, generally speaking, they work upon
productive lodes only. An interesting illustration
of these strange beings is given in Carne's ' Tales of
the West,' wherein we read how ' the rolling of the
barrows, the sound of the pickaxes, and the fall of
the earth and stones, are distinctly heard through
the night, often, no doubt, the echo of their own
labours ; but sometimes continued long after the

labour has ceased, and occasionally voices seem to mingle with them.'

In Wales, when a mysterious thumping, not produced by any human being, is heard, and when, in examining the spot from whence the sound proceeded, indications of ore oftentimes are detected, the sturdiest incredulity is shaken.[1] In such cases, 'science points out that the noise may be produced by the action of water upon the loose stones in fissures and pot-holes of the mountain limestone, and does actually suggest the presence of metals.' Furthermore, as the late Mr. Wirt Sikes rightly suggests, 'in the days before a Priestley had caught and bottled that demon which exists in the shape of carbonic acid gas, when the miner was smitten dead by an invisible foe in the deep bowels of the earth, it was natural that his awe-struck companions should ascribe the mysterious blow to a supernatural enemy. When the workman was assailed suddenly by what we now call fire-damp, which killed him and his companions upon the dark rocks, scorching, burning, and killing, those who survived were not likely to question the existence

[1] See Hunt's *Popular Romances of West of England.*

of the mine-fiend.' Hence, too, originated the superstition of basilisks in mines, which destroyed with
their terrible gaze.[1]

In the 'Colliery Guardian' for May 13, 1863,
many strange superstitions are described, in which
it is stated that the pitmen in the Midland Counties
have or had a belief unknown to the north, in
aerial whistlings warning them against the pit.
Who or what the invisible musicians were, nobody
pretended to know, but they generally consisted of
seven, as the 'Seven Whistlers' is the name they
bear to this day.[2] An instance of this superstition
is given in the 'Times' of September 21, 1874.
Owing to certain nocturnal sounds, a large number
of the men employed at some of the Bedworth
collieries in North Warwickshire refused to descend
the coal-pits in which they were employed. During
Sunday it was stated that these sounds had been
distinctly heard in the neighbourhood of Bedworth,
and the result was that on the following morning,
when labour should have been resumed, the men
pointedly refused to work.

[1] Wirt Sikes : *British Goblins*, p. 26.
[2] See Chapter 'Phantom Animals.'

The Northern mines were supposed to be haunted by two goblins. One was a spiteful elf, who indicated his presence only by the mischief he perpetrated. He rejoiced in the name of ' Cutty Soams,' and appears ' to have amused himself by severing the rope-traces or soams, by which an assistant putter, honoured by the title of "the fool," is yoked to the tub. The strands of hemp, which were left all sound in the board at "kenner-time," were found next morning severed in twain. "'Cutty Soams' has been at work," would the fool and his driver say, dolefully knotting the cord.' The other goblin was no other than a ghostly putter, and his name was 'Bluecap.' Sometimes the miners would perceive a light blue flame flicker through the air, and settle on a full coal-tub, which immediately moved towards the rolley way, as though impelled by the sturdiest sinews in the working. Industrious Bluecap was at his vocation, but he required to be paid for his services ; therefore, once a fortnight, his wages were left for him in a solitary corner of the mine. If they were a farthing below his due, the indignant Bluecap would not pocket a stiver ; if they were a farthing above his due, Bluecap left

the surplus where he found it. A hewer was asked
if Bluecap's wages were nowadays to be left for
him, whether they would be appropriated. The
man shrewdly answered he thought they would be
taken by Bluecap, or somebody else.

But as most mines are productive, more or less,
of the same weird echoes, we find similar stories
current in different localities of strange hammerings
and knockings. A story is told in North Ayrshire
of a miner who, day by day, heard the sounds of a
pick on the other side of the coal into which he was
digging, which so terrified him, that at last he
sought the help of a minister to protect him 'from
the machinations of the devil.' The good man
having asked him how many 'holings'—the depth
of coal displaced by one blasting—there were before
the wall between him and the evil spirit could be
broken through, sent him back to work until there
was only one 'holing' between them. Then he was
to take a piece of bread, and crumble it all down in a
train to the mouth of the pit, and again resuming
his pick, to strike through the dividing coal. The
moment this was done, he was to cry 'The hole's
mine!' and make for the mouth of the pit as fast as

he could. These directions the miner carefully followed, but he had a narrow escape, for he had no sooner reached his place of safety than the walls of the pit came close together with a thundering crash.

Another story, recorded in 'Communications with the Unseen World,' tells how, for many years, the overseer of a mine at Whitehaven was a Cumberland man, but being found guilty of some unfair proceedings, he was dismissed by the proprietors from his post, though employed in an inferior one. The new overseer was a Northumberland man, to whom the degraded overseer bore the strongest hatred, and was heard to say that some day he would be his ruin. One day they were both destroyed by fire-damp, and it was believed in the mine that, preferring revenge to life, the ex-overseer had taken his successor, less acquainted than himself with the localities of the mine, into a place where he knew the fire-damp to exist, without a safety lamp, and had thus contrived his destruction. But, ever after, in the place where the two men perished, their voices might be heard high in dispute, the Northumbrian burr being distinctly audible, and also the well-known pronunciation of the treacherous murderer.

The mysterious apparition of a woman who committed suicide was supposed to haunt Polbreen Mine, Cornwall, locally known as 'Dorcas.' She appeared to take a malicious delight in tormenting the miner when at work, calling him by his name, and enticing him from his duties. This was carried on by her to such an extent that when ' a tributer ' had made a poor month, he was commonly asked if he had 'been chasing Dorcas.' On one occasion only, Dorcas is said to have acted kindly. It is stated [1] that two miners, who may be styled Martin and Jacky, were at work in their end, and at the time busily engaged 'beating the borer.' The name of Jack was distinctly uttered between the blows. He stopped and listened—all was still. They proceeded with their task, a blow on the iron rod—'Jacky!' Another blow—'Jacky!' They pause—all is silent. 'Well, thee wert called, Jacky,' said Martin, 'go and see.' Jacky, however, disregarded the sound, work was resumed, and 'Jacky! Jacky! Jacky!' was called more vehemently

[1] Hunt's *Popular Romances of West of England*, p. 354.

and distinctly than before. Jacky threw down his hammer, resolved to satisfy himself as to the person who was calling him. But he had not proceeded many yards from the spot on which he had been standing at work, when a mass of rock fell from the roof of the level weighing many tons, which would have crushed him to death. Martin had been stooping, holding the borer, and a projecting corner of rock just above him turned off the falling mass. He was securely enclosed, but he was extricated without injury. Jack declared to his dying day that he owed his life to Dorcas.

A similar experience is recorded by Mr. John Lean in the 'West Briton,' who relates how, when he was underground hundreds of fathoms distant from any other human being at Wheal Jewell, a mine in the parish of Gwennap, ' as he was walking slowly and silently through the level, his thoughts, as it were, absorbed, examining the rich course of copper ore in the roof or back, he was aroused as though by an audible voice, "You are in the winze!" He at once threw himself flat on his back in the bottom of the level, and on shifting from this posture to that of a sitting one, he discovered that his heels were on the verge of the end of a winze, left exposed and open,

embracing all the width of the gunnis, communicating with the next level, ten fathoms below. At
the moment he received this singular warning, his
foot was lifted for the next step over the mouth of
this abyss, a step to eternity, had it not thus been
prevented.'

On the Continent, similar tales of phantoms
haunting mines are current. In the mines about
Clausthal and Andreasberg a spectre was formerly
seen who went by the name of the 'Bergmönch.'
He was clad as a monk, but was of gigantic stature,
and always carried in his hand a large tallow candle,
which never went out. When the miners entered
in the morning, he would stand at the aperture with
his light, letting them pass under it. It appears
that the Bergmönch was formerly a burgomaster or
director, who took such delight in mining that, when
at the point of death, he prayed that instead of
resting in heaven, he might wander about till the
last day, over hill and dale, in pits and shafts, and
superintend the mining. To those towards whom
he is well disposed he renders many a kind service,
and appears to them in a human form and of
ordinary stature ; while to others he appears in his
true form. His eyes sprout forth flames, and are

like coach-wheels; his legs are like spiders' webs.[1]
Associated, too, with the German miners' superstitious fancies is the belief in the ' Cobal,' or ' Kobold,'
a supernatural being who is generally malicious, and
rarely heard but when mischief is near. But still
more to be feared were the 'Knauff-kriegen,' of
whom Professor Ramazzini of Padua thus writes :

' I took the story of devils haunting mines to be
fabulous, until I was undeceived by a skilful
Hanoverian operator in metals, who is now employed by our duke in tracing the metallic veins in
the mountainous parts of Modena. For this man
told me seriously, that in the Hanoverian mines the
diggers have frequent falls, which they say are occasioned by their being knocked down by devils,
which they call "Knauff-kriegen," and that after
such falls they often die in the space of three or
four days; but if they outlive that time they
recover.'

French mines are haunted, and many tales are
told of a spectral hare which at times is seen. One
story tells how ' a miner was frightened one day by
seeing a white object run and conceal itself in an

[1] Thorpe's *Northern Mythology*, iii. p. 96.

iron pipe. He went forward, and stopped up the two
ends of the tube, and called one of his fellow men to
examine the pipe with him. They did so, but found
nothing within, the hare spirit had vanished.'[1]
' Similarly at Wheal Vor,' says Mr. Hunt,[2] ' it has
always been and is now believed that a fatal
accident in the mine is presaged by the appearance
of a hare, or white rabbit, in one of the engine
houses. The men solemnly declare that they have
chased these appearances till they were hemmed in
apparently, without being able to catch them; and
they tell how the white rabbit on one occasion was run
into a "windbore" lying on the ground, and though
stopped in, escaped.' With this belief may be compared one which was common in Sussex a few years
ago, closely resembling the French superstition of
the Fétiches, animals of a dazzling whiteness which
appear only in the night-time, and vanish as soon
as anyone attempts to touch them. A black-
smith's wife at Ashington, the daughter of a small
farmer, was found one morning much depressed in
mind, and on being questioned as to the cause of it

[1] Jones's *Credulities Past and Present*, p. 138.
[2] *Popular Romances of West of England*, p. 350.]

said, ' I shall hear bad news before the day is over;
for late last night as I was waiting for my husband
what should I see on looking out of the window,
lying close under it, but a thing like a duck, yet a
great deal whiter than it ought to have been, whiter
than any snow.' It was suggested that it might
have been a neighbour's cat, and that it looked
whiter than usual on account of the moonlight.
' Oh, dear no!' she replied, ' it was no cat, nor
anything alive; those white things were sent as
warnings,' but no sad news came as she expected.[1]
She nevertheless remained firmly convinced that a
warning of some kind had been supernaturally sent
to her.

[1] *Folk-lore Record*, i. p. 54.

CHAPTER XX

THE BANSHEE

ONE of the grandest and wildest legends of Ireland is that relating to the Banshee—a mysterious personage, generally supposed to be the harbinger of some approaching misfortune. The name of the Banshee 'is variously pronounced Banshi and Benshee, being translated by different scholars, the "Female Fairy," the "Woman of Peace," the "Lady of Death," the "Angel of Death," the "White Lady of Sorrow," the "Nymph of the Air," and the "Spirit of the Air."' The many romantic incidents in which this weird figure has, at different times, made its appearance are treasured up among the household stories of our Irish peasantry. It must not be forgotten that in a country abounding in natural beauties such a superstition would harmonise with the surroundings of the picturesque scenery, and

T

so gain a firm hold on the mind of the inhabitants.

Unlike, also, many of the legendary beliefs of
this kind, the popular accounts illustrative of it are
related on the evidence of all sections of the community, many an enlightened and well-informed
advocate being enthusiastic in his vindication of its
reality. It would seem, however, that no family
which is not of an ancient and noble stock is
honoured with this visit of the Banshee, and hence
its non-appearance has been regarded as an indication of disqualification in this respect on the part of
the person about to die. 'If I am rightly informed,'
writes Sir Walter Scott, 'the distinction of a Banshee is only allowed to families of the pure Milesian
stock, and is never ascribed to any descendant of
the proudest Norman or boldest Saxon who followed
the banner of Strongbow, much less to adventurers
of later date who have obtained settlements in the
Green Isle.' Thus, an amusing story is contained
in an Irish elegy to the effect that on the death of
one of the Knights of Kerry, when the Banshee was
heard to lament his decease at Dingle—a seaport
town, the property of those knights—all the

merchants of this place were thrown into a state of
alarm lest the mournful and ominous wailing
should be a forewarning of the death of one of
them, but, as the poet humorously points out, there
was no necessity for them to be anxious on this
point. Although, through misfortune, a family
may be brought down from high estate to the rank
of peasant tenants, the Banshee never leaves
nor forgets it till the last member has been
gathered to his fathers in the churchyard. The
MacCarthys, O'Flahertys, Magraths, O'Neils,
O'Rileys, O'Sullivans, O'Reardons, have their
Banshees, though many representatives of these
names are in abject poverty.[1]

'The Banshee,' says Mr. McAnally, 'is really a
disembodied soul, that of one who in life was
strongly attached to the family, or who had good
reason to hate all its members. Thus, in different
instances, the Banshee's song may be inspired by
different motives. When the Banshee loves those
whom she calls, the song is a low, soft chant, giving
notice, indeed, of the close proximity of the angel of
death, but with a tenderness of tone that reassures

---

[1] McAnally: *Irish Wonders*, p. 112.

T 2

the one destined to die, and comforts the survivors ;
rather a welcome than a warning, and having
in its tones a thrill of exultation, as though the
messenger spirit were bringing glad tidings to him
summoned to join the waiting throng of his ancestors.'   To a doomed member of the family of the
O'Reardons the Banshee generally appears in the
form of a beautiful woman, 'and sings a song so
sweetly solemn as to reconcile him to his approaching fate.'   But if, during his lifetime, the Banshee
was an enemy of the family, the cry is the scream
of a fiend, howling with demoniac delight over the
coming death agony of another of his foes.

Hence, in Ireland, a source of dread to many a
family against which she has an enmity is the
'hateful Banshee.'   'It appears,' adds McAnally,[1]
'that a noble family, whose name is still familiar in
Mayo, is attended by a Banshee of this description
—the spirit of a young girl, deceived, and afterwards murdered by a former head of the family.
With her dying breath she cursed her murderer,
and promised she would attend him and his for
ever.   After many years the chieftain reformed his

[1] *Irish Wonders*, 1888, p. 114.

ways, and his youthful crime was almost forgotten
even by himself, when one night, as he and his
family were seated by the fire, the most terrible
shrieks were suddenly heard outside the castle
walls. All ran out, but saw nothing. During the
night the screams continued as though the castle
were besieged by demons, and the unhappy man
recognised in the cry of the Banshee the voice of
the young girl he had murdered. The next night
he was assassinated by one of his followers, when
again the wild unearthly screams were heard
exulting over his fate. Since that night the " hateful Banshee " has, it is said, never failed to notify
to the family, with shrill cries of revengeful glad-
ness, when the time of one of their number has
arrived.'

Among some of the recorded instances of the
Banshee's appearance may be mentioned one re-
lated by Miss Lefrau, the niece of Sheridan, in the
Memoirs of her grandmother, Mrs. Frances Sheridan.
From this account we gather that Miss Elizabeth
Sheridan was a firm believer in the Banshee, and
firmly maintained that the one attached to the
Sheridan family was distinctly heard lamenting

beneath the windows of the family residence before
the news arrived from France of Mrs. Frances Sheridan's death at Blois.   She added that a niece of Miss
Sheridan's made her very angry by observing that
as Mrs. Frances Sheridan was by birth a Chamber-
laine, a family of English extraction, she had no
right to the guardianship of an Irish fairy, and that
therefore the Banshee must have made a mistake.
Then there is the well-known case related by Lady
Fanshawe, who tells us how, when on a visit in
Ireland, she was awakened at midnight by a supernatural scream outside her window.   On looking
out she saw a young and rather handsome woman,
with dishevelled hair, who eventually vanished with
two shrieks similar to that which had at first
attracted her attention.   On communicating the
circumstance in the morning, her host replied, 'A
near relation of mine died last night in the castle,
and before such an event happens, the female
spectre whom you have seen is always visible.'

This weird apparition is generally supposed to
assume the form of a woman, sometimes young, but
more often old.   She is usually attired in a loose
white drapery, and her long ragged locks hang over

her thin shoulders. As night time approaches she occasionally becomes visible, and pours forth her mournful wail—a sound said to resemble the melancholy moaning of the wind:

> Who sits upon the heath forlorn,
> With robe so free and tresses worn?
> Anon she pours a harrowing strain,
> And then she sits all mute again!
> Now peals the wild funereal cry,
> And now—it sinks into a sigh.

Oftentimes she is not seen but only heard, yet she is supposed to be always clearly discernible to the person upon whom she specially waits. Respecting the history of the Banshee, popular tradition in many instances accounts for its presence as the spirit of some mortal woman whose destinies have become linked by some accident with those of the family she follows. It is related how the Banshee of the family of the O'Briens of Thomond is related to have been originally a woman who had been seduced by one of the chiefs of that race —an act of indiscretion which ultimately brought upon her misfortune and death.

'Sometimes the song of the Banshee is heard,'

writes Mr. McAnally,[1] 'at the beginning of a course
of conduct, a line of action, that has ended fatally.'
A story is told in Kerry of a young girl who engaged
herself to a youth, but at the moment the promise
of marriage was given, the low sad wail was heard
by both above their heads. The young man
deserted her, she died of a broken heart, and, on
the night before her death, the Banshee's ominous
song was heard outside her mother's cottage
window. On another occasion, we are told by the
same authority, one of the Flahertys of Galway
marched out of his castle with his men on a foray,
and, as his troops filed through the gateway, the
Banshee was heard high above the towers of the
fortress. The next night she sang again, and was
heard no more for a month, when he heard the
wail under his window, and on the following day
his followers brought back his corpse. One of the
O'Neils of Shane Castle, Antrim, heard the Banshee as he started on a journey, but while on the
same journey he was accidentally killed. According to Lady Wilde, 'at Lord O'Neil's residence,
Shane's Castle, there is a room appropriated to the

[1] *Irish Wonders*, p. 112.

use of the Banshee, and she often appears there,
sometimes shrouded and in a dark, mist-like cloak.
At other times she is seen as a beautiful young
girl, with long red-gold hair, and wearing a green
kirtle and scarlet mantle, covered with gold, after
the Irish fashion.' She adds that there is no harm
or fear of evil in her mere presence, unless she is
seen in the act of crying. But this is a fatal sign,
and the mournful wail is a sure and certain prophecy that the angel of death is waiting for one of
the family.[1]

Mr. Crofton Croker, in his 'Fairy Legends and
Traditions of the South of Ireland,' has given
several entertaining stories of the Banshee; but
adds, that since these spirits have become amenable
to vulgar laws they have lost much of their
romantic character. The introduction of the Banshee in the following stanza of a 'keening'—an
Irish term for a wild song of lamentation poured
forth over a dead body by certain mourners
employed for the purpose—indicates the popular
feeling on the subject. It was composed on a
young man named Ryan, whose mother speaks—

---

[1] *Ancient Cures, Charms, and Usages of Ireland*, p. 84.

> 'Twas the Banshee's lonely wailing,
>   Well I knew the voice of death,
> On the night wind slowly sailing
>   O'er the bleak and gloomy heath.

If a member of an Irish family dies abroad, the
Banshee notifies his misfortune at home. When
the Duke of Wellington died, the Banshee was
heard wailing round the house of his ancestors,
and during the Napoleonic campaigns she often
announced at home the death of Irish officers and
soldiers—an occurrence which happened on the
night preceding the Battle of the Boyne. 'Indeed,'
says Mr. McAnally, 'the Banshee has given notice at
the family seat in Ireland of deaths in battle fought
in every part of the world; from every point to which
Irish regiments have followed the roll of the British
drums, news of the prospective shedding of Irish
blood has been brought home.'

'The Welsh have also their Banshee, which
generally makes its appearance,' writes Mr. Wirt
Sikes,[1] 'in the most curdling form,' and is regarded
as an omen of death. It is supposed to come after
dusk, and to flap its leathern wings against the

---

[1] *British Goblins*, pp. 212–216.

window where the sick person happens to be. Nor
is this all, for in a broken, howling tone, it calls on
the one who is to quit mortality by his or her name
several times. There is an old legend of the ' Ellyl-
lon,' a prototype of the Scotch and Irish Banshee,
which usually appears as an old crone with streaming hair and a coat of blue, making its presence
manifest by its ominous scream of death. The
Welsh have a further form of the Banshee in the
' Cyhyraeth,' which is never seen, although the
noise it makes is such as to inspire terror in those
who chance to hear it. Thus, in some of the Welsh
villages it is heard passing through the empty
streets and lanes by night groaning dismally, and
rattling the window-shutters as it goes along.
According to the local belief it is only heard ' before
the death of such as are of strayed mind, or who
have been long ill; but it always comes when an
epidemic is about to visit the neighbourhood.' As
an instance of how superstitions are remitted from
one country to another, it is told that in America
there are tales of the Banshee imported from
Ireland along with the sons of that soil.

CHAPTER XXI

SEA PHANTOMS

THE romance of the sea has always attracted interest, and, as Buckle once remarked, ' the credulity of sailors is notorious, and every literature contains evidence of the multiplicity of their superstitions, and of the tenacity with which they cling to them.' This is not surprising, for many of the weird old fancies with which the legendary lore of the sea abounds originated in certain atmospherical phenomena which were once a mystery to our seafaring community. In a ' New Catalogue of Vulgar Errors ' (1761) the writer says : ' I look upon sailors to care as little of what becomes of themselves as any people under the sun ; yet no people are so much terrified at the thoughts of an apparition. Their sea-songs are full of them ; they firmly believe in their existence, and honest Jack

Tar shall be more frightened at the glimmering of
the moon upon the tackling of a ship, than he
would be if a Frenchman were to place a blunder-
bus at his head.' The occasional reflections of
mountains, cities, and ships in mirage gave rise
to many strange stories of spectral lands. Early
instances of this popular fancy occur, and Mrs.
Jameson, in her ' Sacred and Legendary Art,' quotes
an old Venetian legend of 1339, relating to the
ring with which the Adriatic was first wedded.
During a storm a fisherman was required to row
three men, whom he afterwards learns were St.
Mark, St. George, and St. Nicholas, first to certain
churches, and then over to the entrance of the port.
But there a huge Saracen galley was seen with
frightful demons on board, which spectral craft the
three men caused to sink, thus saving the city. On
leaving the boat, the boatman is presented with a
ring. In the Venetian academy is a painting by
Giorgione of this phantom ship, with a demon
crew, who, terrified at the presence of the three
holy men, jump overboard, or cling to the rigging,
while the masts flame with fire, and cast a lurid
glare on the water. Collin de Plancy, in his

' Sacred Legends of the Middle Ages,' tells us how at Boulogne, in 663, while the people were at prayers, a strange ship—without guide or pilot— was observed approaching the shore, with the Virgin on board, who indicated to the people a site for her chapel—delusions which may be classed in the same category as the ' phantom ship.' Novel- ists and poets have made graphic use of such well- known apparitions, variations of which occur in every maritime country. But the author accounts for this philosophically, adding that ' a great deal may be said in favour of men troubled with the scurvy, the concomitants of which disorder are, generally, faintings and the hip, and horrors with- out any ground for them.'

There were few ships in days gone by that ' doubled the Cape ' but owned among the crew some who had seen the ' Flying Dutchman,' a phantom to which Sir Walter Scott alludes as the harbinger of woe. This ship was distinguished from earthly vessels by bearing a press of sail when all others were unable to show an inch of canvas.

The story goes that ' Falkenburg was a noble-

man who murdered his brother and his bride in a
fit of passion, and was condemned to wander towards the north. On arriving at the sea-shore, he
found awaiting him a boat, with a man in it, who
said, " Expectamus te." He entered the boat,
attended by his good and his evil spirit, and went
on board a spectral bark in the harbour. There
he still lingers, while these spirits play dice for his
soul. For six hundred years the ship has wandered the seas, and mariners still see her in the
German Ocean, sailing northwards, without helm
or helmsman. She is painted grey, has coloured
sails, a pale flag, and no crew. Flames issue from
the masthead at night.'[1] There are numerous
versions of this popular legend, and O'Reilly, in his
' Songs of Southern Seas,' says—

Heaven help the ship near which the demon sailor steers !
The doom of those is sealed to whom the phantom ship
    appears,
They'll never reach their destin'd port, they'll see their homes
    no more,
They who see the Flying Dutchman never, never reach the
    shore.

Captain Marryat made this legend the basis of

[1] See Bassett's *Legends and Superstitions of the Sea*, pp. 346
347.

his ' Phantom Ship,' and Longfellow, in his ' Tales of a Wayside Inn,' powerfully tells of—

> A ship of the dead that sails the sea,
> And is called the Carmilhan,
> A ghostly ship, with a ghostly crew.
> In tempests she appears,
> And before the gale, or against the gale,
> She sails, without a rag of sail,
> Without a helmsman steers.
>
> And ill-betide the luckless ship
> That meets the Carmilhan!
> Over her decks the seas will leap,
> She must go down into the deep,
> And perish, mouse and man.

There are, also, a host of stories of spectral ships, some of which are still credited by sailors. The Germans have their phantom ships, to meet which is regarded as an omen of disaster. In one instance, the crew is said to consist of ghosts of condemned sinners, who serve one hundred years in each grade, until each has a short tour as captain. This mysterious vessel is described by Oscar L. B. Wolff in ' The Phantom Ship ' :

> For the ship was black, her masts were black,
>   And her sails coal-black as death;
> And the Evil-One steered at the helm, and laughed,
>   And mocked at their failing breath.

Swedish sailors have a vessel of this kind. She is so large that it takes three weeks to go from poop to prow, and hence orders are transmitted on horseback. Danish folk-lore has its spectral ship, and a Schleswick-Holstein tradition relates how a maiden was carried off by her lover in a spectral ship, as one day she sat on the shore bewailing his absence. In 'Mélusine' for September 1884,[1] it is stated that, ' in many localities in Lower Brittany, stories are current of a huge ship manned by giant human forms and dogs. The men are reprobates guilty of horrible crimes; the dogs, demons set to guard them and inflict on them a thousand tortures. Such a vessel wanders ceaselessly from sea to sea, without entering port or casting anchor, and will do so to the end of the world. No vessel should allow it to fall aboard, for its crew would suddenly disappear. The orders, in this strange craft, are given through huge conch-shells, and, the noise being heard several miles off, it is easy to avoid her. Besides, there is nothing to fear, if the " Ave Maria " is repeated, and the Saints appealed to, especially St. Anne d'Auray.'

[1] Quoted in Bassett's *Legends of the Sea*, p. 351.

U

Stories of phantom ships are found, more or less, all over the world, and are associated with many a romantic and tragic tale. Bret Harte [1] relates how some children go on board a hulk to play, but it breaks away from its moorings, drifts out to sea, and is lost. Yet at times there are heard:

> The voices of children, still at play,
> In a phantom hulk that drifts away
> Through channels whose waters never fail.

And Whittier [2] tells how the young captain of a schooner visits the Labrador coast where, in a certain secluded bay, two beautiful sisters live with their mother. Both fall in love with him, and, just as the younger is about to meet her lover and fly with him, she is imprisoned in her room by her mother, whereupon her elder sister goes in her stead, and is carried to sea in the vessel. The disappointed lover, on learning the deception, returns only to find his loved one dead. But the schooner, adds Whittier, never returned home and:

> Even yet, at Seven Isle Bay,
> Is told the ghastly tale

[1] Poems: *A Greypoint Legend, 1797.*
[2] *The Wreck of the Schooner Breeze.*

Of a weird unspoken sail.
She flits before no earthly blast,
With the red sign fluttering from her mast,
The ghost of the Schooner Breeze.

In Dana's 'Buccaneer,' the pirate carries a
lady to sea, who jumps overboard, and on the
anniversary of her death:

A ship! and all on fire! hull, yards, and mast,
Her sails are sheets of flame; she's nearing fast!

Occasionally a spectre ship is seen at Cap
d'Espoir, in the Gulf of St. Lawrence, which is
commonly reported to be the ghost of the flag-
ship of a fleet sent to reduce the French forts by
Queen Anne, and which was wrecked here, and
all hands. On this phantom ship, which is
crowded with soldiers, lights are seen, and on the
bowsprit stands an officer, pointing to the shore with
one hand, while a woman is on the other side. The
lights suddenly go out, a scream is heard, and the ill-
fated vessel sinks. Under one form or another, the
phantom ship has long been a world-wide piece of
folk-lore, and even in an Ojibway tale, when a
maiden is on the eve of being sacrificed to the spirit

u 2

of the falls, a spectral canoe, with a fairy in it, takes her place as a sacrifice.

Dennys, in his 'Folk-lore of China,' gives a novel variety of the phantom ship. The story goes that a horned serpent was found in a tiger's cage near Foochow by a party of tiger-hunters. They tried to ship it to Canton, but during the voyage the serpent escaped, through a flash of lightning striking the cage and splitting it. Thereupon the captain offered a thousand dollars to anyone who would destroy the monster, but its noxious breath killed two sailors who attempted the task. Eventually the junk was abandoned, and is still believed to cruise about the coast, and cautious natives will not board a derelict junk.

One of the chief features of many of these phantom-ship stories is the idea of retribution for evil deeds, as in the following, told by Irving in the 'Chronicles of Wolfert's Roost.' A certain Ramnout van Dam had 'danced and drank until midnight —Saturday—when he entered his boat to return home. He was warned that he was on the verge of Sunday morning, but he pulled off, swearing that he would not land until he reached Spiting Devil,

if it took him a month of Sundays. He was never
seen afterwards, but may be heard plying his oars,
being the Flying Dutchman of the Tappan Sea,
doomed to ply between Kakiot and Spiting Devil
until the day of judgment.' Moore in his account
of the phantom ship seen in the description of Dead-
man's Island, where wrecks were once common,
writes :

> To Deadman's Isle, on the eve of the blast,
> To Deadman's Isle, she speeds her fast,
> By skeleton shapes, her sails are furled,
> And the hand that steers is not of this world.

Turning to our own country, similar phantom
vessels have long been supposed to haunt the coast,
and Mr. Hunt [1] describes one that visited the
Cornish shores on the occasion of a storm, and to
rescue which delusive bark help was despatched :
' Away they pulled, and the boat which had been
first launched still kept ahead by dint of mechanical
power and skill. At length the helmsman cried,
" Stand by to board her." The vessel came so close
to the boat that they could see the men, and the
bow oarsman made a grasp at the bulwarks. His

[1] *Romances of West of England*, pp. 362–364.

hand found nothing solid and he fell. Ship and light then disappeared. The next day the " Neptune " of London was wrecked, and all perished. The captain's body was picked up after a few days, and that of his son also.' Among other Cornish stories may also be mentioned those known as the ' Pirate-wrecker and the Death Ship ; ' and the ' Spectre Ship of Porthcurno.' Occasionally off the Lizard a phantom lugger is seen, and Bottrell [1] tells how, at times, not only spectral ships, but the noise of falling spars, &c., are heard during an incoming fog.

Scotch sailors have their stories of phantom ships. Thus a spectral vessel—the ghostly bark of a bridal party maliciously wrecked—is said to appear in the Solway, always hovering near a ship that is doomed to be wrecked ; and Cunningham [2] has given a graphic account of two phantom pirate ships. The story goes that, for a time, two Danish pirates were permitted to perform wicked deeds on the deep, but were at last condemned to perish by wreck for the evil they had caused. On a certain night they were seen approaching the shore—the

[1] *Traditions and Fireside Stories of West Cornwall.*
[2] *Traditional Tales of the English and Scottish Peasantry,* p. 338.

one crowded with people, and the other carrying on its deck a spectral shape. Then four young men put off in a boat that had been sent from one ship, to join her, but, on reaching the ship, both vessels sank where they were. On the anniversary of their wreck, and before a gale, these two vessels are supposed to approach the shore, and to be distinctly visible. A Highland legend records how a large ship —the 'Rotterdam'—which went down with all on board, is seen at times with her ghostly crew, a sure indication of disaster. But perhaps this superstition has been most firmly riveted in the popular mind by Coleridge's 'Ancient Mariner,' wherein an ominous sign is seen afar off prefiguring the death of himself and his comrades. It is a spectre ship in which Death and Life-in-Death play at dice for the possession of the crew—the latter winning the mariner.

> Her lips were red, her looks were free,
> Her locks were yellow as gold ;
> Her skin was white as leprosy,
> The night-mare Life-in-Death was she,
> Who thicks man's blood with cold.

Stories of ghosts having appeared at sea have been told from early days, and have everywhere been a fruitful source of terror to sailors. But this is not surprising for, as Scot says,[1] 'innumerable are the reports of accidents unto such as frequent the seas, as fishermen and sailors, who discourse of noises, flashes, shadows, echoes, and other things, nightly seen or heard upon the waters.' Brand,[2] for instance, narrates an amusing tale of a sea ghost. The ship's cook, who had one of his legs shorter than the other, died on a homeward passage and was buried at sea. A few nights afterwards his ghost was seen walking before the ship, and the crew were in a panic. It was found however that the cause of this alarm was part of a maintop, the remains of some wreck floating before them that simulated the dead man's walk. On another occasion a ship's crew fancied they had not only seen but 'smelled' a ghost—a piece of folly which so enraged the captain that he ordered the boat-swain's mate to give some of the sailors a dozen lashes, which entirely cleared the ship of the ghost during the remainder of the voyage. It was afterwards ascertained that the smell proceeded from a dead rat

[1] *Discoverie of Witchcraft.*
[2] *Pop. Antiq.* iii. p. 85.

behind some beer-barrels. In the same way, many a ghost story might be explained which, proceeding from natural causes, has been the source of superstitious dread among the seafaring community. Cheever, in his 'Sea and Sailor,' referring to the credulity of sailors, says: 'The sailor is a profound believer in ghosts. One of these nocturnal visitants was supposed to visit our ship. It was with the utmost difficulty that the crew could be made to turn in at night. You might have seen the most athletic, stout-hearted sailor on board, when called to take his night-watch aloft, glancing at the yards and tackling of the ship for the phantom. It was a long time, in the opinion of the crew, before the phantom left the ship.' It may be remembered that Sir Walter Scott [1] relates how the captain of an English ship was assured by the crew that the ghost of a murdered sailor, every night, visited the ship. So convinced were the sailors of the appearance of this phantom that they refused to sail, but the mystery was cleared up by the discovery of a somnambulist.

Occasionally, the ghost of a former captain is

[1] *Letters on Demonology and Witchcraft*

supposed to visit a vessel and to warn the crew of an approaching storm. Symondson in his 'Two Years abaft the Mast' records the appearance of such an apparition, at one time 'to prescribe a change of course, at another, in wet and calm weather, quietly seated in his usual place on the poop deck.'[1] Sometimes similar warnings have come from other sources. Thus a curious occurrence is told by Mary Howitt, which happened in 1664 to Captain Rogers, R.N., who was in command of the 'Society,' a vessel bound from England to Virginia. The story goes that 'he was heading in for the capes, and was, as he reckoned, after heaving the lead, three hundred miles from them. A vision appeared to him in the night, telling him to turn out, and look about. He did so, found all alert, and retired again. The vision appeared again, and told him to heave the lead. He arose, caused the lead to be cast, and found but seven fathoms. Greatly frightened, he tacked ship, and the daylight showed him to be under the capes, instead of two hundred miles at sea.[2] With this

[1] Quoted by Bassett in his *Legends and Superstitions of the Sea*, p. 288.
[2] *Ibid.* p. 286.

story may be compared a mysterious story told in the 'Chicago Times' of March, 1885.

It appears that, as two men had fallen from the topmast head of a lake-vessel, the rumour spread that the ship was an unlucky one. Accordingly, writes one of the crew, 'on its arrival at Buffalo, the men went on shore as soon as they were paid off. They said the ship had lost her luck. While we were discharging at the elevator, the story got round, and some of the grain-trimmers refused to work on her. Even the mate was affected by it. At last we got ready to sail for Cleveland, where we were to load coal. The captain managed to get a crew by going to a crimp, who ran them in, fresh from salt water. They came on board two-thirds drunk, and the mate was steering them into the forecastle, when one of them stopped and said, pointing aloft, " What have you got a figurehead on the mast for ? " The mate looked up and then turned pale. " It's Bill," he said, and with that the whole lot jumped on to the dock. I didn't see anything, but the mate told the captain to look for another officer. The captain was so much affected that he put me on another schooner, and then

shipped a new crew, and sailed for Cleveland. He
never got there. He was sunk by a steamer off
Dunkirk.'

Another curious phantom warning to sailors
seen in years gone by was the 'Hooper,' or the
'Hooter,' of Sennen Cove, Cornwall. This was supposed to be a spirit which took the form of a band
of misty vapour, stretching across the bay, so opaque
that nothing could be seen through it. According to
Mr. Hunt,[1] 'it was regarded as a kindly interposition of some ministering spirit, to warn the fisherman against venturing to sea. This appearance
was always followed, and often suddenly, by a
severe storm. It is seldom or never now seen.
One profane old fisherman would not be warned by
the bank of fog, and, as the weather was fine on
the shore, he persuaded some young men to join
him. They manned a boat, and the aged leader,
having with him a threshing-flail, declared that he
would drive the spirit away, and he vigorously beat
the fog with the "threshel," as the flail is called.
The boat passed through the fog, and went to sea, but
a severe storm arose, and no one ever saw the boat

[1] *Romances of West of England*, p. 367.

or the men again, since which time the " Hooper "
has been rarely seen.' Similarly a mist over the
river Cymal, in Wales, is thought to be the spirit
of a traitoress, who lost her life in the lake close
by. Tradition says she had conspired with pirates
to rob her lord of his domain, and was defeated by
an enchanter.[1]

But sailors' yarns are so proverbially remarkable
that the reader must estimate their value for himself, not forgetting how large a factor in their pro-
duction is the imagination, worked upon by nervous
credulity and superstitious fear, a striking instance
of which is recorded by a correspondent of the
'Gentleman's Magazine :' 'My friend, Captain
Mott, R.N., used frequently to repeat an anecdote of
a seaman under his command. This individual, who
was a good sailor and a brave man, suffered much
trouble and anxiety from his superstitious fears.
When on the night watch, he would see sights and
hear noises in the rigging and the deep, which kept
him in a perpetual fever of alarm. One day the
poor fellow reported upon deck that the devil, whom
he knew by his horns and cloven foot, stood by the

[1] Wirt Sikes : *British Goblins.*

side of his hammock the preceding night, and told him that he had only three days to live. His messmates endeavoured to remove his despondency by ridicule, but without effect ; and the next morning he told the tale to Captain Mott, with this addition, that the fiend had paid him a second nocturnal visit, announcing a repetition of the melancholy tidings. The captain in vain expostulated with him on the folly of indulging such groundless apprehensions ; and the morning of the fatal day being exceedingly stormy, the man, with many others, was ordered to the topmast to perform some duty among the rigging. Before he ascended he bade his messmates farewell, telling them that he had received a third warning from the devil, and that he was confident he should be dead before night. He went aloft with the foreboding of evil on his mind, and in less than five minutes he lost his hold, fell upon the deck, and was killed on the spot.'

CHAPTER XXII

PHANTOM DRESS

ACCORDING to a popular ghost doctrine, the spirits of the departed ' generally come in their habits as they lived,' and as George Cruikshank once remarked,[1] 'there is no difference in this respect between the beggar and the king.' For they come—

Some in rags, and some in jags, and some in silken gowns.

And he adds that all narrators agree that ' the spirits appear in similar or the same dresses which they were accustomed to wear during their lifetime, so exactly alike that the ghost-seer could not possibly be mistaken as to the identity of the individual.' Horatio, describing the ghost to Hamlet, says—

A figure like your father,
Armed at all points, exactly cap-à-pé.

[1] *A Discovery Concerning Ghosts*, p. 3.

And it is further stated that the ghost was armed 'from top to toe,' 'from head to foot,' that 'he wore his beaver up;' and when Hamlet sees his father's spirit he exclaims—

> What may this mean,
> That thou, dead corse, again, in complete steel,
> Revisit'st thus the glimpses of the moon?

It is the familiar dress worn in lifetime that is, in most cases, one of the distinguishing features of the ghost, and when Sir George Villiers wanted to give a warning to his son, the Duke of Buckingham, his spirit appeared to one of the duke's servants 'in the very clothes he used to wear.' Mrs. Crowe,[1] some years ago, gave an account of an apparition which appeared at a house in Sarratt, Hertfordshire. It was that of a well-dressed gentleman, in a blue coat and bright gilt buttons, but without a head. It seems that this was reported to be the ghost of a poor man of that neighbourhood who had been murdered, and whose head had been cut off. He could, therefore, only be recognised by his 'blue coat and bright gilt buttons.' Indeed, many

---

[1] *Night Side of Nature.*

ghosts have been nicknamed from the kinds of
dress in which they have been in the habit of
appearing. Thus the ghost at Allanbank was
known as 'Pearlin Jean,' from a species of lace
made of thread which she wore; and the 'White
Lady' at Ashley Hall—like other ghosts who have
borne the same name—from the white drapery in
which she presented herself. Some lady ghosts
have been styled 'Silky,' from the rustling of
their silken costume, in the wearing of which they
have maintained the phantom grandeur of their
earthly life. There was the 'Silky' at Black
Heddon who used to appear in silken attire, oftentimes 'rattling in her silks'; and the spirit of
Denton Hall—also termed 'Silky'—walks about
in a white silk dress of antique fashion. This last
'Silky' 'was thought to be the ghost of a lady who
was mistress to the profligate Duke of Argyll in
the reign of William III., and died suddenly, not
without suspicion of murder, at Chirton, near
Shields—one of his residences. The "Banshee of
Loch Nigdal," too, was arrayed in a silk dress, green
in colour. These traditions date from a period
when silk was not in common use, and therefore

attracted notice in country places.'[1] Some years
ago a ghost appeared at Hampton Court,[2] habited
in a black satin dress with white kid gloves. The
'White Lady of Skipsea' makes her midnight
serenades clothed in long white drapery. Lady
Bothwell, who haunted the mansion of Wood-
houselee, always appeared in white ; and the apparition of the mansion of Houndwood, in Berwick-
shire—bearing the name of ' Chappie '—is clad in
silk attire.

One of the ghosts seen at the celebrated
Willington Mill was that of a female in greyish
garments. Sometimes she was said to be wrapped
in a sort of mantle, with her head depressed and
her hands crossed on her lap. Walton Abbey had
its headless lady who used to haunt a certain
wainscotted chamber, dressed in blood-stained
garments, with her infant in her arms ; and, in
short, most of the ghosts that have tenanted our
country-houses have been noted for their distinctive
dress.

Daniel de Foe, in his ' Essay on the History

[1] Henderson's *Folk-lore of Northern Counties*, p. 270.
[2] See *All the Year Round*, June 22, 1867.

and Reality of Apparitions,' has given many
minute details as to the dress of a ghost. He tells
a laughable and highly amusing story of some
robbers who broke into a mansion in the country,
and, whilst ransacking one of the rooms, they saw,
in a chair, 'a grave, ancient man, with a long full-
bottomed wig, and a rich brocaded gown,' &c.
One of the robbers threatened to tear off his 'rich
brocaded gown'; another hit at him with a fire-
lock, and was alarmed at seeing it pass through the
air; and then the old man 'changed into the most
horrible monster that ever was seen, with eyes like
two fiery daggers red hot.' The same apparition
encountered them in different rooms, and at last
the servants, who were at the top of the house,
throwing some 'hand grenades' down the chimneys
of these rooms, the thieves were dispersed. Without adding further stories of this kind, which may
be taken for what they are worth, it is a generally
received belief in ghost lore that spirits are accustomed to appear in the dresses which they wore
in their lifetime—a notion credited from the days
of Pliny the Younger to the present day.

But the fact of ghosts appearing in earthly

x 2

raiment has excited the ridicule of many philosophers, who, even admitting the possibility of a
spiritual manifestation, deny that there can be the
ghost of a suit of clothes. George Cruikshank,
too, who was no believer in ghosts, sums up the
matter thus : ' As it is clearly impossible for spirits
to wear dresses made of the materials of the earth,
we should like to know if there are spiritual out-
fitting shops for the clothing of ghosts who pay
visits on earth.' Whatever the objections may be
to the appearance of ghosts in human attire, they
have not hitherto overthrown the belief in their
being seen thus clothed, and Byron, describing the
' Black Friar ' who haunted the cloisters and other
parts of Newstead Abbey, tells us that he was always

arrayed
In cowl, and beads, and dusky garb.

Indeed, as Dr. Tylor remarks,[1] ' it is an habitual
feature of the ghost stories of the civilised, as of
the savage, world, that the ghost comes dressed,
and even dressed in well-known clothing worn in
life.' And he adds that the doctrine of object-souls

---

[1] *Primitive Culture,* i. p. 480.

is held by the Algonquin tribes, the islanders of
the Fijian group, and the Karens of Burmah—it
being supposed that not only men and beasts have
souls, but inorganic things. Thus, Mariner describing the Fijian belief, writes : ' If a stone or
any other substance is broken, immortality is
equally its reward ; nay, artificial bodies have
equal good luck with men, and hogs, and yams.
If an axe or a chisel is worn out or broken up,
away flies its soul for the service of the gods. The
Fijians can further show you a sort of natural well,
or deep hole in the ground, at one of their islands,
across the bottom of which runs a stream of water,
in which you may clearly see the souls of men
and women, beasts and plants, stocks and stones,
canoes and horses, and of all the broken utensils
of this frail world, swimming, or rather tumbling
along, one over the other, pell-mell, into the regions
of immortality.[1] As it has been observed, animistic
conceptions of this kind are no more irrational than
the popular idea prevalent in civilised communities
as to spirits appearing in all kinds of garments.

[1] See Letourneau's *Sociology*, p. 250; Sir John Lubbock's
Origin of Civilisation, and Primitive Condition of Man, 1870,
p. 246.

CHAPTER XXIII

HAUNTED HOUSES

A jolly place, said he, in days of old,
But something ails it now : the spot is curst.
WORDSWORTH.

A VARIETY of strange causes, such as secret murder,
acts of treachery, unatoned crime, buried treasures,
and such-like incidents belonging to the seamy side
of family history, have originated, at one time or
another, the ghostly stories connected with so many
a house throughout the country.   Robert Browning
has graphically described the mysteries of a haunted
house :

At night, when doors are shut,
And the wood-worm picks,
And the death-watch ticks,
And the bar has a flag of smut,
And a cat's in the water-butt—

And the socket floats and flares,
    And the house-beams groan,
    And a foot unknown
Is surmised on the garret stairs,
    And the locks slip unawares.

Although in some cases centuries have elapsed
since a certain house became haunted, and several
generations have come and passed away, still, with
ceaseless persistency, the restless spirit hovers about
in all kinds of uncanny ways, reminding us of Hood's
romance of 'The Haunted House.'

For over all there hung a cloud of fear,
A sense of mystery the spirit daunted,
And said, as plain as whisper in the ear,
The place is haunted !

Corby Castle, Cumberland, was famous for its
'Radiant Boy;' Peel Castle had its 'Mauthe Doog;'
and Dobb Park Lodge was noted for 'the Talking
Dog.' Cortachy Castle, the seat of the Earl of Airlie,
is noted for its 'Drummer;' and a noted Westmore-
land ghost was that of the 'bad Lord Lonsdale,'
locally known as Jemmy Lowther, which created
much alarm at Lowther Hall; but of recent years this
miscreant spirit has been silent, having, it is said,

been laid for ever under a large rock called Wallow
Crag.   Strange experiences were associated with
Hinton Ampner Manor House, Hampshire,[1] and
when, in 1797, it was pulled down, ' under the floor
of the lobby was found a box containing bones, and
what was said to be the skull of a monkey.   No
regular inquiry was made into the matter, and no
professional opinion was ever sought as to the real
character of the relic.'   Wyecoller Hall, near Colne,
is visited once a year by a spectre horseman; and
some years ago Hackwood House, an old mansion
near Basingstoke, purchased from Lord Bolton by
Lord Westbury, was said to have its haunted room,
the phantom assuming the appearance of a woman
clothed in grey.   Ramhurst Manor House, Kent,
was disturbed by weird and mysterious noises, and
at Barton Hall, Bath, in 1868, a phantom is said
to have appeared, displaying a human countenance,
but devoid of eyes.

Allanbank, a seat of the Stuarts—a family of
Scotch baronets, has long been haunted by 'Pearlin
Jean,' one of the most remarkable ghosts in Scot-
land.   On one occasion, seven ministers were called

[1] See Ingram's *Haunted Homes*, 2nd S. pp. 159-180.

in to lay this restless spirit, but to no purpose.
Creslow Manor House, Buckinghamshire, has its
ghost, and Glamis Castle has its famous 'Haunted
Room,' which, it is said, was walled up. At Hilton
Castle there was the time-honoured 'Cold Lad,'
which Surtees would lead us to suppose was one of
the household spirits known as 'Brownies.' But,
according to one local legend, in years gone by a
servant-boy was ill-treated and kept shut up in a
cupboard, and is supposed to have received the
name of 'Cold Lad' from his condition when discovered. Sundry apparitions seem to have been
connected with Newstead Abbey, one being that of
'Sir John Byron the Little, with the Great Beard,'
who was wont to promenade the state apartments
at night. But the most dreaded spectre was the
'Goblin Friar,' previously alluded to, who—

> appeared,
> Now in the moonlight, and now lapsed in shade,
> With steps that trod as heavy, yet unheard.

This strange, weird spectre has been thought to
forebode evil to the member of the family to whom
it appears, and its uncanny movements have been
thus pictured by the poet:

By the marriage-bed of their lords, 'tis said,
 He flits on the bridal eve;
And 'tis held as faith, to their bed of death
 He comes—but not to grieve.

When an heir is born, he is heard to mourn,
 And when aught is to befall
That ancient line, in the pale moonshine
 He walks from hall to hall.

His form you may trace, but not his face,
 'Tis shadowed by his cowl;
But his eyes may be seen from the folds between,
 And they seem of a parted soul.

Holland House has had the reputation of being haunted by the spirit of the first Lord Holland; and, in 1860, there was published in 'Notes and Queries,' by the late Edmund Lenthal Swifte, Keeper of the Crown Jewels, the account of a spectral illusion witnessed by himself in the Tower. He says that in October, 1817, he was at supper with his wife, her sister, and his little boy, in the sitting-room of the jewel-house. To quote his own words: 'I had offered a glass of wine and water to my wife, when, on putting it to her lips, she exclaimed, "Good God! what is that?" I looked up, and saw a cylindrical figure like a glass tube,

seemingly about the thickness of my arm, and
hovering between the ceiling and the table; its
contents appeared to be a dense fluid, white and
pale azure. This lasted about two minutes, when
it began to move before my sister-in-law; then,
following the oblong side of the table, before my
son and myself, passing behind my wife, it paused
for a moment over her right shoulder. Instantly
crouching down, and with both hands covering her
shoulder, she shrieked out, "O Christ! it has
seized me!" It was ascertained,' adds Mr. Swifte,
' that no optical action from the outside could have
produced any manifestation within, and hence the
mystery has remained unsolved.' Speaking of the
Tower, we learn from the same source how 'one
of the night sentries at the jewel-office was alarmed
by a figure like a huge bear issuing from underneath the jewel-room door. He thrust at it with
his bayonet which stuck in the door. He dropped
in a fit and was carried senseless to the guard-
room. . . . In another day or two the brave and
steady soldier died at the presence of a shadow.'
Windsor Castle, as report goes, was haunted by
the ghost of Sir George Villiers, who appeared to

an officer in the king's wardrobe and warned him of the approaching fate of the Duke of Buckingham.[1]

According to Johnson, the ' Old Hummums ' was the scene of the 'best accredited ghost story' that he had ever heard, the spirit of a Mr. Ford, said to have been the riotous parson of Hogarth's ' Midnight Conversation,' having appeared to a waiter; and Boswell, alluding to a conversation which took place at Mr. Thrale's house, Streatham, between himself and Dr. Johnson, thus writes : ' A waiter at the Hummums, in which house Ford died, had been absent for some time, and returned, not knowing that Ford was dead. Going down to the cellar, according to the story, he met him ; going down again, he met him a second time. When he came up he asked some of the people of the house what Ford could be doing there. They told him Ford was dead. The waiter took a fever, and when he recovered he said he had a message from Ford to deliver to some women, but he was not to tell what, or to whom. He walked out, he was followed, but

[1] See Lord Clarendon's *History of the Rebellion,* and *Notes and Queries,* July 1860.

somewhere about St. Paul's they lost him. He
came back, and said he had delivered the message,
and the women exclaimed, "Then we are all un-
done."' There is the so-called 'Mystery of Berkeley
Square,' No. 50 having been reputed to be haunted.
But a long correspondence on the subject in the
pages of 'Notes and Queries' proved this to be a
fallacy, the rumour, it would seem, having arisen
from ' its neglected condition when empty, and the
habits of the melancholy and solitary hypochondriac
when occupied by him.' Lord Lyttelton, however,
wrote in 'Notes and Queries' of November 16,
1872, thus: 'It is quite true that there is a house
in Berkeley Square (No. 50) said to be haunted,
and long unoccupied on that account. There are
strange stories about it, into which this deponent
cannot enter.' What these strange stories were
may be gathered from 'Mayfair' of May 10,
1879—an interesting illustration of how rapidly
legendary stories spring up on little or no basis.
'The house in Berkeley Square contains at least one
room of which the atmosphere is supernaturally
fatal to body and mind. A girl saw, heard, and
felt such horror in it that she went mad, and

never recovered sanity enough to tell how or why. A gentleman, a disbeliever in ghosts, dared to sleep in it, and was found a corpse in the middle of the floor, after practically ringing for help in vain. Rumour suggests other cases of the same kind, all ending in death, madness, or both, as the result of sleeping, or trying to sleep, in that room. The very party walls of the house, when touched, are found saturated with electric horror. It is uninhabited, save by an elderly man and woman who act as caretakers; but even these have no access to the room. That is kept locked, the key being in the hands of a mysterious and seemingly nameless person, who comes to the house once every six months, locks up the elderly couple in the basement, and then unlocks the room and occupies himself in it for hours.'

Berry Pomeroy Castle, Devonshire, was long said to be haunted by the daughter of a former baron, who bore a child to her own father, afterwards strangling the fruit of their incestuous intercourse; and all kinds of weird noises are heard at Ewshott House, Hampshire. Bagley House, near Bridport, is haunted by the ghost of a Squire

Lighte, who committed suicide; and at Astwood Court, once the seat of the Culpepers, was an old oak table, removed from the side of the wainscot in 1816, respecting which tradition declares that it bore the impress of the fingers of a lady ghost who, it has been suggested, probably tired of appearing to no purpose, at last struck the table in a rage and vanished for ever. Holt Castle was supposed, in bygone years, to be haunted by a mysterious lady in black who, in the still hours of the nigh occasionally walked in a certain passage near the attics. It was likewise said that the cellar had been occupied by an ill-favoured bird like a raven, which would sometimes pounce upon any person who ventured to approach a cask for drink, and, having extinguished the candle with a horrid flapping of wings, would leave its victims prostrate with fright. A solution, however, has been given to this legend that 'would imply a little cunning selfishness on the part of the domestics who had the care of the ale and cider *depôt*.' [1]

At Althorp, the seat of Earl Spencer, is said to have appeared the ghost of a favourite groom, and

[1] *Gentleman's Magazine*, 1855, pt. ii. pp. 58, 59.

Cumnor Hall, the supposed scene of the murder
of Lady Ann Robsart, was haunted by her apparition.   According to Mickle—

> In that Manor now no more
>   Is cheerful feast and sprightly ball;
> For, ever since that dreary hour,
>   Have spirits haunted Cumnor Hall.
>
> The village maids, with fearful glance,
>   Avoid the ancient moss-grown wall;
> Nor ever lead the merry dance
>   Among the groves of Cumnor Hall.
>
> Full many a traveller oft hath sighed
>   And pensive wept the Countess's fall,
> As, wandering onward, they espied
>   The haunted towers of Cumnor Hall.

Powis Castle had once its ghost, and Cullaby Castle,
Northumberland, the seat of Major A. H. Browne,
is haunted.   According to a correspondent,[1] in the
older part of the castle, which was the pele-tower
of the Claverings, there was known to be a room
walled up, 'which Mrs. Browne, during her husband's
absence, had broken into;' but the room was
ound to be quite empty.   She says, however, that

[1] *More Ghost Stories*, p. 64.

'she let a ghost out who is known as " The Wicked
Priest." Ever since they have been annoyed with the
most unaccountable noises, which are sometimes so
loud that one would think the house was being blown
down. I believe the ghost has been seen—it is a
priest with a shovel hat.' The seat of the Trevelyans
is haunted with the incessant wailing of a spectral
child, and the ruins of Seaton Delaval Castle are
said to be haunted. Churton Hall, at one time
the seat of the Duke of Argyll, 'has marked
Tyneside with the ghost of the Duke's mistress,
who is locally known as " Silky." ' 'Tyneside,'
writes Mr. W. T. Stead, 'abounded with stories of
haunted castles; but, with the doubtful exception
of Dilston, where Lady Derwentwater was said to
revisit the pale glimpses of the moon to expiate the
restless ambition which impelled her to drive Lord
Derwentwater to the scaffold, none of them were
leading actors in the tragedies of old time.'

Bisham Abbey, report says, is haunted by the
ghost of Lady Hoby, who treated her son by her
first husband so unmercifully, on account of his
antipathy to study, that he died. As a punishment for her unnatural cruelty she glides through

Y

a certain chamber, in the act of washing blood-
stains from her hands.   One of the rooms at Combermere Abbey, Cheshire, formerly known as the
'Coved Saloon,' is tenanted by the ghost of a little
girl, the sister of Lord Cotton, who had died when
fourteen years old.[1]   Then there was the famous
'Sampford Peverell' ghost, which created much
interest at the commencement of the present
century,[2] and Rainham, the seat of the Marquis
Townshend, in Norfolk, has long been haunted by
the 'Brown Lady.'   At Oulton House, Suffolk, at
midnight, a wild huntsman with his hounds,
accompanied by a lady carrying a poisoned cup, is
said to take his ghostly walk; and Clegg Hall,
Lancashire, long had its restless spirits, and the
laying of these 'Clegg Hall boggarts,' as they were
called, is described elsewhere.   At Samlesbury
Hall, near Blackburn, a lady in white attended by
a handsome knight is seen at night;[3] and a
headless lady walked about Walton Abbey.   Hermitage Castle, one of the most famous of the

---

[1] *All the Year Round*, December 24, 1870.
[2] See Ingram's *Haunted Homes*, 2nd S. pp. 226-233.
[3] *Ibid.* see p. 222.

Border keeps in the days of its splendour, has for
years past been haunted, and has been described
as—

Haunted Hermitage,
Where long by spells mysterious bound,
They pace their round with lifeless smile,
And shake with restless foot the guilty pile,
Till sink the mouldering towers beneath the burdened
ground.

The story goes that Lord Soulis, 'the evil hero of Hermitage,' made a compact with the devil, who appeared
to him in the shape of a spirit wearing a red cap,
which gained its hue from the blood of human
victims in which it was steeped. Lord Soulis sold
himself to the demon, and in return he could
summon his familiar whenever he chose to rap
thrice on an iron chest, on condition that he never
looked in the direction of the spirit. Once, however, he forgot or ignored this condition, and his
doom was sealed. But even then Lord Soulis kept
the letter of the compact. Lord Soulis was protected by an unholy charm against any injury from
rope or steel; hence cords could not bind him,
and steel could not slay him. When, at last, he
was delivered over to his enemies it was found

necessary to adopt the ingenious and effective expedient of rolling him up in a sheet of lead and
boiling him to death :

> On a circle of stones they placed the pot,
> On a circle of stones but barely nine ;
> They heated it red and fiery hot,
> And the burnished brass did glimmer and shine.

> They rolled him up in a sheet of lead—
> A sheet of lead for a funeral pall ;
> They plunged him into the cauldron red,
> And melted him, body, lead, bones and all.

This was the end of Lord Soulis's body, but his
spirit still lingers on the scene.   Once every seven
years he keeps tryst with Red Cap on the scene of
his former devilries :

> And still when seven years are o'er
> Is heard the jarring sound,
> When hollow opes the charmèd door
> Of chamber underground.[1]

Hugh Miller, in his 'Schools and Schoolmasters,'
says that, while working as a stonemason in a

---

[1] *More Ghost Stories*, W. T. Stead, 1892, p. 63.

remote part of Scotland, he visited the ruins of
Craighouse, a grey fantastic rag of a castle, which
the people of the neighbourhood firmly believed to
be haunted by its goblin—a miserable-looking,
grey-headed, grey-bearded old man, who might be
seen, late in evening and early in the morning,
peering out through a narrow slit or shot-hole at
the chance passenger. He further adds that he
met with a sunburnt herd-boy who was tending his
cattle under the shadow of the old castle wall. He
asked the lad whose apparition he thought it was
that could continue to haunt a building whose last
inhabitant had long been forgotten. 'Oh, they're
saying,' was the reply, 'it's the spirit of the man
who was killed on the foundation-stone, soon after
it was laid, and then built intil the wa' by the
masons that he might keep the Castle by coming
back again; and they're saying that a' varra auld
hooses i' the country had murderit men builded
intil them i' that way, and that all o' them hev
their bogie!'

Among Irish haunted houses may be noticed the
castle of Dunseverick, in Antrim, which is believed to
be still inhabited by the spirit of a chief, who there

atones for a horrid crime; while the castles of
Dunluce, of Magrath, and many others are similarly
peopled by the wicked dead. In the abbey of Clare
the ghost of a sinful abbot walks, and will continue
to do so until his sin has been atoned for by the
prayers he unceasingly mutters in his tireless
march up and down the aisles of the ruined
nave.

The 'Cedar Room' at Ashley Hall, Cheshire,
was said to be tenanted by the figure of a white
lady, reminding us of similar so-called apparitions
at Skipsea and Blenkinsopp Castles. At Burton
Agnes Hall, the family seat of Sir Henry Somer-
ville Boynton, there is a spirit of a lady which
haunts the ancient mansion, known in the neighbourhood as 'Awd Nance.' The skull of this lady
is preserved at the Hall, and so long as it is left
quietly in its resting-place all goes well, but should
any attempt be made to remove it, all kinds of
unearthly noises are raised in the house, and last
until it is restored.[1] Denton Hall has for many
years past attracted interest from being inhabited
by a spirit known by the names of 'Old Barbery'

[1] Henderson's *Folk-lore of Northern Counties*, pp. 314, 315.

and 'Silky,' and Waddow Hall, Yorkshire, is
haunted by a phantom called 'Peg O'Nell.' Bridge
End House, Burnley, was said to have its ghost;
Crook Hall, near Durham, has its 'White Ladie;'
South Biddick Hall, its shadowy tenant, 'Madam
Lambton;' and Netherby Hall, a 'Rustling Lady'
who walks along a retired passage in that mansion,
her dress rustling as she moves along.[1] There
was the famous Willington Mill, alluded to in the
previous chapter, which some years ago became
notorious in the North of England, having been
haunted, it is said, by a priest and a grey lady
who amused themselves at their victims' expense
by all kinds of strange acts.[2] A correspondent
of 'Notes and Queries' (4th S. x. 490) referring
to the Willington ghost says: 'The steam flour
mill, with the house, was in the occupation then
of Messrs. Proctor and Unthank; the house was
separated from the mill by a space of a few
feet, so that no tricks could be played from
the mill. The partners alternately lived in the
house. A relation of mine asked one of those

---

[1] Henderson's *Folk-lore of Northern Counties*, pp. 314, 315.
[2] See *Ibid.* p. 315; Ingram's *Haunted Homes*, pp. 266–277;
More Ghost Stories, W. T. Stead.

gentlemen if there was any truth as to the current rumours. He remarked, " Well, we don't like to speak of it; my partner certainly cannot live comfortably in the house, from some unexplained cause, but as to myself and family we are never disturbed." '

Several parsonages have had their ghosts. Southey, in his 'Life of Wesley,' speaking of Epworth parsonage, which appears to have been haunted in the most strange manner, and alluding to the mysterious disturbances that happened in it, says : 'An author who, in this age, relates such a story, and treats it as not utterly incredible and absurd, must expect to be ridiculed, but the testimony upon which it rests is far too strong to be set aside because of the strangeness of the relation.' In the '' Gentleman's Magazine ' is recorded an account of an apparition that appeared at Souldern Rectory, Oxfordshire, to the Rev. Mr. Shaw, who had always ridiculed the idea of ghosts, announcing to him that his death would be very soon, and very sudden. Suffice it to say that shortly afterwards he was seized with an apoplectic fit while reading the service in church, and died

almost immediately. This strange affair is noticed
in the register of Brisly Church, Norfolk, under
December 12, 1706: 'I, Robert Withers, M.A.,
Vicar of Gately, do insert here a story which I
had from undoubted hands, for I have all the
moral certainty of the truth of it possible.'

The old parsonage at Market, or East, Lavington,
near Devizes—now pulled down—was reputed to be
haunted by a lady supposed to have been murdered,
and, it has been said, a child came also to an
untimely end in the house. Previous to 1818, a
correspondent of 'Notes and Queries' (5 S. i. 273)
says: 'A witness states his father occupied the
house, and writes "that in that year on Feast
Day, being left alone in the house, I went up to my
room. It was the one with marks of blood on the
floor. I distinctly saw a white figure glide into
the room. It went round by the washstand by
the bed, and there disappeared."' It may be
added that part of the road leading from Market
Lavington to Easterton, which skirts the grounds
of Fiddington House, used to be looked upon as
haunted by a lady, who was known as the
'Easterton Ghost.' In 1869, a wall was built

round the road-side of the pond; and, close to the
spot where the lady was seen, two skeletons were
disturbed—one of a woman, the other of a child.
The bones were buried in the churchyard, and
no ghost, it is said, has been seen since.

Occasionally, churches have been haunted.
The famous phantom nun of Holy Trinity Church,
Micklegate, York, has excited a good deal of interest—an account of which is given by Mr. Baring-
Gould in his 'Yorkshire Oddities.' The story
goes that during the suppression of religious
houses before the Reformation, a party of soldiers
came to sack the convent attached to the church.
But having forced an entry they were confronted
by the abbess, a lady of great courage and
devotion, who declared that they should only pass
it over her body, and that should they slay her
and succeed in their errand of destruction, her
spirit would haunt the place until the time came
that their sacrilegious work was expiated by the
rebuilding of the holy house. Many accounts
have been published of this apparition, the following being from the 'Ripon and Richmond
Chronicle' (May 6, 1876): 'In the middle of the

service,' writes a correspondent, 'my eyes, which
had hardly once moved from the left or north
side of the [east] window, were attracted by a
bright light, formed like a female, robed and
hooded, passing from north to south with a rapid
gliding motion outside the church, apparently at
some distance. There are four divisions in the
window, all of stained glass, but at the edge of
each runs a rim of plain transparent glass, about
two inches wide, and adjoining the stone-work.
Through this rim especially could be seen what
looked like a form transparent, but yet thick (if
such a term can be used) with light. The robe
was long and trailed. About half an hour later it
again passed from north to south, and, having
remained about ten seconds only, returned with
what I believe to have been the figure of a young
child, and stopped at the last pane but one, and
then vanished. I did not see the child again,
but a few seconds afterwards the woman reappeared, and completed the passage behind the
last pane very rapidly.' It is said to appear
very frequently on Trinity Sunday, and to bring
two other figures on to the scene, another female,

called the nurse, and the child. Likewise, on one
of the windows of the Abbey Church, Whitby, was
occasionally seen—

> The very form of Hilda fair,
> Hovering upon the sunny air.

According to a correspondent of the 'Gentleman's Magazine,' a ghost appeared for several
years, but very seldom, only in the church porch
at Kilncote, Leicestershire. Folk-lore tells us that
ghosts are occasionally seen in the church porch,
and, in years gone, it was customary for young
people to sit and watch here on St. Mark's
Eve, from 11 at night till 1 o'clock in the
morning. In the third year, for the ceremony
had to be gone through three times, it was supposed the ghosts of all those about to die in the
course of the ensuing year would pass into the
church. It is to this piece of superstition that
James Montgomery refers in his 'Vigil of St.
Mark':

> ' 'Tis now,' replied the village belle,
>   ' St. Mark's mysterious Eve ;
> And all that old traditions tell
>   I tremblingly believe.

'How, when the midnight signal tolls,
   Along the churchyard green
A mournful train of sentenced souls
   In winding sheets are seen.

'The ghosts of all whom death shall doom
   Within the coming year,
In pale procession walk the gloom,
   Amid the silence drear.'

A strange illustration of this superstition is found among the Hollis manuscripts in the Lansdowne collection. The writer, Gervase Hollis, of Great Grimsby, Lincolnshire, was a colonel in the service of Charles I., and he professes to have received the tale from Mr. Liveman Rampaine, minister of God's word at Great Grimsby, Lincolnshire, who was household chaplain to Sir Thomas Munson of Burton, in Lincoln, at the time of the incident.[1]

A curious and somewhat unique advertisement of a haunted house appeared some years ago, and ran thus: 'To be sold, an ancient Gothic mansion, known as Beckington Castle, ten miles from Bath, and two from Frome. The mansion

---

[1] Quoted in *Book of Days*, i. p. 549.

has been closed for some years, having been the subject of proceedings in Chancery. There are legends of haunted rooms, miles of subterranean passages, &c., affording a fine field of research and speculation to lovers of the romantic.' It was no doubt true of the ghost of this, as of most other haunted houses—

> We meet them on the door-way, on the stair,
>   Along the passages they come and go,
> Impalpable impressions on the air,
>   A sense of something moving to and fro.

CHAPTER XXIV

HAUNTED LOCALITIES

SPIRITS in most countries are supposed to haunt all kinds of places, and not to confine themselves to any one locality. Local traditions show how the most unlikely spots, which can boast of little or no romance, are supposed to be frequented by ghosts; the wayfarer along some country road having oftentimes been confronted by an uncanny apparition.

Indeed, the superstitious fear of places being haunted by ghosts not only led to the abandonment but even destruction of many a dwelling-place, a practice which, amongst uncultured tribes, not only 'served as a check to material prosperity, but became an obstacle to progress.' [1] But even in civilised countries the same antipathy to a haunted house is often found, and the ghostly tenant is allowed uninterrupted possession owing to the

[1] Dorman's *Primitive Superstitions*, p. 22.

dread his presence inspires. The Hottentots deserted the house after a decease, and the Seminoles at once removed from the dwelling where death had occurred, and from the neighbourhood where the body was buried. Among the South Slavonians and Bohemians, the bereaved family, returning from the grave, pelted the ghost of their deceased relative with sticks, stones, and hot coals. And the Tschuwasche, a tribe in Finland, opened fire on it as soon as the coffin was outside the house. In Old Calabar, it was usual for a son to leave his father's house for two years, after which time it was considered safe to return. If a Kaffir or Maori died before he could be carried out, the house was tabooed and deserted.[2] The Ojibways pulled down the house in which anyone had died, and chose another one to live in as far off as possible. Even with the death of an infant the same fear was manifested. One day, when a friend visited a neighbour whose child was sick, he was not a little surprised to find, on his return in the evening, that the house had disappeared and all its inhabitants gone. Among the Abipones of Paraguay,

[1] See Tylor's *Primitive Culture*, ii. p. 26.
[2] *Contemporary Review*, xlviii. p. 108.

when anyone's life is despaired of, the house is immediately forsaken by his fellow inmates, and the New England tribes would never live in a wigwam in which any person had died, but would immediately pull it down.

If a deceased Creek Indian ' has been a man of eminent character, the family immediately remove from the house in which he is buried, and erect a new one, with a belief that where the bones of their dead are deposited, the place is always attended by goblins.' [1] The Kamtchadales frequently remove from their dwelling when anyone has died, and among the Lepchas the house where there has been a death ' is almost always forsaken by the surviving inmates.' [2] Occasionally, it would seem, the desertion is more complete. After a death, for instance, the Boobies of Fernando Po forsake the village in which it occurred, and of the Bechuanas we read that ' on the death of Mallahawan . . . the town [Lattakoo] was removed, according to the custom of the country.' [3]

[1] Schoolcraft's *Indian Tribes*, v. p. 270.
[2] See Herbert Spencer's *Principles of Sociology*, 1885, i. p. 199.
[3] *Ibid.* p. 199.

338 THE GHOST WORLD

Ghosts are supposed to find pleasure in re-visiting the places where they have experienced joy, or sorrow and pain, and to wander round the spot where they died, and hence all kinds of pre-cautions have been adopted to prevent their returning. In Europe, sometimes, ' steps were taken to barricade the house against him. Thus, in some parts of Russia and East Prussia, an axe or a lock is laid on the threshold, or a knife is hung over the door, and in Germany as soon as the coffin is carried out of the house all the doors and windows are shut.' [1] And conversely, it is a common custom in many parts of England to unfasten every bolt and lock in the house that the spirit of the dying man may freely escape.

But, as Mr. Frazer shows in his interesting paper on the 'Primitive Ghost,' our ancestors knew how to outwit the ghost in its endeavour to find its way back to the house it left at death. Thus the practice of closing the eyes of the dead, he suggests, originated in 'blindfolding the dead that he might not see the way by which he was carried to his last home. At the grave, where he was to rest for ever, there was no motive for concealment;

[1] The *Contemporary Review*, xlviii. p. 109.

hence the Romans, and apparently the Siamese, opened the eyes of the dead man at the funeral pyre. And the idea that if the eyes of the dead be not closed, his ghost will return to fetch away another of the household, still exists in Germany, Bohemia, and England.' With the same object the coffin was carried out of the house by a hole purposely made in the wall, which was stopped up as soon as the body had passed through, so that, when the ghost strolled back from the grave, he found there was no thoroughfare—a device shared equally by Greenlanders, Hottentots, Bechuanas, Samoieds, Ojibways, Algonquins, Laosians, Hindoos, Tibetans, Siamese, Chinese, and Fijians. These ' doors of the dead ' are still to be seen in a village near Amsterdam, and they were common in some towns of Central Italy. A trace of the same custom survives in Thüringen, where there is a belief that the ghost of a man who has been hanged will return to the house if not taken out by a window instead of a door. Similarly, for the purpose of misleading the dead, the Bohemians put on masks, that the dead might not know and therefore might not follow them, and it is a matter of con-

jecture whether mourning customs may not have
sprung from 'the desire to disguise and therefore
to protect the living from the dead.'

Among further methods in use for frustrating the
return of the dead, may be noticed the objection to
utter the names of deceased persons—a superstition
which Mr. Frazer shows has modified whole
languages. Thus, ' among the Australians, Tas-
manians, and Abipones, if the name of a deceased
person happened to be a common name, e.g. the
name of an animal or plant, this name was
abolished, and a new one substituted for it. During
the residence of the Jesuit Missionary Dobritz-
hoffer amongst the Abipones, the name for tiger
was thus changed three times. Amongst the
Indians of Columbia, near relatives of a deceased
person often change their names, under the impression that the ghost will return if he hears the
familiar names.' [1]

The Sandwich Islanders say the spirit of the
departed hovers about the place of its former
resort, and in the country north of the Zambesi
' all believe that the souls of the departed still

[1] The *Contemporary Review*, xlviii. p. 111.

mingle among the living, and partake in some way
of the food they consume.' In the Aleutian
Islands, it is said that 'the invisible souls or shades
of the departed wander about among their children.'

But one of the most favourite haunts of departed spirits is said to be burial-grounds, and especially their own graves, reminding us of Puck's words
in 'A Midsummer Night's Dream' (Act v. sc. 2):

> Now it is the time of night,
>   That the graves all gaping wide,
> Everyone lets forth his sprite,
>   In the church-way paths to glide.

'The belief in ghosts,' writes Thorpe,[1] 'was
deeply impressed on the minds of the heathen
Northmen, a belief closely connected with their
ideas of the state after death. The soul, they
believed, returned to the place whence it sprang,
while the body, and the grosser life bound to it,
passed to the abode of Hel or Death. Herewith
was naturally combined the belief that the soul of
the departed might, from its heavenly home, revisit the earth, there at night-time to unite itself
in the grave-mound with the corporeal shadow

---

[1] *Northern Mythology*, ii. p. 20.

released from Hel. Thus the dead could show themselves in the open grave-mounds in the same form which they had in life.'

Indeed, it has been the current opinion for centuries that places of burial are haunted with spectres and apparitions. Ovid speaks of ghosts coming out of their sepulchres and wandering about, and Virgil,[1] too, quoting the popular opinion of his day, tells us how 'Mœris could call the ghosts out of their tombs.' In short, the idea of the ghost remaining near the corpse is of world-wide prevalence, and, as Dr. Tylor remarks,[2] 'through all the changes of religious thought from first to last in the course of human history, the hovering ghosts of the dead make the midnight burial-ground a place where man's flesh creeps with terror.' We may further compare Hamlet's words (Act iii. sc. 2):

'Tis now the very witching time of night,
When church-yards yawn.

And Puck also tells how, at the approach of Aurora, 'ghosts, wandering here and there, troop home to churchyards.' Tracing this superstition

[1] *Bucolics*, viii. p. 98.   [2] *Primitive Culture*, ii. p. 30.

amongst uncultured tribes, we find the soul of the
North American hovering about its burial-place,
and among the Costa Ricans the spirits of the dead
are believed to remain near their bodies for a year.
The Dayak's burial-place is frequented by ghosts,
and the explorer Swan tells us that when he
was with the North-Western Indians, he was not
allowed to attend a funeral for fear of his offend-
ing the spirits hovering about. From the same
authority we learn how at Stony Point, on the
north-west coast of America, a burial-place of the
Indians was considered to be haunted by spirits,
and on this account no Indian ever ventured there.[1]
This dread of burial-grounds still retains a persistent hold, and is one of those survivals of
primitive belief which has given rise to a host of
strange superstitious practices.

Keppel, in his 'Visit to the Indian Archipelago,'
says that in Northern Australia the natives will not
willingly approach graves at night, alone, 'but when
they are obliged to pass them, they carry a fire-
stick to keep off the spirit of darkness.'

There is still a belief that the ghost of the last

[1] See Dorman's *Primitive Superstitions*, p. 21.

person watches round the churchyard till another
is buried, to whom he delivers his charge. Crofton
Croker says that in Ireland it is the general opinion
among the lower orders that 'the last buried corpse
has to perform an office like that of "fag" in our
public schools by the junior boy, and that the attend-
ance on his churchyard companions is duly relieved
by the interment of some other person.' Serious
disturbances have resulted from this superstition,
and terrific fights have at times taken place to decide
which corpse should be buried first. The ancient
churchyard of Truagh, county Monaghan, is said
to be haunted by an evil spirit, whose appearance
generally forebodes death. The legend runs, writes
Lady Wilde,[1] 'that at funerals the spirit watches
for the person who remains last in the graveyard.
If it be a young man who is there alone, the spirit
takes the form of a beautiful young girl, inspires
him with an ardent passion, and exacts from him
a promise that he will meet her that day month in
the churchyard. The promise is then sealed by a
kiss, which sends a fatal fire through his veins, so
that he is unable to resist her caresses, and makes

---

[1] *Ancient Cures, Charms, and Usages of Ireland*, p. 84.

the promise required. Then she disappears, and
the young man proceeds homewards ; but no sooner
has he passed the boundary wall of the churchyard
than the whole story of the evil rushes on his mind,
and he knows that he has sold himself, soul and
body, for a demon's kiss. Then terror and dismay
take hold of him, till despair becomes insanity, and
on the very day month fixed for the meeting with
the demon bride, the victim dies the death of a
raving lunatic, and is laid in the fatal graveyard
of Truagh.'

The dead, too, particularly object to persons
treading carelessly on their graves, an allusion to
which occurs in one of the songs of Greek out-
lawry : [1]

All Saturday we held carouse, and far through Sunday night,
And on the Monday morn we found our wine expended
    quite.
To seek for more, without delay, the captain made me go ;
I ne'er had seen nor known the way, nor had a guide to
    show.
And so through solitary roads and secret paths I sped,
Which to a little ivied church long time deserted led.
This church was full of tombs, and all by gallant men
    possest ;
One sepulchre stood all alone, apart from all the rest.

[1] *Essay in the Study of Folk-songs*, pp. 14, 15.

I did not see it, and I trod above the dead man's bones,
And as from out the nether world came up a sound of groans.
' What ails thee, sepulchre ?   Why thus so deeply groan and
    sigh ?
Doth the earth press, or the black stone weigh on thee
    heavily ? '
' Neither the earth doth press me down, nor black stone do
    me scath,
But I with bitter grief am wrung, and full of shame and
    wrath,
That thou dost trample on my head, and I am scorned in
    death.
Perhaps I was not also young, nor brave and stout in fight,
Nor wont, as thou, beneath the moon, to wander through
    the night.'

According to the Guiana Indians, ' every place
is haunted where any have died ; ' and in Madagascar the ghosts of ancestors are said to hover about
their tombs. The East Africans ' appear to imagine
the souls to be always near the place of sepulture,'
and on the Gold Coast ' the spirit is supposed to remain near the spot where the body has been buried.'
The souls of warriors slain on the field of battle are
considered by the Mangaians to wander for a while
amongst the rocks and trees of the neighbourhood
in which their bodies were thrown. At length ' the
first slain on each battlefield would collect his

brothers' ghosts, and lead them to the summit of a mountain, whence they leap into the blue expanse, thus becoming the peculiar clouds of the winter.'[1] And the Mayas of Yucatan think the souls of the dead return to the earth if they choose, and, in order that they may not lose the way to the domestic hearth, they mark the path from the hut to the tomb with chalk.[2]

The primitive doctrine of souls obliges the savage, says Mr. Dorman,[3] 'to think of the spirit of the dead as close at hand. Most uncultured tribes, on this account, regard the spot where death has taken place as haunted. A superstitious fear soon instigates worship, and this worship, beginning at the tombs and burial-places, develops into the temple ritual of higher culture.'

The Iroquois believe the space between the earth and sky is full of spirits, usually invisible, but occasionally seen, and the Ojibways affirm that innumerable spirits are ever near, and dwell in all kinds of places. European folk-lore has similar beliefs, it having been a Scandinavian idea

[1] Gill: *Myths and Songs from the South Pacific*, pp. 162, 163.
[2] See Dorman's *Primitive Superstitions*, p. 33. [3] *Ibid.* p. 30.

that the souls of the departed dwell in the interior of
mountains, a phase of superstition which frequently
presents itself in the Icelandic sagas, and exists
in Germany at the present day. 'Of some German
mountains,' writes Thorpe, 'it is believed that they
are the abodes of the damned. One of these is the
Horselberg, near Eisenach, which is the habitation
of Frau Holle; another is the fabulous Venusberg,
in which the Tannhäuser sojourns, and before which
the trusty Eckhart sits as a warning guardian.'[1]

Departed souls were also supposed to dwell in
the bottom of wells and ponds, with which may be
compared the many tales current throughout Germany and elsewhere of towns and castles that have
been sunk in the water, and are at times visible.
But, as few subjects have afforded greater scope for
the imagination than the hereafter of the human
soul, numerous myths and legendary stories have
been invented to account for its mysterious departure in the hour of death. Shakespeare has
alluded to the numerous destinations of the disembodied spirit, enumerating the many ideas prevalent, in his day, on the subject. In 'Measure

[1] *Northern Mythology*, i. p. 286.

for Measure' (Act iii. sc. 1) Claudio pathetically
says :

> Ay, but to die, and go we know not where ;
> To lie in cold obstruction, and to rot ;
> This sensible warm motion to become
> A kneaded clod, and the delighted spirit
> To bathe in fiery floods, or to reside
> In thrilling regions of thick-ribbed ice ;
> To be imprison'd in the viewless winds,
> And blown with restless violence round about
> The pendent world.[1]

Indeed, it would be a long task to enter into the
mass of mystic details respecting ' the soul's dread
journey by caverns and rocky paths and weary
plains, over steep and slippery mountains, by frail
bank or giddy bridge, across gulfs or rushing
rivers,' to its destined home.

According to the Mazovians the soul remains
with the coffin, sitting upon the upper part of it
until the burial is over, when it flies away. Such
traditions, writes Mr. Ralston,[2] ' vary in different
localities, but everywhere, among all the Slavonic
people, there seems always to have prevailed an
idea that death does not finally sever the ties

---

[1] Cf. *Othello*, Act v. sc. 2.
[2] *Songs of the Russian People*, pp. 115, 116.

between the living and the dead. This idea has taken various forms, and settled into several widely differing superstitions, lurking in the secrecy of the cottage, and there keeping alive the cultus of the domestic spirit, and showing itself openly in the village church, where on a certain day it calls for a service in remembrance of the dead. The spirits of those who are thus remembered, say the peasants, attend the service, taking their place behind the altar. But those who are left unremembered weep bitterly all through the day.'

In some parts of Ireland, writes Mr. McAnally, ' there exists a belief that the spirits of the dead are not taken from earth, nor do they lose all their former interest in earthly affairs, but enjoy the happiness of the saved, or suffer the punishment imposed for their sins in the neighbourhood of the scenes among which they lived while clothed in flesh and blood. At particular crises in the affairs of mortals these disenthralled spirits sometimes display joy and grief in such a manner as to attract the attention of living men and women. At weddings they are frequently unseen guests; at funerals they are always present; and sometimes, at

both weddings and funerals, their presence is
recognised by aerial voices, or mysterious music,
known to be of unearthly origin. The spirits of
the good wander with the living as guardian angels ;
but the spirits of the bad are restrained in their
action, and compelled to do penance at, or near, the
place where their crimes were committed. Some
are chained at the bottom of lakes, others buried
underground, others confined in mountain gorges,
some hang on the sides of precipices, others are trans-
fixed on the tree-tops, while others haunt the homes
of their ancestors, all waiting till the penance has
been endured and the hour of deliverance arrives.'

Harriet Martineau, speaking of the English
lakes, says that Souter or Soutra Fell is the mountain on which ghosts appeared in myriads at
intervals during ten years of the last century.
' On the Midsummer Eve of the fearful 1745,
twenty-six persons, expressly summoned by the
family, saw all that had been seen before, and
more. Carriages were now interspersed with
the troops ; and everybody knew that no carriages
had been, or could be, on the summit of
Souter Fell. The multitude was beyond imagina-

tion; for the troops filled a space of half a mile, and marched quickly till night hid them, still marching. There was nothing vaporous or indistinct about the appearance of these spectres. So real did they seem, that some of the people went up the next morning to look for the hoof-marks of the horses; and awful it was to them to find not one footprint on heather or grass.' This spectral march was similar to that seen at Edge Hill, in Leicestershire, in 1707, and corresponds with the tradition of the tramp of armies over Helvellyn, on the eve of the battle of Marston Moor.

With such phantoms may be compared the mock suns, the various appearances of halos and wandering lights, and such a phenomenon as the ' Spectre of the Brocken.' Calmet relates a singular instance at Milan, where some two thousand persons saw, as they supposed, an angel hovering in the air: he cites Cardan as an eye-witness, who says that the populace were only undeceived when it was shown, by a sharp-sighted lawyer, to be a reflection from one of the statues of a neighbouring church, the image of which was caught on the surface of a cloud. The mirage, or water of the desert, owes its appearance to similar laws of refraction. Mountain districts, we know, abound in these illusions, and 'the splendid enchantment presented in the Straits of Reggio by the Fata Morgana' has attracted much notice. At such times, 'minarets, temples, and palaces, have seemed to rise out of the distant waves;' and spectral huntsmen, soldiers in battle array, and gay but mute cavalcades, have appeared under similar circumstances, pictured on the table of the clouds. It was thus, we are told, that the Duke of Brunswick and Mrs. Graham saw the image of their balloon distinctly exhibited on the face of a cumulous cloud, in 1836; and travellers on Mont Blanc have been startled by their own magnified shadows, floating among the giant peaks.[1] It is difficult to say how many of the apparitions which have been supposed to haunt certain spots might be attributed to similar causes.

[1] *Occult Sciences*, 1855; *Apparitions*, pp. 80, 81.

A A

CHAPTER XXV

CHECKS AND SPELLS AGAINST GHOSTS

AMONGST the qualities ascribed to the cock was the time-honoured belief that by its crow it dispelled all kinds of ghostly beings—a notion alluded to by the poet Prudentius, who flourished at the commencement of the fourth century. There is, also, a hymn said to have been composed by St. Ambrose, and formerly used in the Salisbury Missal, in which allusion is made to this superstition. In Blair's 'Grave' the apparition vanishes at the crowing of the cock, and in 'Hamlet,' on the departure of the ghost, Bernardo says:

It was about to speak when the cock crew;

to which Horatio answers:

And then it started like a guilty thing
Upon a fearful summons. I have heard
The cock, that is the trumpet to the morn,

Doth with his lofty and shrill-sounding throat
Awake the god of day ; and, at his warning,
Whether in sea or fire, in earth or air,
The extravagant and erring spirit hies
To his confine : and of the truth herein
This present object made probation.

Whereupon Marcellus adds the well-known lines :

It faded on the crowing of the cock.
Some say that ever 'gainst that season comes,
Wherein our Saviour's birth is celebrated,
The bird of dawning singeth all night long ;
And then, they say, no spirit dares stir abroad ;
The nights are wholesome ; then no planets strike,
No fairy takes, nor witch hath power to charm,
So hallow'd and so gracious is the time.

Even the devil is powerless at the sound of cock-
crow. An amusing story is told on the Continent
of how a farmer's wife tricked the devil by means
of this spell. It appears that her husband was
mourning the loss of his barn—either by wind or
fire—when a stranger addressed him, and said :
'That I can easily remedy. If you will just write
your name in your blood on this parchment, your
barn shall be fixed and ready to-morrow before the
cock crows ; if not, our contract is void.' But
afterwards the farmer repented of the bargain he

A A 2

had made, and, on consulting his wife, she ran out
in the middle of the night, and found a number of
workmen employed on the barn. Thereupon she
cried with all her might, 'Cock-a-doodle-doo!
cock-a-doodle-doo!' and was followed by all the
cocks in the neighbourhood, each of which sent
forth a hearty 'Cock-a-doodle-doo!' At the same
moment all the phantom workmen disappeared, and
the barn remained unfinished. In a pretty
Swedish ballad of 'Little Christina,' a lover rises
from the grave to console his beloved. One night
Christina hears light fingers tapping at the door;
she opens it and sees her betrothed. She washes
his feet with pure wine, and for a long while they
converse. Then the cocks begin to crow, and the
dead get them underground. The young girl
follows her sweetheart through the white forest,
and when they reach the graveyard, the fair hair
of the young man begins to disappear. 'See,
maiden,' he says, 'how the moon has reddened all
at once; even so, in a moment, thy beloved will
vanish.' She sits down on the tomb, and says, 'I
shall remain here till the Lord calls me.' Then
she hears the voice of her betrothed, 'Little

Christina, go back to thy dwelling-place. Every time a tear falls from thine eyes my shroud is full of blood. Every time thy heart is gay, my shroud is full of rose-leaves.' These folk-tales are interesting, as embodying the superstitions of the people among whom they are current.

A similar idea prevails in India, where the cock is with the Hindoos, as with the English peasant, a most potent instrument in the subjugation of troublesome spirits. A paragraph in the ' Carnatic Times' tells us how a Hindoo exorcist tied his patient's hair in a knot, and then with a nail attached it to a tree. Muttering some 'incantatory' lines, he seized a live cock, and holding it over the girl's head with one hand, he, with the other, cut its throat. The blood-stained knot of hair was left attached to the tree, which was supposed to detain the demon. It is further supposed that ' one or a legion thus exorcised will haunt that tree till he or they shall choose to take possession of some other unfortunate.'

It was said that chastity was of itself a safe-guard against the malignant power of bad ghosts ; a notion to which Milton has referred :

Some say no evil thing that walks by night,
In fog or fire, by lake or moorish fen,
Blue meagre hag, or stubborn unlaid ghost,
That breaks the magic chains at curfew-time,
No goblin, or swart faery of the mine,
Hath hurtful power o'er true virginity.

The cross and holy water have, too, generally been considered sacred preservatives against devils and spirits, illustrations of which will be found in many of our old romances.[1]

Fire, like water,[2] has been employed for the purpose of excluding or barring the ghost, and Mr. Frazer writes how 'the Siberians seek to get rid of the ghost of the departed by leaping over a fire. At Rome, mourners returning from a funeral stepped over fire,' a practice which still exists in China. A survival of this custom prevails among the south Slavonians, who, on their return from a funeral, are met by an old woman carrying a vessel of live coals. On these they pour water, or else they take a live coal from the hearth and fling it over their heads. The Brahmans simply touched fire, while in Ruthenia 'the mourners merely look

[1] See E. Yardley's *Supernatural in Fiction*, pp. 29–31.
[2] See Chapter on 'Ghost Laying.'

steadfastly at the stove or place their hands on it.'[1] It is noteworthy that in the Highlands of Scotland and in Burma, the house-fires were always extinguished when a death happened ; for fear, no doubt, of the ghost being accidentally burnt.

The Eskimos drive away spirits by blowing their breath at them,[2] and the Mayas of Yucatan had evil spirits which could be driven away by the sorcerers ; but they never came near when their fetiches were exposed. They had a ceremony for expelling evil spirits from houses about to be occupied by newly married persons.[3] The natives of Brazil so much dread the ghosts of the dead that it is recorded how some of them have been struck with sudden death because of an imaginary apparition of them. They try to appease them by fastening offerings on stakes fixed in the ground for that purpose.[4]

Mutilations of the dead were supposed to keep his ghost harmless, and on this account Greek

[1] *Contemporary Review*, xlviii. p. 112 ; Ralston's *Songs of the Russian People*, p. 319.

[2] Dorman's *Primitive Superstitions*, p. 20.

[3] *Ibid.* p. 29.   [4] *Ibid.* p. 21.

murderers hacked off the extremities of their victims. Australians cut off the right thumb of a slain enemy that his ghost might not be able to draw the bow. And in Arabia, Germany, and Spain, as the ghosts of murderers and their victims are especially restless, everyone who passes their graves is bound to add a stone to the pile.[1]

In Pekin, six or seven feet away from the front of the doors, small brick walls are built up. These are to keep the spirits out, which fly only in straight lines, and therefore find a baulk in their way. Another mode of keeping spirits away in the case of children is to attire them as priests, and also to dress the boys as girls, who are supposed to be the less susceptible to the evil influence. In fact, most countries have their contrivances for counteracting, in one way or another, the influence of departed spirits—a piece of superstition of which European folk-lore affords abundant illustrations.

Thus, in Norway, bullets, gunpowder, and weapons have no influence on ghosts, but at the sight of a cross, and from exorcisms, they must

[1] 'The Primitive Ghost,' *Contemporary Review*, xlviii. p. 107.

retire. The same belief prevails in Denmark, where all kinds of checks to ghostly influence are resorted to. It is said, for instance, to be dangerous to shoot at a spectre, as the bullet will return on him who shot it. But if the piece be loaded with a silver button, that will infallibly take effect. A Danish tradition tells how once there was a horrible spectre which caused great fear and disquietude, as everyone who saw it died immediately afterwards. In this predicament, a young fellow offered to encounter the apparition, and to endeavour to drive it away. For this purpose he went at midnight to the church path, through which the spectre was in the habit of passing, having previously provided himsel with steel in various shapes. When the apparition approached, he fearlessly threw steel before its feet, so that it was obliged instantly to turn back, and it appeared no more.[1] A common superstition, equally popular in England as on the Continent, is that when a horseshoe is nailed over the doorway no spirit can enter. It is also said that 'if anyone is afraid of spectres, let him strew

[1] Thorpe's *Northern Mythology*, ii. p. 205.

flax seed before the door; then no spirit can cross
the threshold. A preventive equally efficacious is
to place one's slippers by the bedside with the heels
towards the bed. Spectres may be driven away by
smoking the room with the snuff of a tallow
candle; while wax-lights attract them.' And at
the present day various devices are adopted by
our English peasantry for warding off from their
dwellings ghosts, and other uncanny intruders.[1]

[1] See Harland and Wilkinson's *Lancashire Folk-lore*, 1867,
p. 63.

CHAPTER XXVI

WRAITH-SEEING

CLOSELY allied to 'second sight' is the doctrine of 'wraiths' or 'fetches,' sometimes designated 'doubles'—an apparition exactly like a living person, its appearance, whether to that person or to another, being considered an omen of death. The 'Fetch' is a well-known superstition in Ireland, and is supposed to be a mere shadow, 'resembling in stature, features, and dress, a living person, and often mysteriously or suddenly seen by a very particular friend. Spiritlike, it flits before the sight, seeming to walk leisurely through the fields, often disappearing through a gap or lane. The person it resembles is usually known at the time to be labouring under some mortal illness, and unable to leave his or her bed. When the 'fetch' appears agitated, or eccentric in

its motions, a violent or painful death is indicated
for the doomed prototype. Such a phantom, too,
is said to make its appearance at the same time,
and in the same place, to more than one person.[1]
Should it be seen in the morning, a happy
longevity for the original is confidently expected;
but if it be seen in the evening, immediate dissolution of the living prototype is anticipated. It
is thought, too, that individuals may behold their
own 'fetches.' Queen Elizabeth is said to have
been warned of her death by the apparition of her
own double, and Miss Strickland thus describes
her last illness: 'As her mortal illness drew
towards a close, the superstitious fears of her
simple ladies were excited almost to mania, even
to conjuring up a spectral apparition of the Queen
while she was yet alive. Lady Guilford, who was
then in waiting on the Queen, leaving her in an
almost breathless sleep in her privy chamber, went
out to take a little air, and met her Majesty, as
she thought, three or four chambers off. Alarmed
at the thought of being discovered in the act
of leaving the royal patient alone, she hurried

[1] *Gentleman's Magazine*, 1865, pt. ii. p. 564.

forward in some trepidation in order to excuse herself, when the apparition vanished away. She returned terrified to the chamber, but there lay the Queen in the same lethargic slumber in which she left her.'

Shelley, shortly before his death, believed he had seen his wraith. 'On June 23,' says one of his biographers, 'he was heard screaming at midnight in the saloon. The Williamses ran in and found him staring on vacancy. He had had a vision of a cloaked figure which came to his bedside and beckoned him to follow. He did so, and when they had reached the sitting-room, the figure lifted the hood of his cloak and disclosed Shelley's own features, and saying "Siete soddisfatto?" vanished. This vision is accounted for on the ground that Shelley had been reading a drama attributed to Calderon, named 'El Embozado, ó el Encapotado,' in which a mysterious personage who had been haunting and thwarting the hero all his life, and is at last about to give him satisfaction in a duel, unmasks and proves to be the hero's own wraith. He also asks, "Art thou satisfied?" and the haunted man dies of horror.' Sir Robert Napier

is supposed to have seen his double, and Aubrey
quaintly relates how 'the beautiful Lady Diana
Rich, daughter to the Earl of Holland, as she was
walking in her father's garden at Kensington
to take the air before dinner, about 11 o'clock, being
then very well, met her own apparition, habit and
everything, as in a looking-glass. About a month
after, she died of small-pox. And it is said that
her sister, the Lady Isabella Thynne, saw the like
of herself also before she died. This account I
had from a person of honour. A third sister,
Mary, was married to the Earl of Breadalbane,
and it has been recorded that she also, not long
after her marriage, had some such warning of her
approaching dissolution.'

The Irish novelist, John Banim, has written
both a novel and a ballad on this subject, one
which has also largely entered into many a tradition and folk-tale.[1] In Cumberland this apparition is known by the peasantry as a 'swarth,'
and in Yorkshire by the name of a 'waff.' The
gift of wraith-seeing still flourishes on the Continent,
and examples abound in Silesia and the Tyrol.

---

[1] See *Popular Irish Superstitions*, by W. R. Wilde, p. 109.

'With regard to bilocation, or double personality,' writes a Catholic priest,[1] 'there is a great deal of very interesting matter in St. Thomas of Aquin, and also in Cardinal Cajetan's "Commentaries of St. Thomas." The substance of the principles is this: Bilocation, properly so called, is defined by the scholastics as the perfect and simultaneous existence of one and the same individual in two distinct places at the same time. This *never* does and never can happen. But bilocation, improperly so called, and which St. Thomas terms *raptus*, does occur, and is identical with the double, as you call it, in the cases of St. Gennadius, St. Ignatius, &c.

'St. Thomas quotes as illustrations or instances, St. Paul being taken up to the Third Heaven. Ezekiel, the prophet, was taken by God and shown Jerusalem, whilst at the same time he was sitting in the room with the ancients of the tribe of Judah before him (Ezekiel viii.), &c. In which the soul of man is not wholly detached from the body, being necessary for the purpose of giving life, but is detached

[1] *More Ghost Stories*, collected and edited by W. T. Stead, 1892, p. 22.

from the *senses* of the body. St. Thomas gives
three causes for this phenomenon: (1) Divine
power; (2) the power of the Devil; and (3),
disease of the body when very violent sometimes.'
Bardinus tells how Marsilius Ficinus appeared at
the hour of his death on a white horse to Michael
Mercatus, and rode away crying, 'O Michael,
Michael, vera, vera sunt illa,' that is, the doctrine
of a future life is true.   Instances of this kind of
phenomenon have been common in all ages of the
world, and Lucretius suggested the strange fancy
that the superficial surfaces of all bodies were
continually flying off like the coats of an onion,
which accounted for the appearance of apparitions;
whilst Jacques Gaffarel suggested that corrupting
bodies send forth vapours which, being compressed
by the cold night air, appear visible to the eye in
the forms of men.[1]

In one of the notes to 'Les Imaginations
Extravagantes de Monsieur Oufle,' by the Abbé
Bordélon, it is said that the monks and nuns,
a short time before their death, have seen the
images of themselves seated in their chairs or stalls.

[1] See Mrs. Crowe's *Night Side of Nature*, 1854, p. 111.

Catharine of Russia, after retiring to her bedroom, was told that she had been seen just before to enter the State Chamber. On hearing this she went thither, and saw the exact similitude of herself seated upon the throne. She ordered her guards to fire upon it.

In Scotland and the northern counties of England it was formerly said that the apparition of the person that was doomed to die within a short time was seen wrapped in a winding-sheet, and the higher the winding-sheet reached up towards the head the nearer was death. This apparition was seen during day, and it might show itself to anyone, but only to one, who generally fell into a faint a short time afterwards. If the person who saw the apparition was alone at the time, the fainting fit did not come on till after meeting with others.

In the 'Statistical Account of Scotland' (xxi. 148), the writer, speaking of the parish of Monquhitter, says, the 'fye gave due warning by certain signs of approaching mortality'; and, again (149), 'the fye has withdrawn his warning.' Some friends observing to an old woman, when in the ninty-ninth year of her age, that, in the course of nature, she could not long survive, she remarked, with pointed indignation, ' What fye-token do you see about me ? '

In the same work (iii. 380) the minister of Applecross, county of Ross, speaking of the superstitions of that parish, says : ' The ghosts of the dying, called " tasks," are said to be heard, their cry being a repetition of the moans of the sick. Some assume the sagacity of distinguishing the voice of their departed friends. The corpse follows the track led by the " tasks " to the place of interment, and the early or late completion of the prediction is made to depend on the period of the night at which the " task " is heard.'

The Scotch wraith and Irish fetch have their parallel in Wales in the Lledrith, or spectre of a person seen before his death. It never speaks, and vanishes if spoken to. It has been seen by miners previous to a fatal accident in the mine. The story is told of a miner who saw himself lying dead and horribly maimed in a phantom tram-car, led by a phantom horse, and surrounded by phantom miners. As he watched this dreadful group of spectres they passed on, looking neither to the right nor the left, and faded away. The miner's dog was as frightened as its master, and ran away howling. The miner continued to work in the pit, and as the days passed on and no harm came to him he grew more cheerful, and was so bold as to laugh at the superstition. But the day he did this a stone fell from the roof and broke his arm. As soon as he recovered he resumed work in the pit; but a stone crushed him, and he was borne maimed and dead in the tram along the road where his 'lledrith' had appeared.[1]

'Examining,' says Dr. Tylor,[2] 'the position of the doctrine of wraiths among the higher races, we find it specially prominent in three intellectual districts : Christian hagiology, popular folk-lore, and modern spiritualism. St. Anthony saw the soul of St. Ammonius carried to heaven in the midst of choirs of angels, the same day that the holy hermit died five days' journey off in the desert of Nitria. When St. Ambrose died on Easter Eve, several newly-baptized children saw the holy bishop and pointed him out to their parents; but these, with their less

[1] Wirt Sikes, *British Goblins*, p. 215.
[2] *Primitive Culture*, 1891, i. p. 448.

pure eyes, could not behold him.' Numerous
instances of wraith-seeing have been chronicled
from time to time, some of which are noteworthy.
It is related how Ben Jonson, when staying at Sir
Robert Cotton's house, was visited by the apparition
of his eldest son, with a mark of a bloody cross
upon his forehead, at the moment of his death by
the plague. Lord Balcarres, it is said, when in
confinement in Edinburgh Castle under suspicion
of Jacobitism, was one morning lying in bed
when the curtains were drawn aside by his friend
Viscount Dundee, who looked upon him steadfastly,
and then left the room. Shortly afterwards the
news came that he had fallen about the same hour
at Killiecrankie. Lord Mohun, who was killed in a
duel in Chelsea Fields, is reported to have appeared
at the moment of his death, in the year 1642, to a
lady in James Street, Covent Garden, and also
to the sister of Glanvill, famous as the author of
'Sadducismus Triumphatus.' It is related how
the second Earl of Chesterfield, in 1652, saw, when
walking, a spectre with long white robes and black
face. Regarding it as an intimation of some illness of his wife, then visiting her father at Net-

worth, he set off early to inquire, and met a servant from Lady Chesterfield, describing the same apparition. Anna Maria Porter, when living at Esher, was visited by an old gentleman, a neighbour, who frequently came in to tea. On this occasion, the story goes, he left the room without speaking; and, fearing that something had happened, she sent to inquire, and found that he had died at the moment of his appearance. Similarly Maria Edgeworth, when waiting with her family for an expected guest, saw in a vacant chair the apparition of a sailor cousin, who suddenly stated that his ship had been wrecked and he himself the only one saved. The event proved the contrary—he alone was drowned.[1]

One of the most striking and best authenticated cases on record is known as the Birkbeck Ghost, and is thus related in the 'Proceedings of the Psychical Research Society': 'In 1789, Mrs. Birkbeck, wife of William Birkbeck, banker, of Settle, and a member of the Society of Friends, was taken ill and died at Cockermouth while returning from a journey to Scotland, which she

[1] *Real Ghost Stories*, W. T. Stead, p. 103.

had undertaken alone—her husband and three children, aged seven, five, and four years respectively, remaining at Settle. The friends at whose house the death occurred made notes of every circumstance attending Mrs. Birkbeck's last hours, so that the accuracy of the several statements as to time as well as place was beyond the doubtfulness of man's memory, or of any even unconscious attempt to bring them into agreement with each other. One morning, between seven and eight o'clock, the relation to whom the care of the children had been entrusted, and who kept a minute journal of all that concerned them, went into their bedroom, as usual, and found them all sitting up in bed in great excitement and delight. "Mamma has been here," they cried; and the little one said, "She called, 'Come, Esther!'" Nothing could make them doubt the fact, and it was carefully noted down to entertain the mother when she came home. That same morning, as their mother lay on her dying bed at Cockermouth, she said, "I should be ready to go if I could but see my children." She then closed her eyes, to reopen them, as they thought, no more. But after ten minutes of perfect stillness she looked up brightly, and said, "I am ready now; I have been with my children;" and at once passed peacefully away. When the notes taken at the two places were compared, the day, hour, and minutes were the same.'

Baxter, in his 'World of Spirits,' records a very similar case of a dying woman visiting her children in Rochester, and in a paper on 'Ghosts and Goblins,' which appeared in the 'Cornhill' (1873, xxvii. 457), the writer relates how, in a house in Ireland, a girl lay dying. Her mother and father were with her, and her five sisters were praying for her in a neighbouring room. This room was well lit, but overhead was a skylight, and the dark sky beyond. One of the sisters, looking towards this skylight, saw there the face of her dying sister looking sorrowfully down upon them. She seized another sister and pointed to the skylight; one after another the sisters looked where she pointed. They spoke no word; and in a few moments their father and mother called them to the room where their sister had just died. But when afterwards they talked together about what had happened that night, it was found that they had all seen the vision

and the sorrowful face. But, as the writer observes,
' in stories where a ghost appears for some useful
purpose, the mind does not reject the event as alto-
gether unreasonable, though the circumstances may
be sufficiently preposterous ; ' but one can conceive
no reason why the vision of a dying sister should
look down through a skylight.

According to a Lancashire belief, the spirits of
persons about to die, especially if the persons be
in distant lands, are supposed to return to their
friends, and thus predict the event. While the
spirit is thus away, the person is supposed to be in
a swoon, and unaware of what is passing. But his
desire to see his friends is necessary ; and he must
have been thinking of them.[1]

It is related from Devonshire, of the well-known
Dr. Hawker, that, when walking one night, he
observed an old woman pass by him, to whom he
was in the habit of giving a weekly charity. As
soon as she had passed, he felt somebody pull his
coat, and on looking round he recognised her, and
put his hand in his pocket to seek for a sixpence,
but on turning to give it to her she was gone. On

[1] Harland and Wilkinson, *Lancashire Folk-lore*, p. 105.

his return home he heard she was dead, but his family had forgotten to mention the circumstance.[1]

A correspondent of 'Notes and Queries' (3rd S. vi. 182) tells how a judge of the Staffordshire County Courts, being on one occasion in the North, went with his sisters into the church of the place to inspect its monuments. While there they were surprised to see a lady, whom they knew to be in Bath, walk in at one door and out through another. They immediately followed, but could neither see nor hear anything further of her. On writing to her friends, it was found that she was dead, and a second letter elicited the fact that she had died at the very same time at which she had been seen by them in the North.

Patrick Kennedy, in his 'Legendary Fiction of the Irish Celt,' speaking of the Irish fetch, gives the following tale of 'The Doctor's Fetch,' based, it is stated, on the most authentic sources: 'In one of our Irish cities, and in a room where the mild moonbeams were resting on the carpet and on a table near the window, Mrs. B., wife of a doctor in good practice and general esteem, looking

---

[1] Quoted by Mrs. Crowe, *Night Side of Nature*, p. 202.

towards the window from her pillow, was startled
by the appearance of her husband standing near
the table just mentioned, and seeming to look with
attention on the book which was lying open on it.
Now, the living and breathing man was by her side
apparently asleep, and, greatly as she was surprised
and affected, she had sufficient command of herself
to remain without moving, lest she should expose
him to the terror which she herself at the moment
experienced. After gazing on the apparition for a
few seconds, she bent her eyes upon her husband
to ascertain if his looks were turned in the direction
of the window, but his eyes were closed. She
turned round again, although now dreading the sight
of what she believed to be her husband's fetch,
but it was no longer there. She remained sleep-
less throughout the remainder of the night, but
still bravely refrained from disturbing her partner.

'Next morning, Mr. B., seeing signs of disquiet
on his wife's countenance while at breakfast, made
some affectionate inquiries, but she concealed her
trouble, and at his ordinary hour he sallied forth to
make his calls. Meeting Dr. C. in the street, and
falling into conversation with him, he asked his

opinion on the subject of fetches. " I think," was
the answer, " and so I am sure do you, that they are
mere illusions produced by a disturbed stomach
acting upon the excited brain of a highly imaginative or superstitious person." " Then," said Dr.
B., " I am highly imaginative or superstitious, for
I distinctly saw my own outward man last night
standing at the table in the bedroom, and clearly
distinguishable in the moonlight. I am afraid my
wife saw it too, but I have been afraid to speak to
her on the subject."

' About the same hour on the ensuing night the
poor lady was again roused, but by a more painful
circumstance. She felt her husband moving con-
vulsively, and immediately afterwards he cried to
her in low, interrupted accents, "Ellen, my dear,
I am suffocating; send for Dr. C." She sprang up,
huddled on some clothes, and ran to his house.
He came with all speed, but his efforts for his
friend were useless. He had burst a large blood-
vessel in the lungs, and was soon beyond human
aid. In her lamentations the bereaved wife frequently cried out, " Oh! the fetch, the fetch! " and
at a later period told the doctor of the appearance

the night before her husband's death.' But, whilst
many stories of this kind are open to explanation,
it is a singular circumstance how even several
persons may be deceived by an illusion such as the
following. A gentleman who had lately lost his
wife, looking out of window in the dusk of evening,
saw her sitting in a garden-chair. He called one
of his daughters and asked her to look out into the
garden. 'Why,' she said, ' mother is sitting there.'
Another daughter was called, and she experienced
the same illusion. Then the gentleman went out
into the garden, and found that a garden-dress
of his wife's had been placed over the seat in such
a position as to produce the illusion which had
deceived himself and his daughters.

In 'Phantasms of the Living'[1] very many
strange and startling cases are recorded, in which
the mysterious ' double ' has appeared, sometimes
speaking, and sometimes without speech, although
such manifestations have not always been omens
of death. Thus the late Lord Dorchester[2] is said to
have seen the phantom of his daughter standing

[1] Messrs. Gurney, Myers, and Podmore.
[2] *Phantasms of the Living*, ii. p. 531.

at the window, having his attention aroused by its shadow, which fell across the book he was reading at the time. She had accompanied a fishing expedition, was caught in a storm, and was distressed at the thought that her father would be anxious on her account.

In Fitzroy's ' Cruise of the Beagle ' an anecdote is told of a young Fuegian, Jemmy Button, and his father's ghost. 'While at sea, on board the " Beagle," about the middle of the year 1842, he said one morning to Mr. Byno, that in the night some man came to the side of his hammock, and whispered in his ear that his father was dead. Mr. Byno tried to laugh him out of the idea, but ineffectually. He fully believed that such was the case, and maintained his opinion up to the time of finding his relations in Beagle Channel, when, I regret to say, he found that his father had died some months previously.' This story is interesting, especially as Mr. Lang says it is the only one he has encountered among savages, of a warning conveyed to a man by a ghost as to the death of a friend.[1]

[1] *Nineteenth Century*, April 1865, p. 629.

CHAPTER XXVII

GHOSTLY TIMES AND SEASONS

SHAKESPEARE, quoting from an early legend, has reminded us that at Christmastide 'no spirit dares stir abroad.' And yet, in spite of this time-honoured belief, Christmas would seem to be one of the favourite seasons of the year for ghosts to make their presence felt in all kinds of odd ways. Many an old baronial hall, with its romantic associations and historic legends, is occasionally, as Christmas-time comes round, disturbed by certain uncanny sounds, which timidity is only too ready to invest with the most mysterious and unaccountable associations. One reason for this nervous credulity may be ascribed to the fact that, as numerous old country seats are supposed to be haunted, Christmas is a fitting opportunity for the ghost to catch a glimpse of the family revelry and mirth. But, judging from the many legendary tales which have been handed down in connection with Christmas, it would seem that these spirit-members of the family intrude their presence on their relatives in the flesh in various ways. In Ireland, the ill-fated Banshee has selected this season on more than one occasion, to warn the family of coming trouble. According to one tale told from Ireland, one Christmas Eve, when the family party were gathered round the festive board in an old castle in the South of Ireland, the prancing of horses was suddenly heard, and the sharp cracking of the driver's whip. Imagining that one of the absent members of the family had arrived, some of the young people moved to the door, but found that it was the weird apparition of the 'headless coach and horseman.'

Many such stories might be enumerated, which, under one form or another, have imparted a dramatic element to the season. With some of our country peasantry, there is a deep-rooted dread of encountering anything either bordering on, or resembling, the supernatural, as sometimes spirits are supposed at Christmastide to be un-friendly towards mankind. In Northamptonshire, for instance, there is a strange notion that the ghosts of unfortunate individuals buried at cross-roads have a particular license to wander about on Christmas Eve, at which time they wreak their evil designs upon defenceless and unsuspecting persons. But conduct of this kind seems to be the exception, and ghosts are oftentimes invoked at Christmastide by those anxious to have a foretaste of events in store for them. Thus, the anxious maiden, in her eager desire to know something of her matrimonial prospects, has often subjected herself to the most trying ordeal of ' courting a ghost.' In many countries, at the ' witching hour of midnight, on Christmas Eve,' the candidate for marriage goes into the garden and plucks twelve sage leaves, ' under a firm conviction that she will be favoured with a glimpse of the shadowy form of her future husband as he approaches her from the opposite end of the garden.' But a ceremony observed in Sweden, in years past, must have required a still more strong-minded person to take advantage of its prophetic powers. It was customary in the morning twilight of Christmas Day, to go into a wood, without making the slightest noise, or uttering a word;

total abstinence from eating and drinking being
another necessary requirement. If these rules were
observed, it was supposed that the individual as he
went along the path leading to the church, would
be favoured with a sight of as many funerals as
would pass that way during the ensuing year.
With this practice may be compared one current in
Denmark, where, it is said, when a family are sitting
together on Christmas Eve, if anyone is desirous of
knowing whether a death will occur amongst them
during the ensuing year, he must go outside, and
peep silently through the window, and the person
who appears at table sitting without a head, will
die before Christmas comes round again. The feast
of St. Agnes was formerly held in high veneration
by women who wished to know when and whom
they should marry. It was required that on this
day they should not eat—which was called ' fasting
St. Agnes' fast '—if they wished to have visions
of delight, a piece of superstition on which Keats
has founded his poem, 'The Eve of St. Agnes:'

> They told me how, upon St. Agnes' Eve,
> Young virgins might have visions of delight,
> And soft adorings from their love receive,
> Upon the honey'd middle of the night

> If ceremonies due they did aright;
> As supperless to bed they must retire,
> And couch supine their beauties, lily white,
> Nor look behind, nor sideways, but require
> Of heaven, with upward eyes, for all that they desire.

Laying down on her back that night, with her hands under her head, the anxious maiden was led to expect that her future spouse would appear in a dream, and salute her with a kiss. Various charms have long been observed on St. Valentine's Eve, and Poor Robin's Almanack tells us how:

> On St. Mark's Eve, at twelve o'clock,
> The fair maid will watch her smock,
> To find her husband in the dark,
> By praying unto good St. Mark.

But St. Mark's Eve was a great day for apparitions. Allusion has been made in a previous chapter to watching in the church porch for the ghosts of those who are to be buried in the churchyard during the following months; and Jamieson tells us of a practice kept up in the northern counties, known as 'ash-ridlin.' The ashes being sifted, or riddled, on the hearth, if any one of the family 'be to die within the year, the mark of the shoe, it is supposed, will be impressed on the ashes; and many a mischievous wight has made some of the credulous family miserable, by slyly coming downstairs after the rest have retired to bed, and marking the ashes with the shoe of one of the members.'

In Peru it is interesting to trace a similar superstitious usage. As soon as a dying man draws his last breath, ashes are strewed on the floor of the room, and the door is securely fastened. Next morning the ashes are carefully examined to ascertain whether they show any impression of footsteps, and imagination readily traces marks, which are alleged to have been produced by the feet of birds, dogs, cats, oxen, or llamas. The destiny of the dead person is construed by the footmarks which are supposed to be discernible. The soul has assumed the form of that animal whose tracks are found.[1]

There is St. John's, or Midsummer Eve, around which many weird and ghostly superstitions have clustered. Grose informs us that if anyone sit in the church porch, he will see the spirits of those destined to die that year come and knock at the church door in the order of their decease. In Ireland there is a popular belief that on St. John's

[1] Dorman's *Primitive Superstitions*, p. 48.

Eve the souls of all persons leave their bodies, and
wander to the place, by land or sea, where death
shall finally separate them from the tenement of
the clay. The same notion of a temporary libera-
tion of the soul gave rise to a host of superstitious
observances at this time, resembling those connected with Hallow Eve. Indeed, this latter night
is supposed to be the time of all others when
supernatural influences prevail. 'It is the night,'
we are told, 'set apart for a universal walking abroad
of spirits, both of the visible and invisible world;
for one of the special characteristics attributed to
this mystic evening is the faculty conferred on the
immaterial principle in humanity to detach itself
from its corporeal tenement and wander abroad
through the realms of space. Divination is then
believed to attain its highest power, and the gift
asserted by Glendower of calling spirits " from the
vast deep " becomes available to all who choose to
avail themselves of the privileges of the occasion.'[1] Similarly, in Germany on St. Andrew's
Eve, young women try various charms in the
hope of seeing the shadow of their sweethearts;

[1] See *Book of Days*, ii. pp. 519–521.

one of the rhymes used on the occasion being
this :

> St. Andrew's Eve is to-day ;
> Sleep all people,
> Sleep all children of men
> Who are between heaven and earth,
> Except this only man,
> Who may be mine in marriage.

The story goes that a girl once summoned the
shadow of her future husband. Precisely as the
clock struck twelve he appeared, drank some wine,
laid a three-edged dagger on the table and vanished.
The girl put the dagger into her trunk. Some
years afterwards there came a man from a distant
part to the town where the girl dwelt, bought
property there, and married her. He was, in fact,
the identical person whose form had appeared to
her. Some time after their marriage the husband
by chance opened the trunk, and there found the
dagger, at the sight of which he became furious.
'Thou art the girl,' said he, 'who years ago forced
me to come hither from afar in the night, and it
was no dream. Die, therefore!' and with these
words he thrust the dagger into her heart.[1]

It may be added, that by general consent night-

---

[1] See Thorpe's *Northern Mythology*, iii. p. 144.

time is the season when spirits wander abroad. The appearance of morning is the signal for their dispersion.

> The flocking shadows pale,
> Troop to the infernal jail;
> Each fettered ghost slips to his several grave,
> And the yellow skirted fays,
> Fly after the night-steeds, leaving their noon-loved maze.

The ghost of Hamlet's father says, 'Methinks I scent the morning air,' and adds:

> 'Fare thee well at once!
> The glow-worm shows the matins to be near.'

According to a popular notion formerly current, the presence of unearthly beings was announced by an alteration in the tints of the lights which happened to be burning—a superstition alluded to in 'Richard III.' (Act v. sc. 3)—where the tyrant exclaims as he awakens:

> 'The lights burn blue. It is now dead midnight,
> Cold fearful drops stand on my trembling flesh.
>
> .   .   .   .
>
> Methought the souls of all that I had murder'd
> Came to my tent.'

So in 'Julius Cæsar' (Act iv. sc. 3), Brutus, on seeing the ghost of Cæsar, exclaims:

> 'How ill this taper burns. Ha! who comes here?'

CHAPTER XXVIII

SPIRIT-HAUNTED TREES

ACCORDING to Empedocles 'there are two destinies for the souls of highest virtue—to pass into trees or into the bodies of lions,' this conception of plants as the habitation of the departing soul being founded on the old idea of transmigration. Illustrations of the primitive belief meet us in all ages, reminding us how Dante passed through that leafless wood, in the bark of every tree of which was confined a suicide; and of Ariel's imprisonment:

> Into a cloven pine, within which rift
> Imprison'd, thou didst painfully remain
> A dozen years. . . .
> . . . Where thou didst vent thy groans,
> As fast as mill-wheels strike.

In German folk-lore the soul is supposed occasionally to take the form of a flower, as a lily or white rose; and, according to a popular belief, one of these flowers appears on the chairs of those

about to die. Grimm [1] tells a pretty tale of a child
who 'carries home a bud which the angel had given
him in the wood; when the rose blooms the child
is dead.' Similarly, from the grave of one unjustly
executed white lilies are said to spring as a token
of the person's innocence, and from that of a
maiden three lilies, which no one save her lover
must gather, a superstition which, under one form
or another, has largely prevailed both amongst
civilised and savage communities. In Iceland it is
said that when innocent persons are put to death,
the sorb or mountain ash will spring over their
grave, and the Lay of Runzifal makes a blackthorn
shoot out of the bodies of slain heathens, and a white
flower by the heads of fallen Christians. The
well-known story of ' Tristram and Ysonde' tells
how ' from his grave there grew an eglantine which
twined about the statue, a marvel for all men to see;
and though three times they cut it down, it grew
again, and ever wound its arms about the image
of the fair Ysonde.' With which legend may be
compared the old Scottish ballad of ' Fair Margaret
and Sweet William ' :

[1] *Teutonic Mythology*, ii. p. 827.

> Out of her breast there sprang a rose,
> And out of his a briar;
> They grew till they grew to the church top,
> And there they tied in a true lover's knot.

It is to this time-honoured fancy that Laertes refers when he wishes that violets may spring from the grave of Ophelia,[1] and Lord Tennyson has borrowed the same idea:

> And from his ashes may be made,
> The violet of his native land.[2]

Some of the North-Western Indians believed that those who died a natural death would be compelled to dwell among the branches of tall trees, and the Brazilians have a mythological character called Mani [3]—a child who died and was buried in the house of her mother. Soon a plant—the Mandioca —sprang out of the grave, which grew, flourished, and bore fruit. According to the Iroquois, the spirits of certain trees are supposed to have the forms of beautiful females; recalling, writes Mr. Herbert Spencer,[4] 'the dryads of classic myth-

---

[1] *Hamlet*, Act v. sc. 1.
[2] See *Folk-lore of Plants*, pp. 12, 13.
[3] Dorman's *Primitive Superstitions*, p. 293.
[4] *Principles of Sociology*, 1885, pp. 357–359.

ology, who, similarly conceived as human-shaped
female spirits, were sacrificed to in the same ways
that human spirits in general were sacrificed to.'
'By the Santals,' he adds, ' these spirits or ghosts
are individualised. At. their festivals the separate
families dance round the particular trees which
they fancy their domestic lares chiefly haunt.'

In modern Greece certain trees are supposed to
have their ' stichios,' a being variously described
as a spectre, a wandering soul, a vague phantom,
occasionally invisible, and sometimes assuming the
most widely different forms. When a tree is
' stichimonious,' it is generally considered dangerous
for anyone ' to sleep beneath its shade, and the
woodcutters employed to cut it down will lie upon
the ground and hide themselves, motionless, and
holding their breath, at the moment when it is
about to fall, dreading lest the stichio at whose
life the blow is aimed with each blow of the axe,
should avenge itself at the precise moment when
it is dislodged.' [1] This idea is abundantly illustrated in European folk-lore, and a Swedish legend

---

[1] *Nineteenth Century*, April, 1882, p. 394; *Superstitions of Modern Greece*, by M. Le Baron d'Estournelles.

tells how, when a man was on the point of cutting
down a juniper tree, a voice was heard saying,
'Friend, hew me not.' But he gave another
blow, when, to his horror and amazement, blood
gushed from the root.

Such spirit-haunted trees have been supposed
to give proof of their peculiar character by certain
weird and mysterious signs. Thus the Australian
bush-demons whistle in the branches, and Mr.
Schoolcraft mentions an Indian tradition of a
hollow tree, from the recesses of which there issued
on a calm day a sound like the voice of a spirit.
Hence it was considered to be inhabited by some
powerful spirit, and was deemed sacred. The holes
in trees have been supposed to be the doors through
which the spirits pass, a belief which reappears
in the German idea that the holes in the oak are
the pathways for elves, and that various diseases
may be cured by contact with these holes. It is not
surprising, too, that the idea of spirit-haunted trees
caused them to be regarded by the superstitious
with feelings of awe. Mr. Dorman tells us [1] of certain West Indian tribes, that if any person going

[1] *Primitive Superstitions*, p. 288.

through a wood perceived a motion in the trees which he regarded as supernatural, frightened at the strange prodigy, he would address himself to that tree which shook the most. Similarly, when the wind blows the long grass or waving corn, the German peasant is wont to say that the 'Grass-wolf,' or the 'Corn-wolf' is abroad. Under a variety of forms this animistic conception is found in different parts of the world, and has been embodied in many a folk-tale—an Austrian Märchen relating, for instance, how there sits in a stately fir-tree a fairy maiden waited on by a dwarf, rewarding the innocent and plaguing the guilty; and there is the German song of the maiden in the pine, whose bark the boy split with a gold and silver horn.

CHAPTER XXIX

GHOSTS AND HIDDEN TREASURES

THE presence of troubled phantoms in certain localities has long been attributed to their being interested in the whereabouts of certain secreted treasures, the disposal of which to the rightful owner having been frustrated through death having prematurely summoned them from their mortal existence. Traditions of the existence of large sums of hidden money are associated with many of our own country mansions. Such a legend was long connected with Hulme Castle, formerly a seat of a branch of the Prestwich family. The hoard was generally supposed to have been hidden either in the hall itself or in the grounds adjoining, and was said to be protected by spells and incantations. Many years ago the hall was pulled down, but, although considerable care was taken to search

every spot, no money was discovered. Secreted
treasure is associated with the apparition of
Madame Beswick, who used to haunt Birchen
Tower, Hollinwood;[1] and an eccentric spectre
known as 'Silky,' which used to play all kinds
of strange pranks in the village of Black Heddon,
Northumberland, was commonly supposed to be
the troubled phantom of a certain lady who had
died before having an opportunity of disclosing
the whereabouts of some hoarded money. With
the discovery of the gold, this unhappy spirit is
said to have disappeared. The story goes that
one day, in a house at Black Heddon, a terrific
noise was heard, which caused the servant to
exclaim, 'The deevil's in the house! the deevil's
in the house! He's come through the ceiling!'
But on the room being examined where the noise
occurred, a great dog's skin was found on the floor,
filled with gold, after which time 'Silky' was
neither seen nor heard.

Equally strange is the legend related of Swinsty
Hall, which tells how its original founder was a
poor weaver, who travelled to London at a time

---

[1] See Ingram's *Haunted Homes*, 2nd S. pp. 24, 25.

when the plague was raging, and finding many houses desolate and uninhabited, took possession of the money left without an owner, to such an extent that he loaded a waggon with the wealth thus acquired, and, returning to his home, he built Swinsty Hall. But he cannot cleanse himself from the contamination of the ill-acquired gold, and at times, it is said, his unquiet spirit has been seen bending over the Greenwell Spring rubbing away at his ghastly spoil. Mr. Henderson [1] gives the history of an apparition which, with retributive justice, once haunted a certain Yorkshire farmer. An old woman of Sexhow, near Stokesley, appeared after her death to a farmer of the place, and informed him that beneath a certain tree in his apple orchard he would find a hoard of gold and silver which she had buried there ; the silver he was to keep for his trouble, but the gold he was to give to a niece of hers living in great poverty. The farmer went to the spot indicated, found the money, and kept it all to himself. But from that day his conscience gave him no rest, and every night, at home or abroad, old Nanny's ghost dogged his

[1] *Folk-lore of Northern Counties*, p. 322.

steps. At last one evening the neighbours heard him returning from Stokesley market very late ; his horse was galloping furiously, and as he passed a neighbour's house, its inmates heard him screaming out, ' I will, I will, I will ! ' and looking out they saw a little old woman in black, with a large straw hat on her head, clinging to him. The farmer's hat was off, his hair stood on end, as he fled past them uttering his fearful cry, ' I will, I will, I will ! ' But when the horse reached the farm all was still, for the rider was a corpse.

Tradition asserts that the ' white lady ' who long haunted Blenkinsopp Castle, is the ghost of the wife of Bryan de Blenkinsopp, who quarrelled with her husband, and in a fit of spite she concealed a chest of gold that took twelve of the strongest men to carry into the castle. Filled with remorse for her undutiful conduct, the unhappy woman cannot rest in her grave, but her spirit is doomed to wander back to the old castle, and to mourn over the accursed wealth of which its rightful owner was defrauded.

An old farm, popularly known in the neighbourhood as ' Sykes' Lumb Farm,' from having

been inhabited for many generations by a family
of the name of Sykes, was long haunted by an
old wrinkled woman who, one night, being interrogated by an occupier of the farm as to the
cause of her wandering about, made no reply, but
proceeding towards the stump of an old apple tree
in the orchard, pointed significantly to the ground
beneath. On search being made, there was found
buried deep in the earth a jar of money, on the
discovery of which the phantom vanished.

Anecdotes of treasures concealed at the bottom
of wells are of frequent occurrence, and the ' white
ladies' who dwell in the lakes, wells, and seas of
so many countries, are owners of vast treasures,
which they occasionally offer to mortals. Tradition says that in a pool known as Wimbell Pond
at Acton, Suffolk, is concealed an iron chest of
money, and if any person approach the pond and
throw a stone into the water, it will ring against
the chest—a small white figure having been heard
to cry in accents of distress, ' That's mine.' [1]

Scotland has many such stories. It is popularly believed that for many ages past a pot of

[1] *Notes and Queries*, 1st S. v. p. 195.

gold has lain at the bottom of a pool beneath a fall of the rivulet underneath Craufurdland Bridge, about three miles from Kilmarnock. Many attempts have been made to recover this treasure, but something unforeseen has always happened to prevent a successful issue. 'The last effort made, by the Laird of Craufurdland him- self,' writes Mr. Chambers,[1] ' was early in the last century, at the head of a party of his domestics, who first dammed up the water, then emptied the pool of its contents, and had heard their instruments clink on the kettle, when a voice was heard saying :

> Pow, pow !
> Craufurdland tower 's a' in a low !

Whereupon the laird left the scene, followed by his servants, and ran home to save what he could. Of course, there was no fire in the house, and when they came back to renew their operations, they found the water falling over the lin in full force. Being now convinced that a power above that of mortals was opposed to their researches, the laird and his people gave up the attempt. Such is the traditionary story, whether,' adds Mr.

---

[1] *Popular Rhymes of Scotland*, pp. 241-242.

Chambers, 'founded on any actual occurrence, or a mere fiction of the peasants' brain, cannot be ascertained; but it is curious that a later and well authenticated effort to recover the treasure was interrupted by a natural occurrence in some respects similar.'

Vast treasures are said to be concealed beneath the ruins of Hermitage Castle, but, as they are in the keeping of the Evil One, they are considered beyond redemption. Venturesome persons have occasionally made the attempt to dig for them, but a storm of thunder and lightning has generally deterred the adventurers from proceeding, otherwise, of course, the money would have long ago been found. It is ever, we are told, that such supernatural obstacles come in the way of these interesting discoveries. Mr. Chambers relates how 'an honest man in Perthshire, named Finlay Robertson, about a hundred years ago, went with some stout-hearted companions to seek for the treasures which were supposed to be concealed in the darksome cave of a deceased Highland robber, but just as they had commenced operations with their mattocks, the whole party were instan-

taneously struck, as by an electric shock, which
sent them home with fear and trembling, and they
were ever after remarked as silent, mysterious
men, very apt to take offence when allusion was
made to their unsuccessful enterprise.' [1]

In Scotland and the North of England, the
Brownie was regarded as a guardian of hidden
treasure, and 'to him did the Borderers commit
their money or goods, when, according to the
custom prevalent in wild insecure countries, they
concealed them in the earth.' Some form of
incantation was practised on the occasion, such
as the dropping upon the treasure the blood of a
slaughtered animal, or burying the slain animal
with it.[2]

According to the Welsh belief, if a person die
while any hoarded money—or, indeed, metal of
any kind, were it nothing more than old iron—
is still secretly hidden, the spirit of that person
cannot rest. Others affirm that it is only ill-
gotten treasure which creates this disturbance of
the grave's repose ; but it is generally agreed that
the soul's unquiet condition can only be relieved by
finding a human hand to take the hidden metal,

[1] *Popular Rhymes of Scotland*, p. 240.
[2] Henderson's *Folk-lore of Northern Counties*, pp. 247-248.

and throw it down the stream of a river. To throw
it up a stream is useless. The spirit 'selects a·
particular person as the subject of its attentions,
and haunts that person till asked what it wants.'
A story is told of a tailor's wife at Llantwit Major,
a stout and jolly dame, who was thus haunted until
she was worn to the semblance of a skeleton, 'for
not choosing to take a hoard honestly to the
Ogmore'—the favourite river in Glamorganshire for
this purpose. To quote her own words, 'I at last
consented, for the sake of quiet, to take the treasure
to the river, and the spirit wafted me through the
air so high that I saw below me the church loft and
all the houses, as if I had leaned out of a balloon.
When I took the treasure to throw it into the
river, in my flurry I flung it up stream instead of
down, and on this the spirit, with a savage look,
tossed me into a whirlwind, and how ever I got
back to my home I know not.' The bell-ring-
ers found her lying insensible in the Church
lane, on their return from church, late in the
evening.[1]

No piece of folk-lore is more general in Ireland

[1] Wirt Sikes: *British Goblins*, pp. 151–152.

than that gold or silver may be found under nearly all the raths, cairns, or old castles throughout the island. It is always a difficult task to exhume such buried treasure, for some preternatural guardian or other will be found on the alert. These buried treasures are usually deposited in 'a crock,' but whenever an attempt is made to lift it, some awful gorgon, or monster, appears. Sometimes a rushing wind sweeps over the plain, or from the opening made, with destructive force, carrying away the gold-seeker's hat or spade, or even, in various instances, the adventurer himself, who is deposited with broken bones, or a paralysed frame, at a respectful distance from the object of his quest. 'On the banks of a northern river, and near a small eminence,' writes a correspondent of the 'Gentleman's Magazine,'[1] 'is a beautiful green plot, on which two large, moss-covered stones over six hundred feet apart are shown. It is said two immense " crocks " of gold lie buried under these conspicuous landmarks, and that various attempts have been made to dig round and beneath them. In all those instances when a persistent effort has been made,

[1] 1865, pt. ii. pp. 706–707.

a monk appeared in full habit, with a cross in his hand to warn off sacrilegious offenders.'

Similar legends are found in different parts of the world. 'The Isle of Yellow Sands,' says Mr. Dorman,[1] 'derives its chief interest from the traditions and fanciful tales which the Indians relate concerning its mineral treasures and their supernatural guardians. They pretend that its shores are covered with a heavy, shining, yellow sand, which they are persuaded is gold, but that the guardian spirit of the island will not permit any to be carried away. To enforce his commands, he has drawn together upon it myriads of eagles, hawks, and other birds of prey, who, by their cries warn him of any intrusions upon the domain, and assist with their claws and beaks to expel the enemy. He has also called from the depths of the lake, large serpents of the most hideous forms, who lie thickly coiled upon the golden sands, and hiss defiance to the steps of the intruder. A great many years ago, they say, some people driven by stress of weather upon the island, put a large quantity of the glittering treasure in their canoes

[1] *Primitive Superstitions*, p. 310.

and attempted to carry it off; but a gigantic spirit
strode into the water and in a tone of thunder
commanded them to bring it back '—

> Listen, white man, go not there !
> Unseen spirits stalk the air;
> Ravenous birds their influence lend,
> Snakes defy, and kites defend. . . .
> Touch not, then, the guarded lands,
> Of the Isle of Yellow Sands.

The 'Ceylon Times' records a remarkable
instance of superstition among the Tamul popu-
lation employed as labourers on a coffee estate.
'It is the belief of all Orientals,' says the writer,
'that hidden treasures are under the guardianship
of supernatural beings. The Singhalese, however,
divide the charge between demons and cobra da
capellos. Various charms are resorted to by those
who wish to gain the treasures, the demons requiring
a sacrifice. Blood of a human being is the most
important, but, as far as it is known, the Cappowas
have hitherto confined themselves to the sacrifice of
a white cock, combining its blood with their own,
drawn by a slight puncture in the hand or foot.'

Many curious stories are on record of persons
having been informed by ghosts of the whereabouts

of hidden money, and of their having been directed
to the spot where the hoarded treasure has lain for
years secreted in its undetected recess.

In the 'Antiquarian Repertory' is a singular
narrative of a man named Richard Clarke, a farm-
labourer at Hamington, Northamptonshire, who
was haunted by the ghost of a man who declared
that he had been murdered near his own house
267 years, 9 months, and 2 days ago, and buried
in an orchard. He added that his wife and
children, who had lived in Southwark, never knew
what became of him; that he had some treasures
and papers buried in the cellar of a house near
London, and that he (Clarke) must seek for it,
and that he (the ghost) would meet him in the
cellar, to assist him in the search. The ghost
added that as soon as the money and the writings
were found, and duly delivered to certain relatives
of his in Southwark, at such an address, removed
from him in the fourth generation, he would cease
to visit him, and would leave him in peace.
Clarke went to town, and on London Bridge the
ghost passed him, and conducted him to the
house, where his wife had lived four generations

before.   Clarke found everything answering the
description which the ghost had given him; the
money and the documents were discovered, the
writings on vellum found, but those on paper
decayed.   Clarke divided the money, and acted as
the ghost of the murdered man directed him to
do; and the latter ' lookt chearfully upon him, and
gave him thankes, and said now he should be at
rest, and spoke to those other persons which were
of his generation, relations, but they had not
courage to answer, but Clarke talkt for them.'

CHAPTER XXX

PHANTOM MUSIC

MANY of those weird melodious sounds which romance and legendary lore have connected with the enchanted strains of invisible music have originated in the moaning of the winds, and the rhythmical flow of the waves. In several of their operatic works, our dramatic composers have skilfully introduced the music of the fairies and of other aerial conceptions of the fancy, reminding us of those harmonious sounds which Caliban depicts in the 'Tempest' (Act iii. sc. 2):

> The isle is full of noises,
> Sounds and sweet airs, that give delight and hurt not;
> Sometimes a thousand twangling instruments,
> Will hum about mine ears, and sometimes voices
> That, if I then had waked after long sleep,
> Will make me sleep again.

Most countries have their stories and traditions
of mysterious music which, in many cases, has
been associated with certain supernatural properties.   Under one form or another, the belief
in phantom music has extensively prevailed
throughout Europe, and in many parts of England
it is still supposed to be heard, occasionally as a
presage of death.   It has been generally supposed
that music is the favourite recreation of the
spirits that haunt mountains, rivers, and all kinds
of lonely places.   The Indians would not venture near Manitobah Island, their superstitious
fears being due to the weird sounds produced by
the waves as they beat upon the beach at the
foot of the cliffs, near its northern extremity.
During the night, when a gentle breeze was
blowing from the north, the various sounds heard
on the island were quite sufficient to strike awe
into their minds. These sounds frequently resembled the ringing of distant bells; so close,
indeed, was the resemblance that travellers would
awake during the night with the impression that
they were listening to chimes. When the breeze
subsided, and the waves played gently on the

beach, a low wailing sound would be heard three hundred yards from the cliffs.[1]

Sometimes music is heard at sea, and it is believed in Ireland that when a friend or relative dies, a warning voice is discernible. The following is a rough translation of an Irish song founded on this superstition, which is generally sung to a singularly wild and melancholy air:

> A low sound of song from the distance I hear,
> In the silence of night, breathing sad on my ear.
> Whence comes it? I know not—unearthly the note,
> And unearthly the tones through the air as they float;
> Yet it sounds like the lay that my mother once sung,
> And o'er her firstborn in his cradle she hung.

When ships go down at sea, it is said the death-bell is at times distinctly heard, a superstition to which Sir Walter Scott alludes:

> And the kelpie rang,
> And the sea-maid sang,
> The dirge of lovely Rosabelle.

At the present day, indeed, all kinds of phantom musical sounds are believed to float through the air—sounds which the peasantry, in days past, attributed to the fairies.

[1] Dorman's *Primitive Superstitions*, p. 309.

The American Indians have a similar piece of
legendary lore. Gayarre, in his 'Louisiana,' says that
mysterious music floats on the waters of the river
Pascagoula, 'particularly on a calm moonlight
night. It seems to issue from caverns or grottoes
in the bed of the river, and sometimes oozes up
through the water under the very keel of the boat
which contains the traveller, whose ear it strikes
as the distant concert of a thousand Æolian harps.
On the banks of the river, close by the spot where
the music is heard, tradition says that there
existed a tribe different from the rest of the
Indians. Every night when the moon was visible,
they gathered round the beautifully carved figure
of a mermaid, and, with instruments of strange
shape, worshipped the idol with such soul-stirring
music as had never before blessed human ears.
One day a priest came among them and tried to
convert them from the worship of the mermaid.
But on a certain night, at midnight, there came
a rushing on the surface of the river, and the
water seemed to be seized with a convulsive fury.
The Indians and the priest rushed to the bank of
the river to contemplate the supernatural spec-

tacle. When she saw them, the mermaid turned
her tones into still more bewitching melody, and
kept chanting a sort of mystic song. The Indians
listened with growing ecstasy, and one of them
plunged into the river to rise no more. The rest
—men, women, and children—followed in quick
succession, moved, as it were, with the same irre-
sistible impulse. When the last of the race disappeared, the river returned to its bed. Ever since
that time is heard occasionally the distant music,
which the Indians say is caused by their musical
brethren, who still keep up their revels at the bottom
of the river, in the palace of the mermaid.'

It was a popular belief in years gone by, that
it was dangerous to listen long to the weirdly
fascinating influence of phantom music, or, as it
was sometimes called, 'diabolic music,' as it was
employed by evil-disposed spirits for the purpose
of accomplishing some wicked design. Tradition
tells how certain weird music was long since heard
in an old mansion in Schleswig Holstein. The
story goes that at a wedding there was a certain
young lady present, who was the most enthusiastic
dancer far and near, and who, in spite of having

danced all the evening, petulantly exclaimed, ' If
the devil himself were to call me out, I would not
refuse him.' Suddenly the door of the ball-room
flew open, and a stranger entered and invited her
to dance. Round and round they whirled unceasingly, faster and faster, until, to the horror of
all present, she fell down dead. Every year afterwards, on the same day as this tragic event
happened, exactly at midnight, the mansion long
resounded with diabolic music, the lady haunting
the scene of her fearful death. There are
numerous versions of this story, and one current
in Denmark is known as ' The Indefatigable
Fiddler.' It appears that on a certain Sunday
evening, some young people were merrymaking,
when it was decided to have a little dancing. In
the midst of an animated discussion as to how
they could procure a musician, one of the party
boastingly said, ' Now, that leave to me. I will
bring you a musician, even if it should be the
devil himself.' Thereupon he left the house, and
had not gone far when he met a poverty-looking
man with a fiddle under his arm, who, for a
certain sum, agreed to play. Soon the young

people, spellbound by the fiddler's music, were frantically dancing up and down the room unable to stop, and in spite of their entreaties he continued playing. They must have soon died of exhaustion, had not the parish priest arrived at the farmhouse, and expelled the fiddler by certain mystic words. Sometimes, it is said, the sound of music, such as harp-playing, is heard in the most sequestered spots, and is attributed to supernatural agency. The Welsh peasantry thought it proceeded from the fairies, who were supposed to be specially fond of this instrument; but such music had this peculiarity—no one could ever learn the tune.

Cortachy Castle, the seat of the Earl of Airlie, has long had its mysterious drummer; and whenever the sound of his drum is heard, it betokens the speedy death of a member of the Ogilvie family. The story goes that ' either the drummer, or some officer whose emissary he was, had excited the jealousy of a former Lord Airlie, and that in consequence he was put to death by being thrust into his own drum and flung from the window of the tower, in which is situated the chamber where his music

E E

is apparently chiefly heard. It is said that he threatened to haunt the family if his life were taken,' a promise which he has fulfilled.[1] With this strange warning may be compared the amusing story popularly known as ' The Drummer of Tedworth,' in which the ghost or evil spirit of a drummer, or the ghost of a drum, performed the principal part in this mysterious drama for 'two entire years.' The story, as succinctly given by George Cruikshank,[2] goes that in March 1661, Mr. Monpesson, a magistrate, caused a vagrant drummer to be arrested, who had been annoying the country by noisy demands for charity, and had ordered his drum to be taken from him, and left in the bailiff's house. About the middle of the following April, when Mr. Monpesson was preparing for a journey to London, the bailiff sent the drum to his house. But on his return home, he was informed that noises had been heard, and then he heard the noises himself, which were a ' thumping and drumming,' accompanied by ' a strange noise and hollow sound.' The sign of it when it came was like a hurling in the air over

[1] See Ingram's *Haunted Homes*, p. 53.
[2] *A Discovery Concerning Ghosts*, 1864, pp. 18, 19.

the house, and at its going off, the beating of a drum, like that of the 'breaking up of a guard.' After a month's disturbance outside the house, it came into the room where the drum lay. For an hour together it would beat 'Roundheads and Cockolds;' the 'tattoo,' and several other points of war as well as any drummer. Upon one occasion, when many were present, a gentleman said, ' Satan, if the drummer set thee to work, give three knocks,' which it did at once. And for further trial, he bid it for confirmation, if it were the drummer, to give five knocks and no more that night, which it did, and left the house quiet all the night after. 'But,' as George Cruikshank observes, ' strange as it certainly was, is it not still more strange that educated gentlemen, and even clergy-men, as in this case, also should believe that the Almighty would suffer an evil spirit to disturb and affright a whole innocent family, because the head of that family had, in his capacity as magistrate, thought it his duty to take away a drum from no doubt a drunken drummer, who, by his noisy conduct, had become a nuisance to the neighbour-hood ? '

E E 2

In many parts of the country, phantom bells are supposed to be heard ringing their ghostly peals. Near Blackpool, about two miles out at sea, there once stood, tradition says, the church and cemetery of Kilmigrol, long ago submerged. Even now, in rough weather, the melancholy chimes of the bells may be heard sounding over the restless waters. A similar story is told of Jersey. According to a local legend, many years ago, ' the twelve parish churches in that island possessed each a valuable peal of bells, but during a long civil war the bells were sold to defray the expenses of the troops. The bells were sent to France, but on the passage the ship foundered, and everything was lost. Since then, during a storm, these bells always ring at sea, and to this day the fishermen of St. Ouen's Bay, before embarking, go to the edge of the water to listen if they can hear the bells; if so, nothing will induce them to leave the shore.' With this story may be compared one told of Whitby Abbey, which was suppressed in 1539. The bells were sold, and placed on board to be conveyed to London. But, as soon as the vessel had moved out into the bay' it sank, and beneath the waters the bells may occasionally be heard, a legend which has been thus poetically described :

> Up from the heart of the ocean
>   The mellow music peals,
> Where the sunlight makes its golden path,
>   And the seamew flits and wheels.
>
> For many a chequered century,
>   Untired by flying time,
> The bells no human fingers touch
>   Have rung their hidden chime.

To this day the tower of Forrabury Church, Cornwall, or, as it has been called by Mr. Hawker, 'the silent tower of Bottreaux,' remains without bells. It appears the bells were cast and shipped for Forrabury, but as the ship neared the shore, the captain swore and used profane language, whereupon the vessel sank beneath a sudden swell of the ocean. As it went down, the bells were heard tolling with a muffled peal; and ever since, when storms are at hand, their phantom sound is still audible from beneath the waves :

> Still when the storm of Bottreaux's waves
> Is waking in his weedy caves,
> Those bells that sullen surges hide,
> Peal their deep tones beneath the tide—

> ' Come to thy God in time,'
> Thus saith the ocean chime ;
> ' Storm, whirlpool, billow past,
> Come to thy God at last.'

Legends of this kind remind us of Southey's ballad of the ' Inchcape Bell,' founded on a tragic legend. The abbots of Aberbrothock (Arbroath) fixed a bell on a rock, as a kindly warning to sailors, that obstruction having long been considered the chief difficulty in the navigation of the Firth of Forth. The bell was so fastened as to be rung by the agitation of the waves, but one day, Sir Ralph the Rover ' cut the bell from the Inchcape float,' and down sank the bell with a gurgling sound. Afterwards,

> Sir Ralph the Rover sailed away,
> He scoured the sea for many a day,
> And now grown rich with plundered store,
> He steers his course for Scotland's shore.

But the night is dark and hazy, and—

> They hear no sound, the swell is strong,
> Though the wind hath fallen they drift along,
> Till the vessel strikes with a shivering shock.
> ' O Christ ! It is the Inchcape rock ! '

But it is too late—the ship is doomed:

Sir Ralph the Rover tore his hair ;
He cursed himself in his despair.
The waves rush in on every side ;
The ship is sinking beneath the tide.

But even in his dying fear
One dreadful sound could the rover hear,
A sound as if with the Inchcape bell,
The devil below was ringing his knell.

Indeed, there are all kinds of whimsical stories
current of phantom bells, and according to a
tradition at Tunstall, in Norfolk, the parson and
churchwardens disputed for the possession of some
bells which had become useless because the tower
was burnt. But, during their altercation, the arch-
fiend quickly travelled off with the bells, and being
pursued by the parson, who began to exorcise in
Latin, he dived into the earth with his ponderous
burden, and the place where he disappeared is a
boggy pool of water, called 'Hell Hole.' Notwithstanding the aversion of the powers of darkness
to such sounds, even these bells are occasionally
permitted to favour their native place with a
ghostly peal. Similarly, at Fisherty Brow, near
Lonsdale, there is a sort of hollow where, as the
legend runs, a church, parson, and congregation

were swallowed up. On a Sunday morning the
bells may be heard ringing a phantom peal by
anyone who puts his ear to the ground.

Occasionally, it is said, phantom music, by way
of warning, is heard just before a death, instances
of which are numerous.

Samuel Foote, in the year 1740, while visiting
at his father's house in Truro, was kept awake by
sounds of sweet music. His uncle was at about
the same time murdered by assassins. This strange
occurrence is thus told by Mr. Ingram.[1] Foote's
maternal uncles were Sir John Goodere and Captain
Goodere, a naval officer. In 1740 the two brothers
dined at a friend's house near Bristol. For a long
time they had been on bad terms, owing to certain
money transactions, but at the dinner-table a recon-
ciliation was, to all appearance, arrived at between
them. But, on his return home, Sir John was waylaid by some men from his brother's vessel, acting
by his brother's authority, carried on board, and
deliberately strangled, Captain Goodere not only
unconcernedly looking on, but furnishing the rope
with which the crime was committed. The

[1] *Haunted Homes*, p. 253.

strangest part of this terrible tale, however, remains to be told. On the night the murder was perpetrated, Foote arrived at his father's house in Truro, and he used to relate how he was kept awake for some time by the softest and sweetest strains of music he had ever heard. At first he tried to fancy it was a serenade got up by some of the family to welcome him home, but not being able to discover any trace of the musicians, he came to the conclusion that he was deceived by his own imagination. He shortly afterwards learnt that the murder had been consummated at the same hour of the same night as he had been haunted by the mysterious sounds.

CHAPTER XXXI

PHANTOM SOUNDS

THE deceptiveness of sound in olden times was very little understood, and hence originated, in most countries, a host of traditionary tales descriptive of sundry mysterious noises which were generally attributed to supernatural agencies. Hence, it is impossible to say how many a ghost story would long ago have found a satisfactory solution if only attention had been paid to the properties of sound. But by disregarding the laws which regulate the conditions upon which sound is oftentimes more or less audible, the imagination has frequently conjured up the most fantastic reasons for some mysterious rumbling which has suddenly trespassed on the silence of the night. Thus, Dr. Tyndall has proved how the atmosphere is occasionally in an unusual degree more transparent or opaque to sound as well as to light, and supported this theory by referring to the audibility of fog-signals, which vary according to the state of the weather. Facts of this kind are of the utmost importance in accounting, it may be, for some apparently inexplicable sound. It is sometimes forgotten, too, that sounds are far more audible at night time than during the day, and what would fail to attract notice, even if heard during the hours of sunlight, would probably be treated in a different aspect when once the darkness of evening had set in. There is perhaps no superstition so deeply rooted in the popular mind as the belief in what are generally termed ' death-warnings '; the common opinion being that death announces its approach by certain mysterious noises, a powerful illustration of which occurs in ' Macbeth ' (Act ii. sc. 3), where Lennox graphically describes how, on the awful night in which Duncan is murdered—

Our chimneys were blown down: and, as they say
Lamentings heard i' the air; strange screams of death:
And prophesying, with accents terrible,
Of dire combustion, and confused events,
New hatch'd to the woeful time.

Modern folk-lore holds either that a knocking or rumbling in the floor is an omen of death about to happen, or that dying persons themselves announce their dissolution to their friends in such strange sounds.[1]

In recent years one of the most interesting instances of a phantom voice occurred in connection with the death of Mr. George Smith, the well-known Assyriologist. This eminent scholar died at Aleppo, on August 19, 1876, at about six o'clock in the afternoon. On the same day, and at about the same time, as Dr. Delitzsch—a friend and fellow-worker of Mr. Smith—was passing within a stone's throw of the house in which he had lived when in London, he suddenly heard his own name uttered aloud ' in a most piercing cry,' which a contemporary record of the time said ' thrilled him to the marrow.' The fact impressed Dr. Delitzsch so much that he looked at his watch, made a note of the hour, and recorded the fact in his note-book, this being one of those straightforward and unimpeachable coincidences which, even to an opponent, is difficult to explain.

There can be no doubt that many of the unearthly noises heard near and in lonely houses

[1] Tylor's *Primitive Culture*, i. p. 145.

on the coast were produced by an illicit class of
spirits, that is, through the agency of smugglers,
' in order to alarm and drive all others but their
accomplices from their haunts.' Thus, in a house
at Rottingdean, Sussex, all kinds of strange noises
were heard night after night, when suddenly they
ceased. Soon afterwards one of a gang of smugglers confessed to their having made a secret
passage from the beach close by the house, and that,
wishing to induce the occupiers to abandon it, they
had rolled at the dead of night tub after tub of
spirits up the passage, and so had caused it to be
reported that the place was haunted.[1] George
Cruikshank tells how, in the wine cellar of a house
somewhere near Blackheath, there were sometimes
heard strange noises in the evening and at night-
time, such as knocking, groaning, footsteps, &c.
The master of the house at last determined ' to lay
the ghost ' if possible, and one evening, when these
noises had been heard, went with his servants to
the cellar, where they discovered an under-gardener
in a drunken state. It seems that he had tunnelled

---

[1] Mrs. Latham's ' West Sussex Superstitions,' *Folk-lore
Record*, i. p. 21.

a hole from the tool-house through the wall into
the cellar.

In numerous cases, too, there can be no doubt
that strange noises heard in the silent hours of the
night have been due to some cleverly-devised trick
for the purpose, in many cases, of keeping the
house uninhabited, and thereby benefiting, it may
be, some impecunious care-taker. A story is told
of a ghost—which turned out to be the trick of
a Franciscan friar—that answered questions by
knocking in the Catholic church of Orleans, and
demanded the removal of the provost's Lutheran
wife, who had been buried there.[1] But one of the
most eccentric instances of spiritual antics was
the noises said to have been heard at Epworth
Parsonage in the time of the Rev. Samuel Wesley,
these sounds having consisted of ' knockings ' and
' groanings,' of ' footsteps,' and ' rustling of silk
trailing along,' ' clattering of the iron casement,'
and ' clattering of the warming pan,' and all sorts
of frightful noises, which frightened even a big
dog, a large mastiff, who used, at first, when he
heard the noises, ' to bark, and leap, and snap on

[1] See Tylor's *Primitive Culture*, i. p. 146.

one side and the other, and that frequently before anyone in the room heard the noises at all; but after two or three days he used to creep away before the noise began, and by this the family knew it was at hand.' Mr. Wesley at one time thought it was rats, and sent for a horn to blow them away. But this made matters worse, for after the horn was blown the noise came in the daytime as well. Some of the Wesley family believed it to be supernatural hauntings, and explained the cause of it thus: at morning and evening prayers, 'when the Rev. Samuel Wesley commenced prayer for the king, a knocking began all round the room, and a thundering knock attended the *Amen.*' Mr. Wesley observed that his wife did not say '*Amen*' to the prayer for the king, but Mrs. Wesley added she could not, for she did not believe that the Prince of Orange was king.[1] Ewshott House, Hampshire, was disturbed by equally strange sounds, and Glamis Castle, with its secret room, has long been famous for the mysterious noises, knocking, and hammering heard at night-time, which a lady once remarked reminded her of the erection of a scaffold.

[1] See Southey's *Life of Wesley.*

The miscreant ghosts of wicked people are supposed to make all kinds of unearthly noises, for as they cannot enjoy peace in their graves, they delight in annoying the occupants of their mortal haunts. Lowther Hall, the residence of the 'bad Lord Lonsdale,' was disturbed by such uncanny sounds that neither men nor animals were permitted to rest, and many of the ghost stories told of our old country houses describe the peculiar noises made by their ghostly tenants. The mother of the premier, George Canning, used to tell her experiences of a haunted house in Plymouth, where she stayed during a theatrical engagement. Having learnt from a Mr. Bernard, who was connected with the theatre, that he could obtain comfortable apartments for her at a moderate price, she accepted his offer. 'There is,' said he, 'a house belonging to our carpenter that is reported to be haunted, and nobody will live in it. If you like to have it you may, and for nothing, I believe, for he is so anxious to get a tenant; only you must not let it be known that you do not pay any rent for it.' It turned out as Mr. Bernard had informed her, for night after night she heard all such noises as are wont to proceed from a workshop, although, on examining every part of the house herself, she found nothing to account for this extraordinary series of noises.

Occasionally, it is said, before the perpetration of any dreadful crime, as murder, a supernatural sound is heard. A murder was committed, for instance, at Cottertown, of Auchanasie, near Keith, on January 11, 1797, in connection with which the following facts have been recorded: 'On the day on which the deed was done, two men, strangers to the district, called at a farmhouse about three miles from the house in which lived the old folk that were murdered. Shortly before the tragic act was committed, a sound was heard passing along the road the two men were seen to take, in the direction of the place at which the murder was perpetrated. So loud and extraordinary was the noise that the people left their houses to see what it was that was passing. To the amazement of every one, nothing was to be seen, though it was moonlight, and moonlight so bright that it aroused attention. All believed something dreadful was to happen, and some proposed to follow the sound. About the time this discussion was

going on, a blaze of fire arose on the hill of
Auchanasie. The foul deed had been accomplished,
and the cottage set on fire. By next day all knew
of what the mysterious sound had been the fore-
runner.'[1] At Wheal Vor Mine an unaccountable noise
has been generally supposed to be a warning. On
Barry Island, near Cardiff, it is said that certain
ghostly noises were formerly heard in it—sounds
resembling the clanking of chains, hammering of
iron, and blowing of bellows, and which were supposed to be made by the fiends whom Merlin
had set to work to frame the wall of crags to
surround Carmarthen.

The following extract from Lockhart's 'Life of
Sir Walter Scott' records a strange noise which
was heard while the new house at Abbotsford was
being built, the novelist living in an older part,
close adjoining: 'Walter Scott to Daniel Terry,
April 30, 1818. . . . The exposed state of my
house has led to a mysterious disturbance. The
night before last we were awakened by a violent
noise, like drawing heavy boards along the new
part of the house. I fancied something had

---

[1] Walter Gregor ; _Folk-lore of North-East of Scotland_, pp. 205,
206.

fallen, and thought no more about it ; this was about *two* in the morning. Last night, at the same witching hour, the very same noise occurred. Mrs. S., as you know, is rather timbersome, so up I got, with Beardie's broad sword under my arm—

> Bolt upright,
> And ready to fight.

But nothing was out of order, neither can I discover what occasioned the disturbance.' Mr. Lockhart adds : ' On the morning that Mr. Terry received the foregoing letter in London, Mr. William Erskine was breakfasting with him, and the chief subject of their conversation was the sudden death of George Bullock, which had occurred on the same night, and nearly as they could ascertain at the very hour when Scott was aroused from his sleep by the "mysterious disturbance " here described. This coincidence, when Scott received Erskine's minute detail of what had happened in Tenterdon Street (that is, the death of Bullock, who had the charge of furnishing the new rooms at Abbotsford), made a much stronger impression on his mind than might be gathered from the tone of an ensuing commu-

nication.' It seems that Bullock had been at
Abbotsford, and made himself a great favourite
with old and young. Sir Walter Scott, a week or
two afterwards, wrote thus to Terry: 'Were you
not struck with the fantastical coincidence of our
nocturnal disturbances at Abbotsford, with the
melancholy event that followed? I protest to
you the noise resembled half a dozen men at
work, putting up boards and furniture, and
nothing can be more certain than that there was
nobody on the premises at the time. With a few
additional touches, the story would figure in
Glanville or Aubrey's collection. In the mean-
time you may set it down, with poor Dubisson's
warnings, as a remarkable coincidence coming
under your own observation.'

In a paper by Mrs. Edwards, in 'Macmillan's
Magazine,' entitled 'The Mystery of Pezazi,' an
account is given of constant disturbing sounds of
nocturnal tree-felling heard near a bungalow in
Ceylon, where examination proved that no trees
had been felled. Mrs. Edwards, her husband, and
their servants were on several occasions disturbed
by these sounds, which were unmistakable and

distinct. The Singhalese attribute these noises to a Pezazi, or spirit. A description of precisely the same disturbances occurs, writes Mr. Andrew Lang,[1] in Sahagun's account of the superstitions of the Aztecs, and it seems that the Galapagos Islands, ' suthard of the line,' were haunted by the midnight axe. ' De Quincey,' adds Mr. Lang, ' who certainly had not heard the Ceylon story, and who probably would have mentioned Sahagun's had he known it, describes the effect produced by the midnight axe on the nerves of his brother, Pink: " So it was, and attested by generations of sea-vagabonds, that every night, duly as the sun went down and the twilight began to prevail, a sound arose—audible to other islands, and to every ship lying quietly at anchor in that neighbourhood—of a woodcutter's axe. . . . The close of the story was that after, I suppose, ten or twelve minutes of hacking and hewing, a horrid crash was heard, announcing that the tree, if tree it were, that never yet was made visible to daylight search, had yielded to the old woodman's persecution. . . . The woodcutter's axe began to intermit about the earliest approach of dawn, and as light

[1] *Nineteenth Century*, vol. xvii. p. 627.

strengthened it ceased entirely, after poor Pink's ghostly panic grew insupportable." '

Among the American Indians all the sounds that issued from caverns were thought to be produced by their spiritual inhabitants. The Sonora Indians say that departed souls dwell among the caves and nooks of their cliffs, and that echoes often heard there are their voices. Similarly, when explosions were heard, caused by the sulphurous gas from the rocks around the head-waters of Lake Ontario, the superstitious Indians attributed them to the breathing of the Manitones.[1] The modern Dayaks, Siamese, and Singhalese agree with the Esths as to noises being caused by spirits. European folk-lore has long ascribed most of the unexplained noises to the agency of spirits, and to this day Franconian damsels go to a tree on St. Thomas's Day, knock three times, and listen for the indwelling spirit to inform them from raps within what kind of husbands they are to have. Hence the night is known as 'Little Knocker's Night.' There is the Poltergeist of the German, a mischievous spirit, who wanders about the house at night making all kinds of strange noises.

[1] Dorman's *Primitive Superstitions*, p. 302.

INDEX

ABB

ABBOT, ghost of, in Abbey of Clare, 326
Abbotsford, 434–436
Abipones, superstitions of, 89, 336, 340
Accidents, ghosts appear at scene of, 168
African beliefs, 30, 90–91, 182, 346
Agnes', St., Fast, 385
Alaska belief, 10
Albans, St., Duchess of, 100
Aleutian islanders, 341
Algonquin Indians, 40, 309, 339
Allanbank, ghost at, 312
Allhallow Eve, 118
Althorp, apparition seen at, 319
American Indian beliefs, 6, 23, 37, 89, 143, 217, 343, 414, 438
Ancestor worship, 102
Andaman islanders, 110
Andrew's Eve, St., 388
Angel of death, 273
Angola, belief in, 182
Animal ghosts, 102–126
Arabian belief, 360
Ash-ridlin, 386
Ashley Hall, Cheshire, 326
Assiniboins, belief of, 66
Astwood Castle, 319
Australian beliefs, 21, 33, 45, 67, 165, 340, 343, 360, 395
Awd Nance, ghost so called, 326

BES

Aztec legend of Creation, 36
— belief, 90, 437

BAD Lord Lonsdale, 311, 432
Bagley House, 318
Bahrgeist, 114
Balcarres, Lord, 372
Banshee, 221, 271–283, 305, 383
Barguest, 114
Barton Hall, haunted, 312
Basutos, belief of, 3
Baxter, R., story told by, 250
Bean-geese, 120
Bear, soul as, 111
Becklington Castle, 333
Bees, soul in form of, 161
Bell, passing, 15
Bells, legends of, 420
— phantom, 420
— tolling of, 227
Belludo, Spanish ghost, 147
Benedictine nun, ghost of, 219
Benjie Gear, ghost so called, 195
Ben Jonson, 372
Benshee, 273
Bergmouch, spectre so called, 269
Berkeley Square, mystery of, 317–318
Berry Pomeroy Castle, 318
Bertha of Rosenberg, 228
Beswick, Madame, ghost of, 131, 399

BIB

Bible in ghost laying, 192, 197
Biddick Hall, South, 327
Bilocation, or double personality, 367
Birchen Tower, Hollinwood, 398
Bird near sick-room, 97
Birds as soul bearers, 96
— phantom, 85–101
— singed, souls as, 96
— the way of, 96
Birkbeck ghost, 372–373
Birraark, 165–166
Birth, superstitions relating to, 97
Black dog, spectral, 107–108
— friar, ghost of, 221, 308
— Heddon, Northumberland, 398
Bleeding nun, ghost of, 44
Blenkinsopp Castle, 326, 400
Bloodstains, indelible, 146
Bloody hand, spectre of, 220
Bluecap, 264
— lights, 390
Bodach au Dun, 220
— Gartin, 221
— Glas, 220
Boggan, 114
Boggart, at Clegg Hall, 199
Boguest, 114
Bohemian belief, 86, 160, 183, 211, 228, 336, 339
Boleyn, Lady Ann, 147
Bolivia, Yuricares of, 37
Bolles pit, 203
Bolotu, 28
Bones of dead preserved, 36–37
Booty's ghost, 241–244
Borneo, Dayaks of, 18, 438
Bothwell, Lady, ghost of, 74, 308
Bottle imps, 185
Bottreaux, bells of, 421
Brandenburg, Elector of, 229
Brazil, Indians of, 33, 41, 45, 90, 359, 393
Brides, ghosts of, 61

CHU

Bridge End House, 327
Brocken, spectre of, 352
Brougham, Lord, 245
Brownies, 313, 404
Brown lady at Rainham, 312
Bulgarian belief, 86, 160, 189
Bull, ghost as a, 104
Burial-grounds, haunted, 343
Burma, 359
Burton Agnes Hall, 326
Butterflies, phantom, 156–162
Byron, Lord, 210, 221
— Sir John, the Little, 313

Caistor Hall, ghost at, 150
Calabar superstition, 336
Californian beliefs, 15, 35, 90
Candles in ghost laying, 190
— snuff of, taken for ghost laying, 362
— spectral, 139
Canning, George, 432
Capelthwaite, 114
Cassioway, 111
Castle, sunken, 348
Cedar room at Ashley Hall, 326
Chappie, ghost so called, 306
Chartley Park, 224
Chasse Macabee, 125
Checks against ghosts, 354–362
Chevalier de Saxe, 171
Chiancungi, fortune-tellers, 173
Chibehas, 184
Chinese belief, 6, 19, 33, 53, 55, 6? 65, 66, 72, 195, 211, 292, 339, 35
Choctaw belief, 29, 37
Chough, King Arthur in form o 94
Christmastide, ghosts at, 302–30?
Church ghosts, 330–331
— lamb, 126
— porch, 332–333, 387
— yard spectres, 69

CHU

Churton Hall, 321
Clegg Hall boggart, 199, 322
Clock superstition, 227
Cloud, soul as white, 4
Cobal, ghost so called, 270
Cock-crow, 354-356
Cocks' feathers hinder exit of soul, 12
Cold lad, 313
Colt, ghost as a, 103
Combermere Abbey, 322
Compacts between living and dead, 245-256
Copeland, lady of, 133
Corby Castle, ghost at, 311
Cornish beliefs, 103, 108, 120, 128, 201, 207, 208, 262, 294, 300, 421
— legend of King Arthur, 94
Cornwolf, 396
Corpse candle, 139-140
Cortachy Castle haunted, 311, 417
Courting a ghost, 384
Coved saloon at Combermere Abbey, 322
Cows, ghosts in form of, 109
Craighouse, 325
Creslow Manor House, 313
Criminals, ghosts of, 69
Crook Hall haunted, 327
Cross, check against evil spirits, 358, 361
Cross-roads, ghosts at, 61, 383
Cruikshank, George, 429
Cullaby Castle, 320
Cumberland, 76, 78, 266, 366
Cumnor Hall, 77, 320
Cutty Soams, 264
Cwn y Wybe, 118
Cyprus, 183

Dandy dogs, 118, 120, 121
Danish superstitions, 8, 48, 61, 88,

DYT

97, 126, 183, 215, 289, 361, 385, 416
Dead, mutilation of, 359-360
— unburied, 43-49
— worship of, 63
Death bell, 413
— birds presage of, 97-98
— warnings, 12, 13, 219, 232, 427
Delitzsch, Dr., 428
Demon, soul as, 62
Denis, St., 145
Denton Hall, 326
Departed, Bay of the, 206
Derwentwater, Lady, 321
Desert, water of, 352
Devil, compact with Lord Soulis, 323
— powerless at cock-crow, 355
— tries to seize soul at death, 14
Devonshire beliefs, 97, 98, 376
Diedrick of Bern, 125
Dishonesty in life causes soul to wander, 51
Doe, White, of Rylstone, 108
Dogs of hell, 122
— spectral, 105-106
— the sky, 122
Donart's Castle, St., 76
Doors unfastened at death, 6
Dorcas, ghost so called, 267
Dorchester, Lord, 380
Dorsetshire, 149
Doves in ghost-lore, 94, 98
Doyle, Bishop, death of, 100
Dreams, proof of soul's existence, 17, 18
Dress, phantom, 303-309
Drowned, ghosts of, 206-213
Drummer, mysterious, 311
— of Tedworth, 317
Duck, soul as, 87
Durham, 151
Dutch belief, 8-9
Dyterbjernat, 125

EAG

EAGLE, 94, 96
Easterton ghost, the, 329
Ebb of tide, death at, 15–16
Edge Hill, strange phenomenon at, 351
Edgewell oak, 222
Edgeworth, Maria, 372
Effigy, burial in, 49
Elixir of life, 175
Elizabeth, Queen, and her fetch, 364
Elymas, the sorcerer, 164
Epworth Parsonage haunted, 328, 430
Eskimo belief, 6, 111, 143, 359
Essex, 111
Ewshott House haunted, 318, 431
Exorcism, 88, 166
Eye, soul in the, 3, 4

FAIRY music, 413
Fata Morgana, 352
Feathers, game, hinder exit of soul, 11–12
Female fairy, 273
Fetches, 363–364
Fiddler, the indefatigable, 416
Fijian beliefs, 19, 23, 27–28, 182, 217, 309, 339
Finland, custom in, 336
Fire, check against ghosts, 358
Fish animated by souls, 111
Flame, soul in, 137
Flax-seed, charm against ghosts, 362
Flies, souls as, 161
Flying Dutchman, 286, 293
Foot of the Fawn, 99
Foote, Samuel, 424
Foundation sacrifices, 30
French beliefs, 5, 109, 125, 133, 231, 270, 289, 291

HAI

Furious host, 136
Fye, or wraith, 369

GABRIEL hounds, 117, 136
— Ratchets, 118–119
Galicia, belief in, 37
Game feathers hinder exit of soul, 11–12
German beliefs, 5, 6, 8, 9, 56, 86, 97, 99, 123, 135–136, 155, 183, 212, 227, 260, 338, 341, 348, 360, 388, 391, 396
Ghosts and hidden treasures, 397–410
— checks against, 354–362
— different classes of, 41
— headless, 33, 53, 69, 144–158, 306, 383
— times of appearing, 382–390
— why they wander, 50–63
Ghost laying, 104, 179–205
— of the Hill, 220
— raising, 163–178
— seers, 214–218
Glamis Castle haunted, 313, 431
Gnat, soul as, 161
Goblin friar, 313
Golden mountain, 146
Gould, Madame, 98
Grass-wolf, 396
Grave-sow, 126
Graves, haunted, 341
— treading on, 345
Gray sow, 126
Greece, beliefs in, 25, 183, 394
Greenland, beliefs in, 23, 29, 339
Grief causes soul to wander, 61
Gunpowder and ghosts, 360–361
Gurlinheg, family of, 221

HACKWOOD HOUSE haunted, 32
Hairy left hand, girl with, 221

HAL

Hallow Eve, 388
Hamilton, Lady, of Bothwellhaugh, 74
Hanged, ghosts of, 53
Hare, ghost as, 103, 271
Harlequin, 125
Haunted houses, 310–334
— localities, 335–353
Headless ghosts, 33, 53, 69, 144–158, 306, 383
Heart, seat of soul, 2, 3
Hell Hole, 423
Henequin, 125
Herburt family, 94
Hermitage Castle, 322, 403
Herring piece, 93
— spear, 93
Hidden treasures and ghosts, 397–410
Hilton Castle, 313
Hindu beliefs, 339
— dirge, 11
Hinton Ampner Manor House, 312
Hoby, Lady, 321
Holland House, 145, 314
Holly and ghost laying, 188
— charm against evil spirits, 358
Holt Castle, 319
Hooper of Sennen Cove, 300
Horse, spectre as, 125
— shoe, 361
Hottentot customs at death, 336, 339
Hound, ghost as, 105
House-fire put out at death, 359
Houses, haunted, 310–334
Howard, Lady, ghost of, 104
Hugh Capet, 125
Hulme Castle, treasures at, 397
Hungary, belief in, 61
Hunt, spectral, 124–125
Huntsman, wild, 125
Hurons of America, belief of, 67
Hyssington Church, ghost at, 104

LAM

Ignes Fatui, ghost as, 50–51
Incantations against ghosts, 164
Inchcape Bell, 422–423
India, beliefs in, 12, 62, 67, 96, 99, 109, 110, 340, 343, 346, 357, 393, 395, 412, 414
Insect life, 102
Irish superstitions, 11, 94, 137, 146, 153, 156–157, 226, 274–275, 344, 350, 370, 377, 383, 405, 413
Iroquois of North America, beliefs of, 44, 347, 393
Italian belief, 358
— burial custom, 339

Jackals, ghosts as, 9
Japanese ghost story, 72
— mode of raising ghost, 166
Jeffrey, Lady, ghost of, 187
Jemmy Lowther, 311
Juniper, spirit-haunted tree, 395

Kaffir beliefs, 2, 336
Kaneka superstition, 230–231
Karens, beliefs of, 45, 67, 160, 309
Kendal, Duchess of, 100
Kilncote church porch, 332
Kinchardines, 220
Kirk-grim, 125
Knauff-Kriegen, 270
Knockers, 262

Lady of Copeland, 133
— of Death, 273
— of the Golden Casket, 129
— of the Lantern, 128
— Winter's walk, 156
Lamb buried under altar, 126
— church, 126
Lambton, Madame, 327

LAN

Lancashire, 4–5, 14, 74–75, 91–92, 112, 198, 214, 376
Lavington, East, parsonage, 329
Lightfoot, Lady, 77
Lights, phantom, 127–143
Lily, soul as, 391–392
Lincolnshire, 129
Lion, 226
Little Knocker's Night, 438
Lledwith, 370
Locks unfastened at death, 5, 7
Lowther Hall haunted, 432
Ly-erg, 220
Lyttelton, Lord, 100

Madagascar, beliefs in, 23, 346
Madge Figg's chair, 129
Madness causes soul to wander, 61
Magic circle, 167
Malay belief, 3
Malevolent spirits, 70
Manes worship, 63
Manx fishermen, 93
Maori belief, 336
Mark's, St., Eve, 332, 386
Martyrs, ghosts of, 86
Mary Wray, spectre so called, 152
Mauthe Doog, 116–117, 311
May Moulach, 221
Mazarine, Duchess of, 254
Mermaid, 415
Mexican belief, 89
Midsummer Eve, 387
Milky-way, the, 96
Miners' ghosts, 257–272, 370–371
Mines, ghosts in, 108, 262–263
Mirage, 352
Mohin, Lord, 372
Money hidden by ghosts, 460–469
Monkey, soul as, 110
Mountain, abode of spirits, 348
Mourning customs, 340

OWL

Mouse, soul as, 110
Mouth, escape of soul from, 2–5
Murder discovered through ghos 81–84
— preceded by supernatura sounds, 433–434
Murdered, ghosts of, 33, 64–84
Murderers, ghosts of, 52–53, 54, 36
Music, phantom, 411–425
— at sea, 413

Necromancy, 165
Netherby Hall, 327
Newstead Abbey, 313
New Zealanders, beliefs of, 3, 35 182
Nix, river spirit, 202
Norfolk, 112, 148, 149, 208, 423
Northamptonshire, 383–384, 409 410
Northumberland, 150, 398
Norwegian beliefs, 68, 76, 360
Nostrils, exit of soul through, 3
Nun, bleeding, 44
— of Walton, spectre so called 154
Nymph of air, 273

Oak, holes in, 395
Obrick's colt, 103
Ojibway, beliefs in, 30, 162, 184 185, 217, 291, 336, 339, 347
Old Barbery, ghost so called, 326 327
— Hummums, 316
Orleans, Catholic church of, 430
Ottawas, beliefs of, 45, 68
Oulton House, Suffolk, 322
Ouse, river, 225
Owls and Arundel of Wardour, 95 222
— as souls, 94–95

OXE

Oxenham family, death-omen of, 98

PADFOIT, 113
Papuans of New Guinea, belief of, 110
Parsonages, haunted, 328–329
Passing bell, 15
Pawcorance, small bird, 95
Pearlin, Jean, 305
Peel Castle haunted, 116–117, 311
Peg O'Nell, ghost so called, 200, 327
Percy, Sir Josceline, 150
Personality, double, 367
Peruvian beliefs, 36, 257, 387
Pezazi, mystery of, 436–437
Phantom bells, 420–421
— birds, 85–101
— butterflies, 159–162
— dress, 303–309
— lights, 127–143
— music, 411–425
— sounds, 426–438
Philosopher's stone, 175
Pig, ghost as, 125
Pigeon feathers hinder exit of soul, 11–12
— ghost as a, 86
Pigott, Madame, 197
Pileck family, 94
Pirate wrecker, 294
Polish legend, 94
Poltergeist, a spectre in Germany, 438
Polynesian belief, 45
Pomerania, belief in, 183
Porter, Anna Maria, 373
Potawatomies, 184
Powis Castle, 320
Prophecy at death, 13–14
Pysling, form of ghost, 70

SEV

RABBIT, 271
Radiant boy, 129, 311
Rainham, story Marquis of Townshend, 312
Ramhurst Manor House, 312
Ravens as ghosts of the murdered, 48, 88
— omens of death, 100
Red Sea, ghosts laid in, 201, 203–204
Redwing, noise caused by, 93
Rich, Lady Diana, 366
Robin redbreast, 100–101
Robsart, Amy, 77, 202, 320
Roof, hole made in for exit of soul, 6
Rose, white, soul as, 392
Roslin Chapel, 141
Rothiemurcus, 220
Roumenian legend, 31
Rufus, William, fetch of, 34
Russia, Catharine of, 369
Russian beliefs, 2, 12, 32, 137, 159, 161, 338, 349, 358
Rustling lady, the, 327

SACRIFICES, foundation, 30
— to souls of departed, 62
Samlesbury Hall, 322
Sampford Peverel ghost, 322
Sandwich Islanders, 340
Scotch beliefs, 6, 7, 11, 61, 73, 125, 129, 169, 180, 194, 230, 239, 258, 265, 312, 359, 369, 370, 401–402
Scott, Sir Walter, 434–435
Seals, spectral, 106
Sea-phantoms, 284–302
Seaton Delaval Castle, 321
Second sight, 22, 233–244
Seminoles of Florida, 4, 336
Serpent comes out of mouth, 109
Servian belief, 160
Seven whistlers, 91

SEX

Sexhow, ghost at, 399
Shadow sight, 233
— soul as, 29–32
Sheep, ghosts as, 109
Shelley and his wraith, 365
Shell fire, 137
Shrieking woman, the, 71
Shropshire, 55, 61, 103–104, 151–153, 181–187, 190
Shuck's Lane, 112
Siamese superstitions, 67, 212, 339–438
Siberian belief, 358
Silky, name of a ghost, 130, 305, 321, 327, 398
Silky's bridge, 131
Simon Magus, 164
Singed birds, souls as, 96
Singhalese superstitions, 408, 437–438
Skipsea Castle, 326
Skull at Agnes Burton Hall, 326
Smellie, W., 252
Smith, George, the Assyriologist, 428
Smoke, soul as, 2
Smugglers, 429
Snakes, ghosts in form of, 62–109
Sneezing, explanation of, 22
Soul-bringer, 97
Soul, appearance of, 40–41
— bringing back of, 19
— destination of, 348
— duplex nature of, 27
— existence of depends on manner of death, 33–35
— exit of, 1–16
— materiality of, 24–27
— nature of, 24–42
— temporary exit of, 17–23, 338
— voice of, 39–40
— weight of, 38–39
Souldern Rectory, 328
Souter, or Soutra, Fell, 351

TON

Spanish beliefs, 5, 360
Spectral child, 321
— dogs, 111
— hunt, 124–5
— ships, 288–9, 294
Spells against ghosts, 354–362
Spirit of air, 273
Staffordshire rhyme, 51
Steam, soul as, 3
Stichios, a kind of spectre, 394
Storks, 95, 97
Stradling, Lady, 76
Strand varsler, 48
Striker, 112
Sturgeon, death omen, 222
Suffolk belief, 149, 184–198
Suicides, ghosts of, 53
Sunday children, 215
Sunken towns, 348
Sunrise, ghosts disappear at, 390
Sussex beliefs, 11, 37, 156, 429
Swallow, ghost as, 86
Swan, soul in form of, 88
Swarth or fetch, 366
Swedish beliefs, 88, 125, 135, 229, 289, 356, 384–395
Swinsty Hall, 398
Switzerland, 161
Sykes Lumb Farm, 400–401

Tahiti beliefs, 3, 182
Talking dog, 311
Tasks, or wraiths, 370
Tasmanian belief, 340
Tears hinder exit of soul, 8–11
Tedworth, drummer of, 418
Thomas's Day, St., 438
Thuringia, Duke Louis of, sign of his death, 99
Tibetan belief, 339
Tide, life goes out with, 15–16
Tipperahs of Chittagong, 181
Tongan belief, 29

TOW

Tower of London haunted, 314–315
Trash, spectre dog so called, 112
Treasures and ghosts, 397–410
— guarded by evil spirits, 257–258
Trees, spirit-haunted, 391–396
Trevelyan, seat of, haunted, 321
Trinity Church, York, ghost at, 330
Tulloch Gorms, 221
Tyrolese superstitions, 4

UNBAPTIZED, souls of, 136

VALENTINE's Eve, St., 386
Vampires, 189
Vapour, soul as, 3
Vingoes, death token of, 221
Violets spring from graves, 393

WADDON HALL, 327
Waff, or fetch, 366
Wallow Crag, ghost laid under, 312
Walton Abbey, 306, 322
Warwickshire, 263
Water, relation of ghosts to, 181–182
Weasel, soul as, 110
Wells, haunted, 348
Welsh superstitions, 53, 116, 122, 140, 185, 189, 260–261, 404–405, 417

ZUL

Wheal Vor, mine haunted at, 260, 434
Whistlers, the seven, 91
Whistling, voice of souls, 40
Whitby Abbey, 420
White-breasted bird, 97, 223
White Doe of Rylstone, 108
— lady, 98, 227–229, 305, 326–327
— — of Skipsea, 306
— — of Sorrow, 273
Wicked priest, 321
Willington Mill, 306, 327
Willow tree, anecdote connected with, 223
Wimbell Pond haunted, 401
Wisk hounds, 118
Witchcraft, 7, 106
Woman of peace, 273
Worcestershire, 62, 100, 156, 192, 200, 226
Wraith-seeing, 363–381
Wren, superstition connected with, 93
Wyecoller Hall, 312

YELLOW Sand, Isle of, 407
Yesk hounds, 118
Yeth hounds, 118–119
Yorkshire, 12, 91, 108, 129–130, 150, 154, 159, 215, 366

ZAMBESI superstition, 341
Zulus, beliefs of, 30, 40, 109